PETER STUBLEY

CALENDAR OF
CRIME

The
History
Press

365 TRUE CASES FROM BRITISH HISTORY

First published 2014

The History Press
The Mill, Brimscombe Port
Stroud, Gloucestershire, GL5 2QG
www.thehistorypress.co.uk

© Peter Stubley, 2014

The right of Peter Stubley to be identified as the Author
of this work has been asserted in accordance with the
Copyright, Designs and Patents Act 1988.

All rights reserved. No part of this book may be reprinted
or reproduced or utilised in any form or by any electronic,
mechanical or other means, now known or hereafter invented,
including photocopying and recording, or in any information
storage or retrieval system, without the permission in writing
from the Publishers.

British Library Cataloguing in Publication Data.
A catalogue record for this book is available from the British Library.

ISBN 978 0 7509 5654 3

Typesetting and origination by The History Press
Printed in Great Britain

Introduction

The Calendar of Crime covers nearly 1,000 years of British criminal history, from the assassination of King Edward the Martyr in 978 to the obscenity case over *Lady Chatterley's Lover* in 1960. It features many of the most notorious crimes during that period, ranging from pickpocketing to murder. There will no doubt be many omissions and in some cases no specific date could be found (such as the supposed trial for the murder of a statue of the Virgin Mary in Hawarden, Wales, in AD 946). The cut-off date of 1960 also means no mention of the Yorkshire Ripper, the Great Train Robbery and other modern crimes which are perhaps too fresh in the memory.

Sources

This book relies heavily on original newspaper accounts (available digitally via the British Library), the *Newgate Calendar* (available online at www.exclassics.com) and the *Proceedings of the Old Bailey* website. Many, many other books and websites have been a great help in identifying crimes worthy of inclusion and the relevant dates. Some limited examples: *Brewer's Rogues, Villains and Eccentrics*, www.executedtoday.com, www.rictornorton.co.uk, the *Murderer's Who's Who* by Gaute and Odell, *The Criminal Recorder* by A.F (1815), www.murderpedia.com, *501 Most Notorious Crimes* by Paul Donnelly and *The Book of Days* by Robert Chambers.

1 January

On the evening of 1 January 1845, the electric telegraph operator at Paddington railway station received this message:

A MURDER HAS GUST BEEN COMMITTED
AT SALT HILL AND THE SUSPECTED
MURDERER WAS SEEN TO TAKE A
FIRST CLASS TICKET TO LONDON BY THE
TRAIN WHICH LEFT SLOUGH AT 742 PM
HE IS IN THE GARB OF A KWAKER
WITH A GREAT COAT ON WHICH REACHES
NEARLY DOWN TO HIS FEET HE IS
IN THE LAST COMPARTMENT OF
THE SECOND CLASS COMPARTMENT

The operator, not realising that 'Kwaker' referred to Quaker (the system did not use J, Q or Z), asked for the communication to be repeated before passing it to police. By the time the train arrived at 8.20 p.m., a police officer was waiting to identify and follow the suspect. John Tawell, 60, was arrested and charged with the murder of his second wife Sarah Hart by poisoning her glass of stout with Scheele's Prussic Acid, a treatment for varicose veins which contained hydrogen cyanide. Tawell claimed his wife had inadvertently killed herself by eating too many apple pips but was convicted and sentenced to death. He became known as 'The Man Hanged by the Electric Telegraph'.

2 January

The MP and baronet Sir John Hotham was beheaded
on this day in 1645 after making the mistake
of defying both the king and Parliament during
the English Civil War. He was first declared a
traitor after barring Charles I from entering
Hull to make use of its stockpile of weapons
in April 1642, forcing the king to move to
Nottingham. Hotham then seems to have had a
disastrous change of heart as the Royalists
initially got the better of the early exchanges
with the Parliamentarian forces. Together with
his eldest son – Captain John Hotham the younger,
who served under Thomas Fairfax – he began secret
negotiations to hand over the Hull stronghold to
the Royalists. The deception was discovered and
Parliament ordered the arrest of both Hothams in
June 1643. Sir John attempted to escape but was
arrested in Beverley in Yorkshire and taken to
London for court martial. Both Sir John and his
son (who blamed his father for the betrayal) were
convicted of treason and executed on successive
days at Tower Hill. According to one account,
Sir John's 'unwillingness to die appeared by his
many delays and no doubt but that he had thoughts
of pardon till the last'.

3 January

The 'Siege of Sidney Street' in the East End of London in 1911 pitted two Latvian anarchists against 200 police officers, a company of Scots Guards and

Home Secretary Winston Churchill. The Latvians were believed to be responsible for the murder of three policemen in Houndsditch two weeks earlier on 16 December and detectives had received a tip-off that the gang was hiding out at No. 100 Sidney Street. At 2 a.m., the building was surrounded by armed officers. For the next six hours gunfire echoed around the street until the hideout mysteriously caught fire. Churchill, who was famously photographed peering around a corner at the battle, ordered the firefighters not to intervene and, when the blaze died down, two bodies were recovered. Neither of them was the legendary 'Peter the Painter', the supposed leader of the gang. Nobody knows his true identity – or if he even existed at all. As for Churchill, the future war leader was widely mocked in Parliament for risking his life and taking control of the operation. He would later admit in his diaries that curiosity got the better of him: 'I should have done better to have remained quietly in my office.'

4 January

English history might have been very different if King Charles I had not attempted to arrest five MPs for treason on this day in 1642. Seeking to impose his royal authority, Charles marched into the House of Commons with armed soldiers only to find that the troublesome 'Five Members' – John Pym, John Hampden, Denzil Holles, Arthur Haselrig and William Strode – had already left. Taking the Speaker's chair, Charles told the remaining MPs: 'So long as those persons that I have accused are here, I cannot expect that this House will be in the right way I do heartily wish it.' When he asked Speaker William Lenthall if he knew where the five men were, the Speaker (on bended knee) defiantly replied: 'I have neither eyes to see nor tongue to speak in this place but as this House is pleased to direct me.' After a long silence, the king replied: 'Well, since I see all my birds are flown I do expect from you that you will send them unto me as soon as they return hither.' Six days later, Charles fled from London for his own safety and began to prepare for the outbreak of the Civil War.

5 January

Ten-year-old Mona Tinsley left school in Newark
in Nottinghamshire at 4 p.m. on 5 January 1937.
She never arrived home. By 9 p.m., a full police
search was underway. There were several sightings:
a schoolboy saw Mona with a man at the bus station,
a bus driver reported that a man and a girl travelled on the 4.45 p.m. to Retford, and at Retford
there was a sighting of a young girl in the back
garden of the home of Frederick Nodder. Another
witness had seen Nodder – a former lodger with
the Tinsley family – waiting outside the school in
Newark. At Nodder's house, police found drawings
and writing by Mona. But there was no sign of the
girl. With no body to prove murder, Nodder was
charged with abduction and jailed for seven years
at Warwick Assizes. The judge told him: 'it may
be that time will reveal the dreadful secret
which you carry in your breast.' Five months later,
a family rowing in the River Idle discovered
Mona's body floating in the water. Nodder, who
claimed he had put Mona on a bus to Sheffield, was
convicted of murder at Nottingham Assizes. He was
hanged on 30 December 1937.

6 January

Evelyn Foster was dying. As she lay in bed, her body so badly burnt it was obvious she had only hours to live, she told her story: on the evening of 6 January 1931, she was driving a Hudson Super Six taxi back to her father's garage in Otterburn, Northumberland, when she was flagged down by a smart man in a bowler hat. She agreed to take him to Ponteland, but he took over the wheel, knocked her unconscious and indecently assaulted her. Then he set the car on fire. She managed to clamber away from the vehicle and was found a short while later by a passing bus driver. Evelyn died the following morning, aged 27. Nobody was ever charged and the police seem to have dismissed her version of events. At the inquest, the jury were provided with two alternative theories: either Evelyn was murdered by this mysterious stranger, or she accidentally set herself on fire as well as the car, perhaps in order to claim on the insurance. Although a post-mortem found no evidence of an assault, the jury returned a verdict of wilful murder. So who was the 'dandy in the bowler hat'?

7 January

The 'Christmas Cutpurse', John Selman, was hanged
on 7 January 1612 after he was caught stealing a
purse in the presence of King James I. It was a
daring, but foolish attempt: Selman, disguised in
a handsome black velvet cloak, sneaked into the
King's Chapel in Whitehall as a crowd of nobles
watched the monarch take Communion on Christmas
Day. But the promise of rich pickings soon evapo-
rated after he was caught red-handed with a bag
of shillings lifted from a lord's servant. Selman
confessed and agreed to give evidence against
other thieves in return for a Christian burial.
In his dying speech from the gallows at Charing
Cross, he declared:

> I have deserved death long before this time,
> and deservedly now I suffer death. The offense
> I die for, was high presumption, a fact done even
> in the Kings Majesty's presence, even in the Church
> of God, in the time of divine Service, and the
> celebration of the Sacred Communion, for which if
> forgiveness may descend from God's tribunal Throne,
> with penitence of heart I desire it.

Such was Selman's fame that Ben Jonson quickly
wrote the 'Christmas Cutpurse' into his masque
Love Restored.

8 January

The last man to be hanged for blasphemy in Britain
was a young Scottish student who ridiculed the
Bible as a fable and claimed Jesus was nothing
more than a third-rate magician. The year was 1697,
and the state was determined to make an example
out of Thomas Aikenhead, the 20-year-old son of
a chirurgeon from Edinburgh. According to the
indictment, Aikenhead not only dismissed Christ's
miracles as pranks, but also described his disci-
ples as 'blockish fisher fellows whom he knew had
strong imaginations'. Further claims included his
rejection of the Holy Trinity, his preference for
the prophet Mohammed over Jesus and his confident
belief that Christianity would be eradicated by
the beginning of the nineteenth century. In a
plea for mercy written before his trial, Aikenhead
insisted that he was a Christian who believed
in both the Old and New Testament and was only
repeating 'the sentiments and opinions of some
atheisticall writers whose names I can particularly condescend upon'. He was convicted of the
charge on the evidence of five fellow students and
on 8 January 1697 he was hanged on a gibbet on the
road between Edinburgh and Leith. The blasphemy
law was finally abolished in 2008.

9 January

> Although his hands were warm with blood,
> He down to supper sat,
> And passed the time in merry mood,
> With drink and songs and chat.

This, according to a local ballad, was how John Thurtell celebrated disposing of his victim William Weare on 24 October 1823. Thurtell, a mayor's son, former Royal Marine and boxer, decided to do away with Weare, a solicitor, to avoid paying a gambling debt of £300. He invited Weare to a weekend of games and alcohol with his friends at a cottage in Radlett, Hertfordshire. Shortly before reaching their destination in a horse-drawn carriage, Thurtell shot Weare in the face with a pistol. When this failed to extinguish his life, Thurtell slashed his throat with a knife and battered his brains out with the gun. After hiding the corpse in a pond, Thurtell enjoyed a supper of pork chops and a drunken singalong. But the crime was soon discovered and both Thurtell

and his friend Joseph Hunt were convicted of murder. Thurtell was hanged on 9 January 1824, aged 29, but Hunt was spared the death sentence and transported to Australia.

10 January

The notorious eighteenth-century pickpocket Mary Young was such a talented thief that she was nicknamed Diving Jenny (or Jenny Diver, also a character in *The Beggar's Opera*). Her nimble fingers first demonstrated their worth at the age of 10, when she was taught needlework by her foster mother in Ireland. At 15 she decided to head for London, where, having failed to earn a living from sewing, she fell in with a gang of thieves and learnt the tricks of the trade. One of her favourite escapades involved disguising herself as a pregnant lady and fainting in the middle of the crowds at St James's Park in London, allowing her accomplices to lift as many valuables as possible from the distracted spectators. Jenny was convicted twice under different names and transported to the American colonies, only to return to London. Her luck ran out on 10 January 1741, when one of her victims managed to grab hold of her hand in mid-pick and refused to let go even after being punched in the face. This time the court was aware of her previous offences and sentenced her to death. Jenny was hanged at Tyburn on 18 March.

11 January

On 11 January 1920, Hannah Calladine and her two
children left the market town of Glossop, never
to be seen alive again. Their mysterious disappearance was only solved three years later, when
a 4-year-old boy living in the same neighbour-
hood also went missing. This time a huge search
was mounted by the police and local volunteers.
One of the willing hands, 62-year-old farm
labourer Albert Burrows, the bigamous husband
of Mrs Calladine, told officers he took young
Tommy Wood for a walk through the fields; while
he was trying to catch a rabbit, the boy ran off.
Suspicious of his account, detectives kept him
under watch. When Tommy's body was found at the
bottom of a disused mineshaft, Burrows attempted
to flee across the moors, followed by an angry
mob of spectators. He was found hiding under a
holly bush and driven away, past hordes of baying
locals, to the police station. Two months later,
while Burrows was awaiting trial for murder,
the mineshaft was drained of water to reveal the
bodies of Mrs Calladine, her 15-month-old son and
her 4-year-old daughter. Burrows was hanged in
Nottingham on 8 August 1923.

12 January

The original Great Train Robbery took place in
1855 on the South Eastern Railway between London
and Folkestone. It was only when the cargo reached
its destination in Paris that it was discovered
200lb of gold (then worth £12,000) had been
removed from the bullion safe in the guard's van
and replaced with lead weights. Although railway
staff were suspected, the case remained unsolved
until the following year when one of the thieves,
Edward Agar (who had since been sentenced to
penal transportation for life for forging a
cheque for £700), decided to tell police the full
story. With the help of three railway employees –
former ticket printer William Pierce, office clerk
William Tester and guard James Burgess – he
created replica keys to the bullion safe, tested
them, and performed several dry runs before
choosing a target. After successfully removing
the gold before the train reached Folkestone, Agar
melted it down and sold some of it to pay off his
conspirators. On 12 January 1857, after a trial at
the Old Bailey, Burgess and Tester were sentenced
to transportation for fourteen years and Pierce
was imprisoned for two years.

13 January

The Victorian eccentric Dr William Price was
a Welsh nationalist, a Chartist, a vegetarian,
an archdruid, an advocate of 'free love' and a
naked rambler. Even when clothed he refused to
wear socks and insisted on washing any coins
that were given to him. Dr Price also pioneered
cremation at a time when burial was thought to
be the only proper way of dealing with a dead
body. On 13 January 1884, following the tragic
death of his 5-month-old son Iesu Grist (Welsh
for Jesus Christ), he built a pyre near his
home in Llantrisant, Glamorgan. The fire was
quickly spotted by local residents and police
officers had to rescue Price from an angry mob.
An autopsy confirmed that the baby boy had died
of natural causes but Price, then aged 83, was
arrested and put on trial at Cardiff Assizes for
illegally disposing of a dead body. The judge
agreed with his argument that the law did
not explicitly outlaw cremation and Price was
released. On 14 March, Price was allowed to
perform a full cremation on his son in a druidic
ceremony. The first official cremation, of Jeannette
Pickersgill, took place in Woking on 26 March 1885.

14 January

At the back of the Adelphi Theatre in London's West End, a plaque marks the location of a sensational murder:

WILLIAM TERRISS
1847 – 1897
HERO OF THE ADELPHI MELODRAMAS
MET HIS UNTIMELY END OUTSIDE THIS THEATRE
16 DECEMBER 1897

Terriss, an established and popular actor, had just arrived at the theatre for his performance that night when a man ran up and stabbed him twice in the back. Terriss turned to face his attacker, only to be stabbed in the chest. He bled to death within minutes. The killer, 32-year-old Richard Prince (also known as Mad Archer), was arrested nearby and explained: 'Mr Terriss would not allow me to have any employment and I did it in revenge.' Terriss had previously helped the young actor find work but Prince was notoriously unstable and had been fired from his job at the Adelphi. He had become jealous of the older man's success, and was heard to make comments like 'fools often succeed in life where men of genius fail'. On 14 January 1898, Prince was found 'guilty of murder but insane' at the Old Bailey and remained at Broadmoor Asylum until his death thirty-nine years later.

15 January

Whiteabbey, Belfast, Northern Ireland. 1953.
Iain Hay Gordon, a 21-year-old RAF clerk, was
arrested and charged with the murder of
19-year-old judge's daughter Patricia Curran.
He replied: 'it was not wilful murder' but was
brought before a special court and remanded in
custody to await trial. The case against him was
based on his confession: in the early hours of
13 November 1952, he met Patricia as she walked
home university and asked for a kiss. She resisted
his advances and called him a beast. He lost
control and stabbed her thirty-seven times.
The confession resulted in a verdict of 'guilty
but insane' and he spent the next seven years
locked up in a psychiatric hospital. In 1993 he
began a legal fight to clear his name, based on
contradictory evidence, police misconduct and
an unfair trial. How come there was hardly any
blood at the scene despite the severity of the
injuries? Why was Gordon told by police that if he
didn't confess they would tell his mother about
his friendship with a gay man? Why did his lawyers
insist on putting forward the insanity defence?
Only in 2000 would he succeed in having the
conviction quashed by the Northern Ireland Court
of Appeal.

16 January

On 16 January 1673, the 'German Princess'
Mary Carleton (aka Henrietta Maria van Wolway)
was called before a judge at the Old Bailey to
explain herself. Was she the same woman who had
been banished to Jamaica a few years before for
stealing a silver tankard? Mary admitted that she
was, and the following day was condemned to death.
Her execution on 22 January brought an end to the
life of a highly successful identity fraudster.
For Mary Carleton was not a real German princess.
She was in fact born in Canterbury, her father
was a chorister rather than a lord and her first
husband was a shoemaker in her home town. In 1663
she arrived in London in the guise of an orphan
princess reduced to 'exposing her body to the
pleasure of every bidder'. Her unfortunate tale
attracted the offer of marriage from John Carleton,
an 18-year-old lawyer's clerk, but she was soon
exposed and prosecuted for bigamy. Incredibly,
she was acquitted after the prosecution failed to
locate her first husband. Carleton then perfected
her ploy of seducing wealthy men and running off
with their valuables while they slept – until that
fateful conviction for stealing a tankard.

17 January

The 'notorious Impostor' Lodowicke Muggleton
was sentenced to stand in the pillory for three
days after being convicted of creating his own
religion. According to a report of the trial at the
Old Bailey, in 1651 Muggleton and his confederate
William Reeve declared that they were 'the last
two Witnesses of God on Earth' mentioned in the
Book of Revelation. As such these two humble
tailors had the power to pronounce the power of
salvation and damnation upon anyone they chose,
being respectively the Blessing Prophet and the
Cursing Prophet. Muggleton's 14-year-old wife Sarah
was the first to be blessed. Following Reeve's
death, he 'seduced divers weak
and unstable people (especially
of the Female Sex) to become
his Proselytes' (also known
as Muggletonians). He accused
the Quakers of witchcraft
and wrote a book cursing
one of their members and in
August 1776 was arrested for
blasphemy. He was convicted by
the jury on 17 January 1677 and
sent to jail until he paid a
£500 fine. During Muggleton's
three days in the pillory
(two hours a time at Temple
Gate, the Royal Exchange
and Smithfield Market), his
books were burnt over
his head.

18 January

Fifteen years before the birth of Frankenstein's monster in the novel by Mary Shelley, an experiment was carried out on the body of a hanged man. Two conducting rods, linked to a powerful

A GALVANISED CORPSE

LC-USZ62-69619

battery, were pressed against his face. To the shock of the assembled audience, his jaw began to quiver, an eye opened and his limbs shook as if he had been brought back to life. One observer is said to have died of fright. The subject of this 'Galavanic' experiment (the process is named after the Italian physicist who carried out similar experiments on frogs) was a convicted murderer who had been hanged outside Newgate Prison earlier that day, 18 January 1803. The unfortunate George Forster was found to have drowned his wife and infant child in the Paddington Canal but there were no eyewitnesses to the actual deed and the evidence was all circumstantial. Guilty or not, his 'reanimation' was said to have proved the value of using electricity to revive victims of drowning or suffocation or to treat mental disorders.

19 January

On 19 January 1326, the nobleman Sir Roger Belers
(or Bellere) was ambushed and murdered near
Rearsby in Leicestershire by a band of outlaws
known as the Folville gang. Their leader, Eustace
Folville, was not a low-born criminal or a poor
peasant but a member of the gentry. His arrest
was ordered by King Edward II but the gang
fled to Wales and France to join Edward's rival,
Sir Roger Mortimer. They were pardoned in 1327
after Mortimer overthrew Edward but over the next
four years, the Folvilles continued to terrorise
the Midlands (to the despair of the Sheriff of
Nottingham) and were blamed for several other
murders and robberies – although, like the
legendary Robin Hood, they remained popular local
figures. In 1332 the gang captured and held to
ransom Sir Richard Willoughby, a Justice of the
King's Bench, but somehow Eustace Folville escaped
arrest and punishment, most likely because of his
political connections and the reputations of his
victims. He was pardoned for a second time by
King Edward III and remained a free man until his
death in 1346. The only Folville to be brought to
justice was his brother Richard, who was beheaded
in 1340.

20 January

The M'Naghten Rules, which established the princi-
ples for the legal defence of insanity, were drawn
up by the House of Lords after the murder of a
man who had been mistaken for the prime minister,
Sir Robert Peel. On 20 January 1843, Peel's personal
secretary Edward Drummond was shot in the back as
he walked from Peel's house in Whitehall Gardens
to the government buildings in Downing Street.
The bullet was removed but Drummond died five days
later, possibly as a result of repeated use of
bloodletting and leeching as a medical treatment.
His attacker was Daniel M'Naghten (or McNaughton),
a 30-year-old Scottish woodturner who blamed the
Tories for persecuting him 'wherever I go'. He was
found not guilty of murder by reason of insanity
after a trial at the Old Bailey but the verdict
was criticised by many (including Queen Victoria).
The House of Lords ruled that for the defence to
succeed, the accused had to have been suffering
from such a disease of the mind 'as not to know
the nature and quality of the act he was doing;
or, if he did know it, that he did not know he was
doing what was wrong'.

21 January

Claude Duval was the model gentleman highway
robber. He was dashing, dangerous and, most
importantly from the perspective of his English
lady admirers, French. Duval not only dressed
well – he was quick-witted, eloquent and courteous
to his victims, played a mean flute and stole any
dancefloor. His most famous exploit, recounted in
the 'memoirs' published by William Pope, involves
him stopping a coach laden with £400. When the
lady in the carriage, endeavouring to keep calm,
played a tune on her wooden flute, Duval took out
his instrument and produced a sweet melody of his
own. Then, with Duval singing a French *courante*,
the pair danced with each other in front of her
husband. After such a charming episode, it was
only right that Duval allowed his victims to keep
£300 of their treasure. But he could be ruthless
when required – this Knight of the Road reputedly
stole a child's silver sucking bottle while on
the rampage in Blackheath. Duval was eventually
captured while drinking at the Hole in the Wall
in Chandos Street. Despite repeated pleas for
mercy to the king from Duval's female fans, he was
hanged at Tyburn on 21 January 1670, aged 27.

22 January

When the 200 settlers on board the *Kennersley Castle* sailed from Scotland on this day in 1823, they believed they were headed for a new colony ripe for exploitation on the other side of the ocean. This untapped paradise of 'Poyais' was, according to the architect of this adventure, to be found in the Bay of Honduras. Yet when the ship arrived two months later, the would-be colonists found only an impenetrable jungle populated by a few nomads and the remnants of a smaller group sent out the previous year. Poyais did not exist – it was the creation of the Scottish conman Gregor MacGregor, who had convinced scores of families to buy land and bonds valued at more than £200,000. Only a few dozen of the settlers managed to return home but somehow, MacGregor managed to escape the wrath of his investors and attempted the same ruse in France. He was still claiming to be the chief or 'cacique' of Poyais when he returned to London in 1826 and continued to operate versions of the same scheme until 1839, when he escaped the attentions of his annoyed investors by emigrating to Venezuela.

23 January

The escape from Broadmoor Asylum in Berkshire had
been planned for weeks. Now, on 23 February 1888,
it was time for action. James Kelly, prisoner 1167,
put on his suit, picked up his violin case and
walked to band practice. Concealed in the case
was a piece of metal that Kelly had found in the
kitchen garden and filed down to match the lock on
the door leading to the courtyard. After finishing
practice at 6.30 p.m. he opened the door, clam-
bered over the 6ft wall and made his way to London.
Kelly, who had been certified insane after stabbing
his 22-year-old wife to death, was now on the
run. He remained at large for another eight years
until he walked into the British Consulate in New
Orleans and offered to sail back to England to
give himself up. Yet when two warders went to meet
his ship at Liverpool, he had vanished. Kelly only
reappeared in 1927, when he knocked on the door of
Broadmoor Asylum and asked to be locked up again.
'I dreaded the idea of dying alone,' he told staff.
Kelly died two years later of pneumonia.

24 January

By 1907, William Whiteley had built up his 'fancy
goods' business into a vast department store
occupying a whole row of shops along Westbourne
Grove in Bayswater, west London. He was a self-
made millionaire with more than 6,000 employees;
a self-styled 'Universal Provider' who boasted
that he could meet any request from his customers,
ranging from a pin to an elephant. But the
smartly dressed young man who entered his store
on 24 January did not want to buy any of his
goods. Horace Rayner, 27, demanded an allowance
as recognition that he was Whiteley's illegitimate
son. Whiteley refused and was shot twice in the
head in front of screaming customers in the lace
department. Rayner then turned the gun on himself,
but succeeded only in blasting out his own right
eye. If anyone doubted his intent, he had left a
message on Whiteley's desk: 'This two-fold tragedy
is due to his refusal of a request which is
perfectly reasonable. RIP.' A pathetically disfigured Rayner was convicted of murder at the newly
opened Central Criminal Court on 22 March and
sentenced to death. The sentence was commuted to
life imprisonment, partly because of overwhelming
public sympathy for the killer.

25 January

If you shoot and kill a man you honestly believe is a ghost, are you still guilty of murder? This was the legal dilemma raised by the case of Francis Smith and the Hammersmith Ghost in 1804. The ghost in question, believed to be the spirit of a suicide victim, had been seen wandering the area for weeks. It had even grabbed a young woman walking through the churchyard, causing her to faint. So it was on the night of 3 January that Francis Smith, 29, set out with his blunderbuss to investigate. Soon enough he spotted a figure dressed in white, passing down a darkened lane. 'Damn you, who are you and what are you?' he warned, but received no reply. Smith fired his weapon, felling the ghost, who turned out to be a mild-mannered plasterer dressed in the lime-streaked overalls. Smith was charged with the murder of Thomas Millwood but insisted that he never meant to kill anyone. The jury, unable to return a manslaughter verdict, found him guilty. He was condemned to death but on 25 January the sentence was reduced to twelve months' hard labour. The legal issue raised by the case was only resolved in 1984.

26 January

On 26 January 1765, Lord Byron (the great-uncle of the poet) shot and killed his cousin William Chaworth in a drunken duel. That evening the pair attended a meeting of the Nottinghamshire Club at the Star and Garter tavern in Pall Mall, London. When the conversation meandered into the upkeep of one's estates, Chaworth insisted on ruthless action against poachers while Byron claimed that doing nothing was the best policy. Tempers frayed and Chaworth boasted that he had more game on 5 acres of land than Lord Byron had on all his manors. Byron wagered 100 guineas. Chaworth declined the bet and offered to give him 'satisfaction'. The duel took place in a room on the first floor. Once the door was closed, Chaworth drew his sword and thrust it through Byron's waistcoat. Thinking he had killed his opponent, he paused, only to be stabbed in the stomach.

Byron celebrated inflicting the fatal wound with the words: 'By God, I have as much courage as any man in England.' In April, the 'Wicked Lord' was tried before his peers in Westminster Hall and convicted of manslaughter rather than murder. Because of his status, he escaped with only a small fine.

LC-USZ62-99928

27 January

For Harry Dobkin, the Blitz seemed like an ideal
opportunity to get rid of his estranged wife.
Who would investigate her disappearance in the
chaos of the war? And who would care about the
finding of another dead body in an area where
dozens had already died from German air raids?
And so, on 11 April 1941, Mrs Rachel Dobkin
disappeared. It was not until 17 July 1942 that
her mummified remains were discovered in the
bomb-damaged ruins of a Baptist chapel in
Vauxhall, south-west London. But something about
the body struck the pathologist as suspicious.
Further investigation revealed that the woman
had been strangled; her limbs had been severed
at the knees and elbows and her head cut off;
the bones showed signs of being burnt. Builder's
lime had been used in a bungled attempt to hasten
decomposition. Dental records and a comparison
of the skull to a photograph of Rachel Dobkin
confirmed her identity. Mr Dobkin, who had been
seen trying to put out a fire at the chapel cellar
three days after Mrs Dobkin's disappearance, was
charged with murder. He was convicted at the
Old Bailey and hanged at Wandsworth Prison on
27 January 1943.

28 January

Bodysnatching was a grim but lucrative profession which involved digging up a corpse from its grave and selling it to medical schools for dissection. Cadavers were in such demand that professors of anatomy were willing to pay £10 each for a fresh one, no questions asked. So it was perhaps only a matter of time before enterprising criminals decided to speed up the process by turning to murder. Most famous of all was William Burke, whose surname was later used to refer to the particular type of suffocation he used to kill his victims. Together with his accomplice William Hare, Burke killed at least sixteen people in the West Port area of Edinburgh, including an 18-year-old man known as 'Daft Jamie'. They were only caught when their lodgers spotted the body of their final victim under a bed and alerted the police. Controversially, it was decided to offer Hare immunity in return for testifying against Burke in court. Burke was convicted of murder and hanged on 28 January 1829 in front of 20,000 people. The next day his body was publicly dissected. His tanned skin was used to cover books and a calling-card case.

29 January

In the London of the 'Roaring Twenties',
Kate Meyrick was the queen of Soho. Her most
famous nightclub, 'The 43' in Gerrard Street,
was (depending on your moral outlook) either a
celebrity hang-out for the rich and famous or a
charnel house of unthinkable depravity populated
by indecent drunks and loose women. Although
Meyrick was an attractive and well-mannered lady
who sent her sons to Harrow, the reputation of
The 43 meant that it was repeatedly raided by the
police, resulting in a series of prosecutions for
running a disorderly establishment. By the late
1920s, she had developed a profitable relationship
with a police officer who would tip her off before
any police visit so she could remove evidence of
after-hours drinking. This practice was exposed
when she was caught paying £155 to Sergeant George
Goddard of the Metropolitan Police. Meyrick
pleaded guilty to bribery and corruption and
was sentenced to fifteen months' hard labour on
29 January 1929. She died of pneumonia, aged
57, four years later. In 1935 her son-in-law
Edward Russell, 26th Baron de Clifford, became the
last peer to be tried at the House of Lords after
killing a man in a car crash.

30 January

King Charles I (reigned 1625–49) famously went to his death wearing two thick shirts to stop him shivering. 'The season is so sharp as probably may make me shake, which some observers may imagine proceeds from fear,' he said. His journey to the executioner's block had begun seven years earlier with the outbreak of the English Civil War in 1642. After his defeat, Parliament charged him with high treason and put him on trial in Westminster Hall on 20 January 1649. Seven days later he was declared guilty and condemned to death. His death warrant, dated 29 January, was signed by the fifty-nine judges, including Oliver Cromwell. The following day, the king was taken from St James's Palace to a scaffold outside the Banqueting House in Whitehall. His last significant words are said to be: 'I go from a corruptible to an incorruptible crown; where no disturbance can be, no disturbance in the world.' The king spent the last moments of his life fretting about the arrangement of his hair and the height of the block. It took only one blow to sever the king's neck. This literal and symbolic decapitation was (according to a witness) greeted by 'such a groan by the thousands then present, as I never heard before and I desire I may never hear again'.

31 January

Daily Journal, 31 January 1721

> On Saturday last a Rat, of an uncommon Size,
> having been taken alive in the South-Sea House,
> the Mob laid violent Hands on the poor Creature,
> and without Proceeding according to Law, carried
> him to a Pillory erected for that purpose,
> in Broad-Street, where they nail'd his Ears,
> and over his Head there was a written, *A DIRECTOR
> of the South-Sea*; this Inscription so exasperated
> the Populace, that the poor Creature was first
> pelted, and afterwards *blown up*.

The collapse of the South Sea Company, founded
in 1711 to consolidate the national debt, ruined
thousands of investors, damaged the British
economy and exposed the corruption at the heart of
government. Amongst its victims was the Chancellor
of the Exchequer, John Aislabie, who was convicted
of corruption by the House of Commons and sent
to the Tower of London in March 1721. The company
cashier, Robert Knight, who had bribed Aislabie
and other influential figures with £1 million worth
of free shares, went into exile in France. Perhaps
the only man to benefit was Robert Walpole, who
came to power in the wake of the scandal and is
now remembered as the first British prime minister.

1 February

In 1762, the phenomenon known as the Cock Lane Ghost was the sensation of London. It was widely reported that 'Scratching Fanny' had returned to haunt her husband William Kent, a moneylender.

Responding to a series of questions (one knock for yes, two for no), the ghost claimed she had been poisoned. Large crowds mobbed the building near central London's Smithfield Market, hoping to witness the mysterious visitations, and some even called for Kent to be arrested and charged with murder. Initial investigations suggested that the ghost had possessed the body of the 12-year-old daughter of Kent's landlord Richard Parsons. So it was that on 1 February Dr Samuel Johnson, the noted dictionary compiler, took up the mantle of paranormal investigator and visited young Elizabeth Parsons at a house in Clerkenwell. 'The girl declared that she felt the spirit like a mouse upon her back, and was required to hold her hands out of bed,' reported Dr Johnson. 'From that time, no evidence of any preternatural power was exhibited.' A few days later Elizabeth was caught concealing a piece of wood in her clothing. The hoax resulted in Richard Parsons being jailed for two years.

2 February

The Norman Ranulf Flambard was not only the first
person to be locked up in the Tower of London,
but also the first to escape from it. A priest's
son, he first rose to prominence during the reign
of William the Conqueror and is thought to have
played a part in the compilation of Domesday
Book. Under William II he became the king's
chief adviser and treasurer despite a reputation for corruption. In 1100, Henry I arrived
on the throne and promptly charged Flambard
with extorting money from the Church and the
nobility, and sent him to the Tower. Flambard
contrived his escape on 2 February 1101, after
arranging a feast for his captors. One version of
the story has Flambard incapacitating his guards
with free wine before abseiling down from the
window using a rope smuggled into his cell in
a flagon. He fled to France and masterminded the
failed invasion of England by Robert, Duke of
Normandy (brother of both William II and Henry I)
in July 1101. The treaty which ended the dispute
gave him a pardon and restored him to the post of
Bishop of Durham.

3 February

The newspaper advertisement stated that Amelia
Sach was a midwife offering 'Accouchement, before
and during. Skilled nursing. Home comforts.'
Her fee was usually £1 1s a week, but Sach's
accomplice Annie Walters eventually hit upon a
scheme that would bring in the money much faster,
and spare her the inconvenience of looking after
a newborn child. In return for £25, she offered
to take the baby and place it with a suitable
foster parent. For desperate young women like
Ada Galley, it meant they could keep their jobs
as maidservants and avoid being stigmatised as
single mothers. Miss Galley's infant was delivered
at Sach's lying-in home in East Finchley, north
London, in November 1902 and quickly passed to
Walters to be silenced with chlorodyne. On the
18th, Walters was caught with a bundle containing
the now lifeless child as she left her lodgings
in Islington. Officers sent to arrest Sach found
300 pieces of baby clothing at her home – enough
for six infants. Both Sach and Walters were
found guilty of murder and sentenced to death.
They were hanged side by side at Holloway Prison
on 3 February 1903. It was the last double hanging
of women in Britain.

4 February

In the 1770s, the slang word 'Macaroni' (as featured in the rhyme *Yankee Doodle*) was used to describe foppish young men who pranced about in extravagant clothing and a feather in their hat. It was just such a taste for dandyish fashion that earned Dr William Dodd, chaplain to King George III, the nickname 'The Macaroni Parson'. But Dodd was to become even more famous as a convicted criminal. On 4 February 1777, he forged a bond for £4,200 in the name of his former pupil Lord Chesterfield in an attempt to pay off his debts. The crime was quickly exposed and he was put on trial at the Old Bailey. Knowing that he faced the death sentence, Dodd begged the court for leniency, arguing that he had already repaid the money in full and was being 'pursued with oppressive cruelty'. The jury took ten minutes to find him guilty but recommended him to mercy. Dodd also received the support of Dr Samuel Johnson, the Lord Mayor and a petition containing 30,000 signatures. It was to no avail. On 27 June 1777 he was carried by mourning coach through the crowded streets of London and hanged at Tyburn.

5 February

The crimes of Mr and Mrs Sloane were so scandalous
that many Victorian newspapers did not dare print
the full details. Most upsetting to the sensitive
disposition of the age was the allegation that
the couple had forced their 16-year-old servant
Jane Wilbred to eat a turnip filled with her own
excrement. Jane, a pauper orphan abandoned in a
union workhouse, had been picked out for service
by Theresa Sloane in July 1849 and taken back to
the family home in Temple, central London. She was
treated well at first but over Christmas was
accused of frightening George Sloane's favourite
songbird to death and placed on starvation rations.
Jane was left out in the cold, made to clean the
stairs in the middle of the night and beaten with a
shoe. By mid-November 1850 she was in such a filthy
and emaciated state that a neighbouring barrister
intervened and took her away to a hospital. She was
covered in bruises and weighed just over 4 stone
(instead of 7 or 8). Mr and Mrs Sloane appeared
at the Old Bailey on 5 February 1851 and were
each sentenced to two years' imprisonment after
pleading guilty to assault.

6 February

The seventeenth-century Scottish lord Patrick
Stewart, grandson of James V, was known as 'Black
Patie' for his oppressive rule. Like many tyrants,
the 2nd Earl of Orkney loved extravagant displays
of wealth and power: he travelled everywhere with
fifty musketeers, insisted on having his dinner
and supper served to the sound of trumpets,
and furnished his homes with a huge collection of
weapons. He made his own laws; forced the poor to
work his land, on his boats and in his quarries;
and banned anyone selling the products of their
labour without his permission. The earl also
became known for using allegations of witchcraft
to seize the lands of anybody he particularly
disliked. Eventually, in 1610, he was accused of
treason for usurping the authority of King James
and imprisoned at Edinburgh Castle. This did not
prevent him ordering his son to return to Orkney
and retake the Earl's Palace. The rebellion was
quickly suppressed and Black Patie was sentenced
to death. He was beheaded on 6 February 1615.

7 February

Twenty-seven-year-old Thomas Sherwood became
a Catholic martyr on this day in 1579 after he
refused to recognise the supremacy of Elizabeth I.
His act of treason was based on a Papal Bull
issued in 1670, which excommunicated the queen
and branded her a heretic and usurper of the
throne (after the death of Catholic Queen Mary).
Sherwood was arrested and tortured on the rack
in the Tower of London in an attempt to make
him give up the name of other Catholics and the
location where he heard Mass. Bede Camm's *Lives of
the English Martyrs* states that by the time his
interrogators finished, he had lost the use of his
limbs. He was then cast naked into 'a very dark
and fetid dungeon'. Sherwood was put on trial for
high treason at the Court of the Queen's Bench
in Westminster on 1 February on the grounds that
he claimed the queen 'is a schismatic and an
heretic, to the very great scandal and derogation
of the person of our said Lady the Queen, and the
subversion of the state of this realm of England'.
For this he was sentenced to be hanged, drawn and
quartered at Tyburn.

8 February

The beheading of Mary, Queen of Scots on this day in 1587 did not exactly go to plan. That morning she was led to the scaffold at the Great Hall at Fotheringhay Castle in Northamptonshire, dressed in a velvet petticoat and black satin bodice. A white veil was placed over her head before she knelt upon a cushion before the block and uttered her last words (in Latin): 'Into your hands, Lord, I commend my spirit.' The executioner then swung his axe, only to miss her neck and hit the back of her skull. It took another two blows to finish the job. But when he tried to pick up her severed head he came away with only her auburn wig, revealing that Mary really had short, grey hair. At that moment the queen's Skye Terrier scampered out from under her skirts, covered in blood. The reason for her execution was her involvement in the Babington plot to install her on the throne as a Catholic Queen of England. The proof of her treason was found in coded letters (deciphered by the spymaster Sir Francis Walsingham) which encouraged the assassination of her Protestant cousin Elizabeth I.

9 February

London, 1942. The city is in total darkness.
Everywhere you look, windows have been blacked
out and the streetlamps turned off so as not to
guide the German bombers to their target. It is
only in the morning light that the people become
aware of the devastation caused by the Blitz. But
today a new killer has emerged, as evidenced by
the discovery of the dead body of Evelyn Hamilton,
a teacher in her 40s, in an air-raid shelter in
Marylebone, not far from Marble Arch. She has been
strangled and her handbag is missing. The next day,
another woman is strangled and sexually mutilated
with a tin-opener in Soho. Two more women are
murdered on the 12th and 13th. On the 14th, the
so-called 'Blackout Ripper' strikes for a fifth time.
This time he is disturbed by a delivery boy and
leaves behind his gas mask with its unique number.
Armed with this clue, detectives arrest Gordon
Frederick Cummins, an RAF serviceman based at
Regent's Park, on the 16th. Cummins was convicted
of murder and sentenced to death. He was hanged at
Wandsworth Prison during an air raid on 25 June.

10 February

The 'Button and Badge' murder case takes its
name from the two crucial clues found next to the
victim's body. Nellie Trew, 16, was found raped
and strangled on Eltham Common on the morning of
10 February 1918. She had disappeared the previous
night on a trip to the library. Detectives had
little to go on, other than an imitation military
badge in the shape of a tiger and a black bone
button left behind at the scene, possibly as the
result of a struggle between the killer and his
victim. Pictures of both were released to the
newspapers in the hope someone might come forward.
A few hours later, 21-year-old former soldier
David Greenwood walked into a police station and
claimed that he had sold his badge to a strange
man on a tram. Officers quickly discovered that
he lived close to Nellie Trew and Eltham Common.
Even more damningly, he had a rip in his overcoat
where a button had been torn out and the piece of
wire found attached to the button was the same
unique type found at his workplace, the Hewson
Manufacturing Company. The evidence was enough to
convict him of murder.

11 February

William Hogarth's series of engravings *The Four Stages of Cruelty* (1751) tell the story of a criminal's journey from cruelty to animals to highway robbery and murder. Although the main character, Tom Nero, is a fictional creation, Hogarth included references to real villains in his engravings. One of them is James Field, an Irishman who gained a reputation as a boxer (albeit not a particularly good one). In May 1750, he and three other men robbed a couple walking through Moorfields in London and got away with 14 shillings, a pair of spectacles and a tobacco box. Warrants were made for Field's arrest but the local constables were so afraid of him and his gang that months passed before they were able to catch him unawares at his den, The Fox pub in Drury Lane. Field was convicted of highway robbery at the Old Bailey and was hanged on 11 February 1751. Hogarth inserted his name into two engravings in his series: on a poster referring to a boxing match between Field and George 'The Barber' Taylor, and above a skeleton in the background of the dissection scene in the fourth picture, 'The Reward of Cruelty'.

12 February

Lady Jane Grey was Queen of England for just nine days before being cast into the Tower of London and charged with high treason. She was beheaded on this day in 1554, aged only 16, and became a martyr for those Protestants persecuted by her successor 'Bloody' Mary. Her reluctant rise to the throne came about when Edward VI (the 15-year-old son of Henry VIII) unexpectedly named her as his successor over his half-sisters Mary and Elizabeth. She was officially crowned on 10 July 1553 but nine days later, while her father-in-law – the powerful Duke of Northumberland – was away from London, the Privy Council proclaimed Lady Mary as the rightful queen. Lady Jane Grey, her husband and her father-in-law (who was rumoured to have poisoned Edward VI) were all arrested. Jane was sentenced to death, either by burning or beheading, but Mary initially decided to spare her life. That all changed when in January 1554 her father, the Duke of Suffolk, and two brothers joined 'Wyatt's Rebellion', a popular revolt against Queen Mary's plan to marry the future Spanish king Philip II.

13 February

The wealthy seventeenth-century landowner Thomas
Thynne (nicknamed Tom of Ten Thousand because of
his rumoured annual income) was murdered not for
his money but for his wife. In February 1682, he
was travelling down London's Pall Mall when three
assassins stopped his coach and shot him with a
blunderbuss. Thynne managed to flee back home to
Cannon Row but died the next morning (the 13th).
The killers were arrested the same day: Captain
Christopher Vratz, George Borowski and John Stern.
Under questioning, Vratz made a partial confession which implicated his employer, Count Karl
Johann von Königsmark of Sweden, who had spent the
previous six months seducing Thynne's 15-year-old
wife Lady Elizabeth Percy while she was staying
with friends in the Netherlands. Determined to
have her for himself (as well as her inheritance),
Königsmark challenged Thynne to a duel but Thynne
refused. All four conspirators were tried at the
Old Bailey: the three assassins were convicted of
murder and condemned to death, while Königsmark
was acquitted of being an accessory, possibly with
the help of a bribed jury. Vratz, Borowski and Stern
were hanged at the scene of the crime on 10 March.

14 February

The sixteenth-century gentlewoman Alice Arden
had been trying to kill her husband for two years.
If she had ever loved Thomas Arden, the feelings
had long turned to hate. Her true passion was for
the low-born servant Mosbie, a 'black and swarthy'
tailor who was a regular visitor to their home
at Faversham Abbey. Alice's first attempt to kill
Thomas failed when he spat out his poisoned milk
in disgust. So she spent ten pounds on a hired
killer with the appropriate name of Black Will.
After a series of botched plots, it was decided
to conceal the hit man in the parlour closet to
await Thomas' return on the evening of Valentine's
Day 1551. At an agreed signal, Black Will emerged
and strangled the unwitting Mr Arden with a towel
before Mosbie battered him over the head with
an iron. Mrs Arden finished the job by stabbing
her husband seven or eight times in the chest.
The corpse, dressed in nightgown and slippers,
was left in a field while the newly widowed wife
shed fake tears. The deceit did not last long.
Confronted with the bloodstained knife, Alice
confessed and was burnt to death in Canterbury.

15 February

Not that many centuries ago it was believed that a victim's corpse would bleed if touched by his or her killer. This 'evidence' was used as late as 1688 at the trial of Philip Stansfield in Edinburgh for the murder of his father, Sir James Stansfield, who was found strangled in a river near his home in Newmilns. It was claimed that when Philip was asked to lift the body, the victim's blood 'defiled all his hands, which struck him with such a terror that he immediately let his father's head and body fall with violence and fled from the body and in consternation and confusion cryed, Lord, have mercy upon me!' This, the King's Advocate argued, was 'God's usual method of discovering murderers'. Stansfield was convicted of murder and sentenced to be hanged at the cross in Edinburgh on 15 February 1688. The judges also ordered that his right hand be cut off as punishment for killing his father, his tongue be cut out for cursing his father, and his body hung in chains on the road between Edinburgh and Leith as punishment for drinking a toast to the downfall of the king, James II.

16 February

In 1811, the women who promenaded up and down the streets of London found themselves the victims of a new and unusual terror. No warning was given, and the effects of the attack were not always felt immediately. The targets only realised something had happened when their muslin, chemises and gowns fell in tatters round their feet, singed and burnt by some strange chemical. On the evening of 16 February, one of the perpetrators of this dangerous practical joke was caught after squirting aqua fortis (nitric acid) over several 'cyprians' (Regency slang for promiscuous women) in Fleet Street. Two months later, Edward Beazley was tried at the Old Bailey for damaging Mary Ann Sutton's cloth pelisse (a type of coat), worth £2. Miss Sutton told the court that Beazley not only burnt her clothing but also slapped her face while she was walking with another single lady. When captured, she claimed, Beazley confessed to attacking six other couples in the same manner. Beazley told the jury: 'I never did it, they told me they would forgive me, that made me say that.' The jury convicted him and he was sentenced to be whipped in prison before being released.

17 February

Ten men were executed on the 'fatal tree' at Tyburn in London on 17 February 1744:

- William Clark, a 50-year-old Englishman, claimed the bite of a mad dog led him to steal silverware, five shirts and a wig from his landlord.
- John Burton and Henry Burrows, aged 21 and 22, forsook their trades as a wagon driver and clog maker for stealing four woollen nightcaps.
- Joseph Isaacs, 19, convicted of stealing a silver plate, a towel, a tablecloth and a napkin.
- Peter Rogers, a 35-year-old French bookkeeper who forged a bill of exchange for £25 after being put out of business.
- Samuel Moses, a 35-year-old Dutch Jew described as 'the Father and Counsellor of a Set of vile young Rogues', and his 19-year-old accomplice Solomon Athorn, for ransacking the home of a silversmith.
- Jacob Cordosa, 24, who escaped from Newgate Prison while awaiting transportation for the burglary of a linen-draper.
- Joseph Leath, 24, a Shropshire-born former soldier convicted of highway robbery.
- Thomas Hill, 29, who counterfeited a seal to evade payment of a sixpence tax on sets of playing cards. He also confessed to living with a woman who was not his wife.

18 February

The conviction and imprisonment of the writer
Oscar Wilde stemmed from a calling card left at
the Albemarle club on this day in 1895:

> For Oscar Wilde, posing somdomite
> Marquess of Queensberry

Wilde, who had celebrated the opening of his
play *The Importance of Being Earnest* four days
earlier, should have ignored the allegation of
sodomy (misspelled on the card). Instead he sued
the Marquess of Queensberry, the father of his
lover Lord Alfred Douglas, for criminal libel.
It resulted in a scandalous trial, during which
Queensberry claimed to be able to call several
male prostitutes as witnesses. Wilde, who had
up to that point claimed that his friendships
with young men were perfectly innocent, dropped
the case. Three weeks later, Wilde found himself
on trial at the Old Bailey for gross indecency.
The case is famous for Wilde's defence of 'the love
that dare not speak its name' but the jury were
unable to reach a verdict. He was convicted at
a second trial and sentenced to two years' hard
labour. After his release in 1897 he spent the next
three years in exile, writing his poem 'The Ballad
of Reading Gaol', before dying on 30 September 1900.

19 February

The legend of 'Spring-heeled Jack' seems to have started in early 1838, following a series of reports about a prankster terrorising the inhabitants of London. Several ladies had fainted as a result and on one occasion he caused a horse-drawn carriage to crash before bounding over a 9ft wall while shrieking with laughter. At the height of the scare, on 19 February that year, a man rang the gate at the home of a Mr Alsop in Bow, east London. When Mr Alsop's teenage daughter Jane answered the door, the figure claimed to have caught Spring-heeled Jack and asked her to bring a candle. Once outside, he threw off his cloak to reveal he was wearing a skintight white oilskin costume and a helmet. His eyes burned a fiery red. As she began to flee, the creature vomited blue and white flame from his mouth and lunged at her with metallic claws, ripping her dress and scratching her arms and shoulder. A week later, another girl was attacked with by a man with a 'blue flame' in Limehouse. Further sightings were reported across London, in Sussex, Devon, Lincoln and Liverpool, but 'Jack' was never identified.

20 February

On 20 February 1677, four witches and a warlock
were executed in Scotland after the mysterious intervention of a 14-year-old deaf girl.
The teenager, viewed by the superstitious of that
time as blessed with gifts from God, had arrived
at the home of Sir George Maxwell, laird of Nether
Pollok near Glasgow, to find him seriously ill
with sharp pains in his right side and shoulder.
Through a kind of sign language she convinced
two servants to follow her to the home of a local
woman, Janet Mathie, whose son had previously
stolen from Sir George's orchard. From behind the
chimney, the girl produced a wax effigy with pins
stuck in the right side and shoulder. The pins
were removed and Sir George recovered. A few
months later, the laird fell ill again: this time
a clay figure was found under the bed of Mathie's
son John Stewart, who soon implicated three other
women and his 14-year-old sister Annabel. Only
Annabel was spared the death sentence; the rest
were hanged and burnt on Gallow Green in Paisley.
Twenty years later, the infamous 'Bargarran
Witches' were executed on the same spot for
bewitching an 11-year-old girl.

21 February

King James I of Scotland was assassinated in
a monastery sewer on this day in 1437 as part
of a failed coup. It was a malodorous end to a
thirty-one-year reign that began at the age of 12,
while he was a prisoner of Henry IV. James spent
the next eighteen years as a hostage, until the
Scots paid a £40,000 ransom. Having extinguished
a rebellion led by his rival 'James the Fat',
the king decided to lay siege to the English-
held Roxburgh Castle in the Scottish Borders.
The wretched failure of this enterprise, and his
attempt to raise taxes to continue the war, seems
to have encouraged a group of plotters led by
Sir Robert Graham. On 21 February James I, dressed
in his nightgown and slippers, was preparing to
retire for the night at Blackfriars in Perth when
a group of armed soldiers attempted to break into
the Royal bedchamber. The queen's ladies-in-
waiting held the door shut while James prised up
a floorboard and crawled into the sewer, only to
discover that the exit was barred (supposedly to
prevent tennis balls being swept away). Cornered
in the tunnel, the king was silenced with sixteen
stab wounds.

22 February

Solicitor Herbert Rowse Armstrong might have got away with the murder of his wife if he had not tried to bump off a rival lawyer a few months later. Mrs Katharine Armstrong died at their home in Hay-on-Wye on 22 February 1921 after a long illness involving delusions, partial paralysis and vomiting. Armstrong, who served in the First World War as a major in the army, had appeared the doting husband, leaving work early to care for her and reading to her in bed. Eight months later he invited another Hay solicitor, Oswald Martin, to afternoon tea, supposedly to discuss a case they were both working on (for opposing sides). During the meeting, Amstrong passed a cake to Martin with the words: 'Excuse fingers'. Martin became sick after eating it and the doctor became suspicious about the similarities between his illness and that of Mrs Armstrong. Police exhumed Mrs Armstrong's body and found that her body contained a large amount of arsenic, inconsistent with suicide. Armstong, who claimed to have bought arsenic to kill dandelions in his garden, was convicted of murdering his wife after a trial in Hereford. He was hanged on 31 May 1922.

23 February

The murderer John Lee became known as 'The Man
They Could Not Hang' after the gallows trapdoor
failed to open three times in a row on this day
in 1885. His execution at Exeter Prison was first
postponed for an official investigation and then
cancelled altogether after the Home Secretary
decided that 'it would shock the feeling of
anyone if a man had twice to pay the pangs of
imminent death'. Lee was sentenced to penal
servitude for life but was given his freedom in
1907. He became an Edwardian celebrity, touring
the country with his story. Almost forgotten was
his crime, the murder of Emma Keyse, who employed
him as a groundskeeper at her home 'The Glen' in
Babbacombe Bay in Devon. In the early hours of
15 November 1884, her dead body was found on the
floor of the dining room. The killer, or killers,
had apparently cut her throat before starting a
number of fires around the house. The evidence
against Lee was circumstantial – he had a suspicious cut to his arm and had previously talked of
taking revenge against Ms Keyse in a dispute over
wages – but he was convicted despite his claim
of innocence.

24 February

Lieutenant General Thomas Picton was a genuine war hero: the most senior officer to die at the Battle of Waterloo. He was also a convicted torturer. The crime dated back to 1801, when Picton was Governor of Trinidad. The victim was 10-year-old Louisa Calderon, who was suspected of robbing her lover's friend (it was apparently common for girls to become mothers at 12). When Louisa refused to confess, Picton authorised her to be subjected to 'picketing' – forcing her to stand with her left big toe on a wooden spike, her right hand tied to her right leg and her left hand suspended from a pulley. She was then placed in irons for eight months. Picton was eventually tried at the King's Bench in London. His defence – that torture was legal under the laws of Trinidad at the time – was rejected by the jury and he was convicted on 24 February 1806. His lawyers sought a retrial on the grounds of the girl's questionable character and Picton's belief that torture was acceptable in Trinidad. At the new hearing a jury acquitted him of the charge of torture, allowing him to continue his army career with the Duke of Wellington.

25 February

The extraordinary life of the career criminal
Charles Peace ended on the gallows on this day
in 1879. Peace, the youngest son of a lion-tamer,
turned to burglary aged 19 after injuring his
leg at an iron mill in Sheffield. He used his first
prison sentence to master playing a one-stringed
violin and following his release from jail
supplemented his ill-gotten income by performing
concerts as 'the modern Paganini'. In 1872, after
serving a six-year sentence for housebreaking,
he attempted to settle down with his wife and
children and earn a living as a picture framer.
Four years later he shot and killed PC Nicholas
Cock while leaving the scene of a burglary in
Manchester, but an innocent man was convicted
of the murder and sentenced to life in prison.
Undeterred, Peace murdered his former neighbour
Arthur Dyson (Peace later claimed he had an
affair with Dyson's wife) in
November 1876. The resulting
manhunt and £100 reward
gripped the country but
Peace remained on the run
until his arrest in London
two years later during yet
another burglary. Peace
attempted to conceal his
true identity but was
convicted of the Dyson
murder and hanged outside
Armley Gaol in Leeds.

CHARLES PEACE.

26 February

The Roman Catholic priest William Sawtrey was the
first person to be burned at the stake for heresy
under the new law of *De heretico comburendo*
(passed during the reign of Henry IV). Sawtrey,
from Lynn in Norfolk, was a follower of the
Lollard sect and was charged on the grounds that
he failed to worship the cross and the saints,
preferred to spend his time preaching instead of
in prayer, believed in consubstantiation (rather
than transubstantiation) and thought the wealth
of the church should be shared with the poor
and needy. He quoted the words of St Augustus,
St Paul and St John to support his position but
was convicted despite appeals to the king and
Parliament. On 26 February 1401, he was condemned
to death and stripped of his status in a bizarre
ceremony that involved removing his robes and his
tonsured hair. Sawtrey was publicly burned alive
at London's Smithfield on 2 March but the severe
punishment did not deter people from 'Lollardy'.
The sect's supporters included John Oldcastle, who
was executed in 1417 after leading a rebellion
against his former friend King Henry V.

27 February

It was 1940. War had been declared but the Battle of Britain was still five months away. Hungry for news, millions of listeners tuned in to the broadcasts of William Joyce, otherwise known as 'Lord Haw-Haw', on Nazi radio:

> The British Ministry of Disinformation has been conducting a systematic campaign of frightening British women and girls about the danger of being injured by splinters from German bombs. The women have reacted to these suggestions and alarms by requesting their milliners to shape the spring and summer hats out of very thin tin plate which is covered with silk, velvet or other draping material.

Joyce continued his broadcasts from Berlin until April 1945. He was captured near the border with Denmark and brought back to London to stand trial for high treason on the basis that he had a British passport (he was in fact Irish-American, but had lived in England since 1921). Joyce, former deputy leader of the British Union of Fascists under Oswald Mosley, was convicted and sentenced to death on 19 September 1945 and executed on 3 January 1946.

28 February

Before her execution on this day in 1608, Margaret
Fernseed confessed that she was a prostitute,
a brothel-keeper and a fencer of stolen goods.
But murder? 'Heaven that knoweth best the
secrets of our hearts, knows that I am innocent.'
Her supposed victim was her husband, the jour-
neyman tailor Anthony Fernseed, who was found
with his throat cut near Lambeth Palace in south
London the previous year. There was a knife in his
hand, but the presence of maggots on the corpse
suggested he had been dumped in the field some
time after death. It was not a robbery – he was
still wearing his rings and had 40 shillings in
his purse. The evidence against his wife was
the turbulent nature of their relationship, her
repeated adultery, her previous attempt to poison
him and her callous attitude when told of his death
(when shown the body she did not cry, but merely
turned her nose up at the smell). It was enough
to secure her conviction. Her punishment was to
be stripped of her clothing, dressed in a cloth
soaked in tar and tied to the stake. She again
refused to confess and was burnt to death.

1 March

The grisly murder of John Hayes on this day in 1726 was solved by publicly exhibiting his severed head on a pole in St Margaret's churchyard in Westminster. Within hours an apprentice to King George I's organ-maker had recognised it as the local carpenter John Hayes, although Hayes' wife Catherine insisted her husband was alive and well.

Two weeks passed before a suspicious relative of Mr Hayes went to view the head, which by now had been pickled in a jar. With the identity confirmed, Mrs Hayes was arrested on suspicion of murder. Keen to prove her innocence, Mrs Hayes asked to see the evidence herself. So, in an extraordinary scene, the head was lifted out of the jar by its hair and presented to the widow. 'Oh, it is my dear husband's head!' she cried, taking it in her arms and kissing it before fainting. But the very same day Mr Hayes' legs and arms were found in a pond in Marylebone Fields. At her trial, she denied plotting with her lover Thomas Billings and her lodger Thomas Wood to kill Mr Hayes but was convicted of petty treason and burnt to death on 9 May.

2 March

The discovery of a human skull in the garden of the TV presenter David Attenborough in 2010 was the last act in a notorious Victorian murder case known as the Barnes Mystery. It belonged to an eccentric widow,

Julia Martha Thomas, who was killed at her home in Richmond on this day in 1879. Neighbours had noticed an unusual smell coming from the house but thought nothing more of it. Three days later, a box of body parts was found on the Thames shore near Barnes Bridge but they were not at first linked to the disappearance. It was only when neighbours alerted police on 18 March that suspicion began to fall on Mrs Thomas' maidservant Kate Webster, a 30-year-old Irishwoman who had been posing as her employer so she could sell off the contents of the house. Webster went on the run, leaving officers to find scorched bones in the hearth and human fat in the laundry copper boiler. She was arrested in Ireland on 29 March and returned to London to stand trial at the Old Bailey. Webster was convicted of murder and confessed a day before her hanging on 29 July.

3 March

The Campden Wonder has been described as the most baffling murder case in English history. It began with the disappearance of 70-year-old William Harrison while collecting rent for Lady Viscountess Campden in Gloucester in August 1660. All that remained were his bloodstained hat, band and comb by the side of the highway. Suspicion fell on his servant John Perry, who eventually confessed that his mother and brother had murdered Harrison for the rent money. They were tried and convicted at the King's Gaol in Gloucester on 3 March 1661 and condemned to death. All three were hanged a few days later. The twist in the tale came the following year, when William Harrison returned to Chipping Camden very much alive. Harrison claimed he had been robbed, kidnapped, transported to Turkey and sold into slavery. Upon the death of his new master, an 87-year-old physician, he bought his passage back to England using a silver bowl. Whether this story is true or not, the 'Campden Wonder' would be used for centuries as an example of the risks involved in trying to prove murder without a body.

4 March

Atomic energy expert Dr Alan Nunn May had just finished giving a physics lecture to his students at King's College University on 4 March 1946 when two Special Branch detectives walked into the theatre and arrested him under the Official Secrets Act. Dr May, a former member of the Communist Party, confessed to providing a report on atomic research to Russian agents while working on a nuclear reactor project in Canada. In return he was given two bottles of whisky and 700 Canadian dollars. 'I only embarked on it because I thought this was a contribution I could make for the safety of mankind,' the 34-year-old scientist told the court. 'I certainly didn't do it for gain.' May's sentence was ten years' imprisonment for giving away what the judge called 'one of the country's most precious secrets'. Four years later, Dr Klaus Fuchs, a German scientist who pledged allegiance to Britain during the war, confessed that he too had passed atomic secrets to the Russians between 1943 and 1947. Fuchs was a witness to the first nuclear test in 1945 and worked on designs for a hydrogen bomb. He was jailed for fourteen years.

5 March

The extraordinary life of the poet and playwright Richard Savage was a mixture of miserable
misfortune and incredible luck. His early years
are shrouded in mystery but in 1718, at the age
of 21, he claimed to be the illegitimate outcast
son of the Countess of Macclesfield and accused
her of cheating him out of a £6,000 inheritance
and attempting to banish him to the West Indies.
This story won him the sympathy and friendship
of influential figures, including Alexander Pope
and Samuel Johnson. It also saved him from the
hangman's noose. In November 1727 he stabbed a man
in the belly with his sword during a brawl in a
coffee shop. The victim, James Sinclair, died the
next day. Savage was convicted of murder at the
Old Bailey the following month and condemned to
death, only to be freed from prison on 5 March 1728
after the Countess of Hertford related his unfortunate history to the queen and secured a royal
pardon. Savage spent the rest of his life in
drunken poverty and died in debtor's prison in
1843. The following year, Samuel Johnson published
his biography *Life of Savage*.

6 March

The Times, 6 March 1929

WOMAN'S MASQUERADE AS A MAN – DISCLOSURE IN PRISON

A woman, who had for some years since the War posed
as an ex-Army officer, was compelled to disclose
her sex a few days ago at Brixton Prison, where she
had been taken as a male prisoner, charged with
contempt of Court in failing to appear for public
examination in bankruptcy. After the disclosure she
was removed to the women's prison in Hollway.

The woman in question was Valerie Arkell-Smith,
a cross-dresser who, having escaped from an
abusive husband, began masquerading as Sir Victor
Barker, a colonel in the RAF. It was in this
guise that she married a woman, Elfrida Hayward,
joined the right wing group 'National Fascisti'
and engaged in boxing matches with fellow
members, and set up a restaurant near London's
Charing Cross Road. When this business venture
failed, Colonel Barker was summoned to bankruptcy proceedings, and her arrest for failing to
attend the court led to the discovery of her true
identity. She was later convicted of making a false
statement on her marriage certificate and jailed
for nine months. Valerie lived as a man for the
rest of her life and died in 1960.

7 March

On 7 March 1811, a middle-aged army officer
and a 16-year-old drummer boy were hanged for
their involvement in the gay sex scandal known
as the 'Vere Street Coterie'. It centred upon
a 'molly house', or homosexual brothel, at which
(it was reported) men consorted as 'bridesmaids and
bridesmen' and as many as four couples consummated
their vows simultaneously. As such activity was
a capital offence at this time, the visitors
attempted to keep their true identities hidden
using pseudonyms such as Lady Godiva, the Duchess
of Gloucester and Blackeyed Leonora. The secret
did not last for long, and in July 1810 the local
constables raided the club at the White Swan in
Vere Street (near London's Clare Market). Six of
the twenty-seven men arrested by police were
sentenced to stand at the pillory while more than
fifty women hurled rotten eggs, vegetables, fish,
dead cats, mud, dung and buckets of blood at their
heads. John Hepburn, 42, and Thomas White, 16,
were not at the club but the publicity led another
soldier to testify that the pair had sex at the
White Swan two months earlier and they were
convicted and sentenced to death.

8 March

The 'Clitheroe Abduction' of 1891 led to a famous legal decision that a husband did not have the power to imprison his wife against her will. The wife in question was 47-year-old Emily Jackson, who had decided not to follow her husband Edmund Jackson to New Zealand to start a new life. Edmund returned to England and obtained a court order for the restitution of his 'conjugal rights' but Emily refused. On 8 March 1891 she was seized by her husband outside Clitheroe Parish Church and held captive at his sister's house in Blackburn. Her friends and relatives went to court in an attempt to free her but two judges ruled that under common law, 'a husband has the right to detain his wife in his house if he chooses'. The issue was finally settled by the Court of Appeal after Emily was granted a private interview with three law lords. They issued a writ of habeas corpus after deciding that a wife could not be a 'mere slave of her husband'. Emily returned to Clitheroe to the disgust of her neighbours, who burnt an effigy of her in the street. She died seven years later.

9 March

Mary Queen of Scots was pregnant with the future
King James I of England when she witnessed the
murder of her private secretary on this day in 1566.
The queen was having supper at Holyrood Palace
in Edinburgh when her husband Lord Darnley and
a group of Protestant rebels led by Lord Ruthven
entered her private chamber and informed her that
David Rizzio had 'offended her Majesty's honour'
(insinuating that they had slept together). Rizzio
attempted to hide behind the queen's skirts but was
dragged away and stabbed fifty-six times. His body
was then hurled down a stairway and stripped of
everything of value. When the queen demanded to
know the reason for this 'wicked deed', Lord Darnley
complained that the queen had stopped coming to his
chamber and preferred to spend the evening playing
cards with Rizzio. The queen replied: 'I shall never
be your wife, nor lie with you; nor shall never like
well, till I gar you have as sore a heart as I have
presently.' Lord Darnley was found strangled in an
orchard the following year.

10 March

John the Painter believed he would become
'the admiration of the world' when he embarked on
a terrorist campaign against Britain during the
American Revolution. Instead, thanks partly to
his incompetence, he quickly sank into obscurity. His real name was James Aitken, although
the 25-year-old Scot was known by many aliases
during his career as a robber, thief, rapist and,
finally, arsonist. Aitken, with the approval of the
American diplomat Silas Deane, came up with a plan
to destroy the crucial and badly guarded Royal
Navy stores in Portsmouth. So in December 1776 he
lit three home-made firebombs in the rope house,
burning it down at a cost of £20,000. The navy
wrote it off as an accident until Aitken started a
series of fires in warehouses in Bristol, which so
alarmed the city that King George III authorised
a large reward. A description of a suspicious
housepainter called John was circulated and, in
February 1777, Aitken was arrested in Odiham.
He eventually confessed his schemes to a Welsh
painter who befriended him during prison visits
and on 10 March Aitken was hanged at a height of
67ft from the mizzenmast of the HMS *Arethusa* in
Portsmouth Dockyard.

11 March

On 11 March 1619, a mother and her two daughters
were executed for using witchcraft to kill the
sons and heirs of the Earl and Countess of Rutland.
The so-called Witches of Belvoir – Joan, Margaret
and Philippa Flower – were employed as servants
at the noble couple's castle near Grantham in
Lincolnshire before being sacked on suspicion of
theft. Vowing revenge (according to one version
of the story), they buried a mitten belonging
to the earl's infant son while chanting 'as the
glove does rot, so will the lord'. The boy died a
short time later and the grieving parents became
convinced that the Flower family were responsible.
Following their arrest, mother Joan Flower died
after choking on a piece of bread and was buried
at a crossroads. The sisters admitted their mother
had pricked the glove, boiled it in water and blood
and used the glove to stroke her familiar, a cat
called Rutterkin. They also confessed that they
were assisted by 'familiars' or animal spirits,
which they suckled from their 'witch's teats'
(an extra nipple which dispensed blood rather
than milk). They were duly condemned to death, but
the curse continued: the earl's second son died the
following year.

12 March

The death of Lady Henrietta Tichborne on this day in 1868 began a mammoth six-year legal battle over her estate that ended with her heir being exposed as an impostor. At the centre of the story was a man who claimed to be Roger Tichborne, who disappeared during an ocean voyage from Brazil to Jamaica in 1854. Convinced he was still alive, Lady Tichborne placed advertisements in newspapers around the world and, in 1865, a bankrupt living in Australia under the name Thomas Castro came forward. Lady Tichborne claimed to recognise him during a meeting in Paris and gave him a yearly allowance of £1,000, to the horror of members of the family, who believed Castro was a fake. After Lady Tichborne's death from heart failure, Castro took the seat assigned for the chief mourner at the funeral. He then launched a civil action to claim his inheritance. The case lasted for ten months and resulted in Castro being charged with perjury. After a ten-month trial in the Queen's Bench in Westminster Hall, during which it was argued he was in fact Arthur Orton, a butcher's son from Wapping, he was convicted and sentenced to fourteen years in jail.

13 March

Hangman John Price ended up swinging on the gallows himself after committing a murder on this day in 1718. His ironic death was perhaps not an unexpected one. As a child, Price was known as a habitual thief and a fearsome cusser. At 18 he robbed a market-woman of 18 shillings near Brentwood in Essex and was sentenced to death, only to be reprieved on the basis that if such a brazen liar had pleaded guilty, he must be innocent. He then spent eighteen years as a sailor, serving on a man-of-war, before taking up a new career as Common Hangman for the County of Middlesex (although Price preferred to call himself 'Finisher of the Law'). Eighteen months later, at the age of 41, he was caught drunkenly attacking a woman in Bunhill Fields while demanding her money and shouting 'Damn you for a Bitch, why don't you take it in your Field and put it in? If you won't put it in I'll rip you up.' The victim, Elizabeth White, a married gingerbread seller, died four days later of her injuries. Price, nicknamed 'Jack Ketch' after the notorious seventeenth-century executioner, was hanged on 31 May.

14 March

The poisoner Frederick Seddon had one last card to play before he was sentenced to death on this day in 1912. He stood in the dock of the Old Bailey, made a Masonic sign with his hand and said: 'I declare before the Great Architect of the Universe I am not guilty, my Lord.' Seddon knew that the judge, Mr Justice Bucknill, was a Freemason. The judge appeared to be on the verge of tears as he replied:

> From what you have said, you and I know we both belong to one Brotherhood and it is all the more painful to me to have to say what I am saying. But our Brotherhood does not encourage crime; on the contrary it condemns it. I pray you again to make your peace with the Great Architect of the Universe.

Seddon's failed bid for mercy had only confirmed his arrogance. This was a man who had gone against the advice of his barrister and given evidence about the painful death of his lodger Eliza Barrow from arsenic poisoning in Islington, north London. So slim was the evidence that many believed he would be acquitted – until Seddon talked himself into the noose.

15 March

London was still reeling from the murders of three policemen by Russian anarchists when a Jewish slum landlord named Leon Beron was found murdered on Clapham Common in 1911. He had been bludgeoned about the head with an iron bar and stabbed repeatedly in the body, but the injuries that attracted most attention were two distinctive, symmetrical S-shaped cuts on either side of the victim's face, described by the police surgeon as 'like the F holes on each side of a violin'. Was this a clue to the identity of the killer? Did the cuts refer to the Russian word 'spic' meaning police spy? Was this murder linked to the mysterious 'Peter the Painter' who had seemingly vanished without trace? The detectives thought not and arrested a 29-year-old Russian baker called Stinie Morrison, who had been seen with Beron the previous night and had spots of blood on his clothing. Although circumstantial, the evidence was enough for a jury to convict Morrison of murder at the Old Bailey on 15 March 1911. Morrison, who maintained his innocence for the rest of his life, was sentenced to death but granted a reprieve by Home Secretary Winston Churchill.

16 March

The case of Frederick Bailey
Deeming unfolded almost simultaneously on opposite sides
of the world. On 16 March 1892,
four days after his arrest
on suspicion of murdering
his second wife in Melbourne,
Australia, detectives discovered the bodies of his first
wife and their five children
under the floor of their home in
Rainhill, Liverpool. Deeming
had killed all but one of
the victims by cutting their
throats, a grisly method which
led newspapers to speculate
whether Deeming was the
unidentified serial killer
'Jack the Ripper'. The investigation established that

Deeming had killed his first wife Marie and their
children (aged between 18 months and 9 years old)
in July 1891 after meeting Emily Mather in Rainhill.
He dug a pit in the kitchen floor, entombed their
bodies in cement and then replaced the flagstones.
Deeming then took Mather to Australia (where he
had spent several years in the 1880s) but ended up
killing her as well, burying her body in cement
under the bedroom floor. It was only discovered
because of the foul smell. In April, Deeming was
convicted murder of Emily Mather and sentenced to
death on 2 May. He was hanged three weeks later.

17 March

Skevington's Daughter was an instrument of torture designed to compress the body into a ball until blood poured from the nose and mouth. The device was invented by the Lieutenant of the Tower of London, Sir Leonard Skeffington, and became known as Scavenger's Daughter (in contrast to the rack, which was known as the Duke of Exeter's Daughter). It is recorded as being used on Thomas Miagh, an Irishman suspected of treason, at the Tower of London, in 1580. According to an official report, dated 17 March that year, Miagh refused to confess 'notwithstanding that they had made trial of him by the torture of Skevington's Irons, and with so much sharpness as was in their judgement for the man and his cause convenient'. Miagh was later tortured with the rack and in 1581 carved his name into the wall of his cell at the Tower along with an inscription which refers to his sufferings:

> THOMAS MIAGH WHICH LIETHE HERE ALONE
> THAT FAYNE WOLD FROM HENS BEGON
> BY TORTURE STRAUNGE MI TROUTH WAS
> TRYED YET OF MY LIBERTIE DENIED

18 March

No worse deed for the English race was done than
this was, since they first sought out the land of
Britain. Men murdered him, but God exalted him.
In life he was an earthly king; after death he is
now a heavenly saint.

Anglo-Saxon Chronicle

On 18 March 978, Edward, the 16-year-old King
of England, was assassinated while visiting his
10-year-old half-brother Ethelred (the Unready) at
Corfe Castle in Dorset. According to one version
of the story, he was stabbed in the back after
he accepted a drink from his stepmother Elfrida.
The king managed to ride away but fell from the
saddle and was dragged along by his horse into a
wood. Other accounts accuse Ethelred's advisers or
even Elfrida herself of delivering the fatal blow,
and claim that his body was thrown into the marsh,
only to be discovered intact and reburied without
royal honours at Wareham. His body was finally
given a ceremonial burial at Shaftesbury Abbey in
980 and by 1001 (while Ethelred was still on the
throne), Edward was regarded as a saint and martyr.
His remains were lost during the Dissolution of
the Monasteries by Henry VIII and were not recovered until 1931.

19 March

The Tolpuddle Martyrs were sentenced to seven years' transportation on this day in 1834. Their crime was not the creation of their trade union, the Friendly Society of Agricultural Labourers (which was then legal), but the 'administering of an unlawful oath'. In reality, it was a deliberate attempt by the local landlords to crack down on the organisation of workers and the potential for strikes against a background of low wages and working-class unrest. 'I am not sentencing you for any crime you have committed, or that it could be proved that you were about to commit,' said the judge, 'but as an example to the working classes of this country.' The severity of the punishment passed on George Loveless, a Methodist lay preacher, his brother James, Thomas Standfield and his son John, James Brine and James Hammett, led to protest meetings, marches and a petition of 800,000 signatures for their release. The pressure led to the Home Secretary granting a free pardon to the group from Tolpuddle in Dorset in 1836, allowing them to return home. Five of the six moved to Essex before deciding to emigrate to London, Ontario. The sixth remained in Tolpuddle until his death.

20 March

Football was first banned in 1314 in London under Edward II because of the noise caused by men and boys 'hustling over large balls from which many evils may arise'. The punishment for playing this game (instead of a more useful sport like archery) was imprisonment. Over the next 200 years, there were repeated attempts to ban it without success. Its potential for hooliganism was also recognised, as may be seen by this entry from the records of the Middlesex court sessions 20 March 1576 in the reign of Queen Elizabeth I:

At Ruyslippe, Arthur Reynoldes husbandman, Robert Batte yoman, Edward Bennett yoman, Richard Gadberrie husbandman, John Murdoxe husbandman, all of Ruyslippe aforesaid, Thomas Darcye of Woxbridge yoman, and William Davye taylor, Roger Okeley yoman, Thomas Harker husbandman, Thomas Kerton harnismaker, Gybbens Alkyns husbandman, William Rayner husbandman, and Richard Parsonne husbandman, all seven of Woxbridge aforesaid, with unknown malefactors to the number of a hundred, assembled themselves unlawfully and played a certain unlawful game, called footeball, by reason of which unlawful game there rose amongst them a great affray, likely to result in homicides and serious accidents.

21 March

Menu
Rump Steak
Potatoes
Poisoned dumplings

On 21 March 1815, the Turner family sat down for
dinner at their home in Chancery Lane in London.
Within minutes Robert Turner, his wife Charlotte,
and father Haldebart fell seriously ill with
stomach pains and vomiting. Arsenic was found in
the pan used to cook the strange black dumplings
and suspicion quickly fell on the 20-year-old cook
Eliza Fenning, who was charged with attempted
murder. At the trial, Charlotte Turner suggested
that Fenning had borne a grudge after being
threatened with dismissal for going into the room
occupied by the young male apprentices while half
undressed. Fenning, who initially claimed that the
poison must have come from the milk supplied by
another maid, had herself become ill from eating
the dumplings and insisted she was innocent.
However, witnesses had seen her using the drawer
where the arsenic was kept on many occasions.
Fenning was found guilty and sentenced to death.
She had to be carried from the dock 'convulsed
with agony and uttering frightful screams'.
Despite widespread popular support for her innocence, she was hanged in her white wedding gown on
26 June alongside two men convicted of sodomy and
child rape.

22 March

John Hilliker is now remembered as a political
martyr who sacrificed himself in the struggle
against the mechanisation of the wool industry
in the early nineteenth century. The apprentice
shearman was accused of burning down a wool mill
in Semington, Wiltshire, in July 1802. Although the
manager identified him as taking part in the riot,
it was widely believed at the time that he was
innocent. Having refused to name the true culprits,
he was hanged in front of Fisherton jail on his
nineteenth birthday on 22 March 1803. The night
before his execution he wrote a last letter to his
family: 'I hope the Lord will save my soul and that
they will put up a tomb stone at my grave – to be
a warning to all young men and against bad advice
which has been my fate.' His body was carried
across Salisbury Plain by his shearmen colleagues
and buried in Trowbridge. The tomb bears the
inscription: 'This tomb was erected at his earnest
request by the cloth making factories of the
counties of York, Wilts and Somerset as a token of
their love to him and veneration for his memory.'

23 March

The upper-class *femme fatale* Madeleine Smith had
both the motive and the opportunity to kill her
lover. The 21-year-old architect's daughter was
desperate to end the secret affair with warehouse
clerk Pierre L'Angelier without her parents finding
out. L'Angelier, hearing of her engagement to
another man, would not accept anything less than
marriage and threatened to blackmail her with his
stash of love letters. Then, in the early hours of
23 March 1857, L'Angelier collapsed and died at his
lodging house in Glasgow, Scotland. He had been
poisoned with arsenic. The love letters, combined
with the fact that Smith had ordered arsenic from
a local drug store, suggested she was the most
likely suspect. There were, however, no witnesses
to any meeting between the two in the weeks before
his death. At her trial, Smith's calmness and
indifference were noted by journalists and it was
remarked that she entered the dock like 'a belle
entering a ballroom'. The jury were unconvinced
of her guilt and returned the special verdict
'not proven'. Smith, according to *The Scotsman*, was
'either the most fortunate of criminals or the most
unfortunate of women'.

24 March

Mary Ann Cotton
She's dead and she's rotten
She lies in her bed
With her eyes wide open.
Sing, sing! Oh, what can I sing?
Mary Ann Cotton is tied up with string.
Where, where? Up in the air
Selling black puddings a penny a pair.

Mary Ann Cotton is thought to have poisoned
three husbands, a lover, eight children and seven
stepchildren before she was hanged on this day
in 1873. Her tried and tested method was to take
out life insurance on a victim before poisoning
them with arsenic. The symptoms (stomach pain,
vomiting, and diarrhoea) were often misdiagnosed
as 'gastric fever' and it was not until the death
of her stepson, Charles Edward Cotton (who died
at her home in West Auckland, Country Durham,
in 1872), that the use of arsenic was confirmed.
She was charged with a single count of murder
(although the press was full of stories about other
potential victims) and went on trial at Durham
Crown Court in May 1873. Cotton remained calm and
composed while maintaining her innocence but when
the guilty verdict was announced, she fainted
in the dock. After her execution, she became the
subject of the nursery rhyme above.

25 March

Until 1772, any suspected criminals who refused to enter a plea to a charge (either guilty or not guilty) were tortured by being crushed to death with heavy weights. Perhaps the most famous victim of this punishment was the martyr Margaret Clitherow, or St Margaret of York.

In 1586 Margaret, a butcher's wife, was arrested for harbouring a Catholic priest at her home in the Shambles in York city centre. At the time this was a treasonous offence. Margaret refused to enter a plea at the York Assizes and was condemned to death by *peine forte et dure* (hard and strong punishment). It is said she reacted to the sentence with gratitude: 'I am not worthy of so good a death as this'. On Lady Day (Good Friday)

1586 she was forced to lie upon a sharp stone while her hands were stretched out and tied to two posts. A heavy door was then placed over her and weighted with rocks. The agony lasted fifteen minutes before she uttered her last words: 'Jesu! Jesu! Jesu! Have mercy on me!' After death, her right hand was cut off and preserved as a relic at St Mary's Convent in York.

26 March

The 'Scottish Maiden', a precursor of the guil-
lotine, was used in executions in Edinburgh from
the mid-sixteenth century until 1716. One of its
victims was Godfrey McCulloch, a lesser noble
who, in 1690, shot a rival landowner in the leg
and trampled his body with a herd of cattle.
On hearing of the man's death, McCulloch went
into exile in France, leaving behind a string of
debts, only to attempt to return to Scotland in
disguise. Predictably, he was recognised by one of
his creditors while attending church and arrested.
On 26 March 1697, McCulloch was taken to the
Mercat Cross for execution. Before the blade fell
he prayed that:

> I may be absolved before the Tribunal of the Great
> God, that in the place of this scaffold I may enjoy
> a Throne of Glory; that this violent death may
> bring me to a Life of Glorious Rest, Eternal in
> the Heavens: and that in the place of all these
> Spectators, I may be accompanied with an innumerable
> Company of Saints and Angels singing, Hallelujah to
> the Great King to all Eternity.

According to legend, his headless body then stood
up and ran 100 yards down the road.

27 March

The murder of Thomas and Ann Farrow on 27 March 1905 was the first in Britain to be solved using fingerprints. Detectives investigating the case had little to go on otherwise. There

Arch.   Loop.   Whorl.

MR. GALTON'S TYPES OF FINGER-PRINTS.

were no witnesses to the crime and the milkman who saw two men leaving the scene in Deptford, south London, at 7 a.m. was unable to identify the killers. Another witness saw two men running down the high street a few minutes later and recognised Alfred Stratton, a 22-year-old layabout. But that was hardly convincing proof that Alfred and his younger brother Albert were responsible for the shocking attack. Shop manager Mr Farrow, 71, was still in his nightclothes when he answered the door of Chapman's Oil and colour store to find two men intent on robbery. He was battered over the head with a crossbar and then left to die as the intruders silenced his 65-year-old wife in her room upstairs. The vital clue was a single thumbprint left on a ransacked cash box. Scotland Yard's fingerprint branch, set up in 1901, was able to prove it matched Alfred Stratton. An Old Bailey jury convicted both brothers of murder and they were executed on 23 May.

28 March

Police dogs are now widely used to catch criminals and detect drugs and dead bodies. The first
recorded use of dogs to capture a murderer took
place after a 7-year-old girl went missing in
Blackburn on this day in 1876. Emily Holland
told her friends she was running an errand for a
friendly man she had just met and was never seen
alive again. Two days later her headless and
armless torso was found in a field, wrapped in
pages of the *Preston Herald* newspaper. A crucial
clue was the discovery of hair clippings from
several different people on the body – suggesting
the girl may have been killed at a barber-
shop. A search of barber William Fish's shop in
Blackburn revealed further copies of the *Herald*
but the damning evidence was only found on
16 April, when the police brought in a Springer
spaniel and a Bloodhound to try and sniff out
Emily's remains. Frenzied barking from the two
dogs near Fish's bedroom fireplace led detectives
to parts of the girl's skull and arms hidden in
the chimney. Fish eventually confessed and was
hanged in Liverpool on 14 August.

29 March

THE RUSH DISGUISE.

On the morning of 29 March 1849, a vast crowd of curious spectators gathered in Norwich for the start of the trial of James Blomfield Rush. By 8 a.m. the court was stuffed with lords, ladies, MPs and bishops as well as those common spectators who were lucky enough to obtain a ticket. In the centre of the room was a model of Stanfield Hall, the scene of a shocking double murder. On 28 November 1848, the landowner, Isaac Jermy, and his son had been shot dead by a mysterious intruder wearing a false beard and wig. Witnesses thought they recognised him as Rush, a neighbouring tenant who owed money to Jermy and had come up with a bizarre plan to take over the estate. Rush, a bailiff, had been heard declaring 'it would not be long before he served Jermy with an ejectment for the other world'. Such was his arrogance that Rush chose to defend himself rather than be represented by a barrister and as a result, the trial lasted six days before the jury retired to consider its verdict. They took just ten minutes to find him guilty. Rush was hanged at Norwich Castle on 21 April 1849.

PORTRAIT OF RUSH.

30 March

The discovery of a dead infant girl in a package floating on the River Thames on 30 March 1896 would provide a vital clue to police on the trial of the notorious 'baby farmer' Amelia Dyer. On the wrapping there was a name and an address: Mrs Thomas, 26 Piggotts Road, Lower Caversham, Reading. Detectives placed the house under surveillance before arresting Dyer – aka 'Mrs Thomas' – on 3 April. A search revealed pawn tickets for children's clothing and letters from parents who had paid Dyer a one-off fee to look after their babies. Dyer had turned the nursing service into a gruesome moneymaking enterprise: the children were either allowed to die of neglect, or, more efficiently, strangled and dumped in the river. This scam had been in operation since at

least 1879, when she was sentenced to six months' hard labour for neglecting a child in her care. It is thought she could have killed as many as 400 children over three decades. At her trial, Dyer relied on the defence of insanity (she told doctors she heard voices urging her to 'Do it'), but the jury convicted her of murder. Dyer was hanged on 10 June 1896.

31 March

Alan Turing is now remembered as a scientific
genius whose code-breaking exploits were a crucial
part of Britain's victory in the Second World
War. But on 31 March 1952, when the 39-year-old
mathematician appeared at Knutsford Sessions
House accused of gross indecency, his most important achievements were still a national secret.
The local newspaper report on his case, which was
based on little more than his confession to having
a homosexual relationship with his lover Arnold
Murray, was headlined 'University Reader put on
probation for a year'. He was given a conditional
discharge on condition he agreed to 'organo-
therapic treatment' or chemical castration, which
involved reducing the libido by taking oestrogen
(resulting in side effects such as breast enlarge-
ment). Turing later wrote to a friend saying:
'Whilst in custody with the other criminals I had
a very agreeable sense of irresponsibility, rather
like being back at school.' Two years later Turing
was found dead in his bed in Wilmslow, Cheshire,
having eaten an apple soaked in cyanide (it is
said his favourite film was *Snow White*). It was
only in 2013 that Turing, the 'father of computer
science', was granted a royal pardon.

1 April

Disguised as a man, the female assassin approached Queen Elizabeth I in her royal gardens in London with two loaded pistols. A few yards from her target, the intruder fumbled, then dropped one of the guns. It fired, discharging its round into the crowd with a fearsome roar. A shriek pierced the air, followed by a thud as something slumped to the ground. Was the queen hit? No, only an innocent peacock. The guards seized the intruder and presented her to the queen for summary justice. Her name was Margaret Lambrun, a Scot who had worked in the household of the catholic Mary Queen of Scots before her execution in 1587. Blaming Queen Elizabeth for the death of her mistress (and that of her husband, who died shortly afterwards), she took on the identity of 'Anthony Sparkes' and set about exacting her revenge. As she explained to Elizabeth: 'There is no vengeance too great to be undertaken by a woman, whose love has a double motive to excite her to revenge.' Queen Elizabeth asked: 'You have done your duty, now what do you think my duty is?' Lambrun impertinently replied: 'You must pardon me.' And with those words, she earned her freedom.

2 April

The last hanging of a woman in public took place at Maidstone Prison on this day in 1868. Frances Kidder, 25, had been convicted of murdering her 11-year-old stepdaughter by drowning her in a ditch in Romney Marsh. Kidder claimed the girl had fallen in accidentally after being frightened by a couple of horses but her dislike of the child was all too clear. 'I mean to get rid of that bitch,' she had confided in a neighbour. 'I hate the sight of her because she is always making mischief … I do not like other people's bastards.' Frances now stood on the gallows before a crowd of 3,000 or 4,000 people. The cap was placed over her head and the noose set around her neck, and then the trapdoor opened. Frances fell a short distance before the rope snapped taut. Her dying moments were spent dangling and kicking as she slowly choked to death. Less than two months later, on 29 May, public hangings were banned under the Capital Punishment Amendment Act. Executions would henceforth be carried out in private behind prison walls.

3 April

On 3 April 1817, a distressed
young woman in Asian-
style clothing arrived
at Almondsbury in
Gloucester. She appeared
not to understand
English and gave her
name only as 'Caraboo'.
News of her mysterious
appearance spread
and she was sent to a
vagrants' ward in Bristol
for further investigation. A visiting
Portuguese sailor claimed he could understand
her strange language and revealed her identity as
Princess Caraboo of Javasu, an island in the Indian
Ocean. Through her interpreter, the princess told a
sensational story: her Chinese father and Malaysian
mother had been killed by black cannibals called
'Boogoos'; she worshipped the god Allah Tallah; she
had been captured by pirates and sold into slavery;
she was washed up in Bristol after jumping overboard. Taking pity on her, the county magistrate
and his wife took the princess into their home.
There she delighted curious visitors by writing
in her own language and dressing up in a feather
headdress, banging a gong and practising swordplay
and archery. Although many people were suspicious
of her claims, the truth did not emerge until her
former landlady recognised her description in a
newspaper. Princes Caraboo was in fact Mary Baker
from Witheridge in Devon.

4 April

It was all a terrible accident. That night he, Theodore Gardelle, a Swiss miniaturist of no small talent, was in the parlour looking at a book on French grammar. The landlady, Mrs Anne King, was standing in  her bedroom doorway, teasing him about one of his portraits. He lost his patience and called her an 'impudent woman'. Mrs King punched him in the chest. He pushed her away and she tripped on the rug. She banged her head on the bedstead and started bleeding, screaming and accusing him of murder. So he picked up a sharp comb and stabbed her repeatedly in the neck until she was dead. What else could he do? He told the staff she had gone to Bath or Bristol, cut up the body, threw the internal organs down the toilet, scattered her flesh in the cock-loft and burnt her bones in the grate. Nobody thought anything of the missing Mrs King until they found the bloodstained sheets soaking in the kitchen water-tub. And that was how he came to be arrested nine days after the murder, and how he came to be hanged before a hissing crowd in London's Haymarket on 4 April 1761.

5 April

The murderer Frederick Field came up with a
bizarre and high-risk way of making money –
confess to an unsolved killing and sell his
exclusive story to a newspaper. So it was that in
1933 he told the *Daily Sketch* that he had strangled
a 20-year-old prostitute, Norah Upchurch, in an
empty shop on London's Shaftesbury Avenue. Field,
who had been working at the building that day,
was charged but retracted his confession before
standing trial at the Old Bailey. With little
other evidence to pin him to the murder, the case
collapsed. A few years later, Field was arrested
for deserting from the RAF and promptly confessed
to suffocating 48-year-old Beatrice Sutton with
a pillow at her home in Clapham on 5 April 1936.
'I was fed up because of lack of money and hadn't
the guts to take my own life,' he said. 'I knew
that by doing this I would put myself on the spot.'
He attempted to withdraw this confession at trial
as well but was convicted of murder and sentenced
to death. Field was hanged at the age of 32 on
30 June 1936.

6 April

'For the sake of decency, gentlemen,
don't hang me high.'

These were the last words
of murderess Mary Blandy
before she was hanged in
her black bombazine dress
before a large crowd of
eager spectators on this
day in 1752. Her case had
divided public opinion: was
she a poor lovesick girl
tricked into poisoning her
father with arsenic, or a
wicked daughter desperate
to remove the only barrier
to her happiness? Blandy, then aged 30 or 31,
had fallen for Captain William Henry Cranstoun,
the son of a Scottish lord. There was a small
problem – her father Frances Blandy objected to
the match because Cranstoun was already married
with a child. So in the summer of 1751, Cranstoun
sent her a white powder to put in her father's
gruel and tea. Frances Blandy suffered a long
illness before finally dying at his home in Henley-
on-Thames on 14 August. His physician, Dr Anthony
Addington, testified in court that the powder was
arsenic (the rudimentary test involved the use
of a hot poker) and Mary Blandy was duly tried
and convicted of murder. Cranstoun managed to
escape justice by fleeing to France but died a
few months later.

7 April

The singer Martha Ray was shot dead as she left the Royal Theatre in Covent Garden (now the Royal Opera House) on this day in 1779. Martha, then in her mid-30s, was the mistress of the much older John

Montagu, Earl of Sandwich, who is remembered as the inventor of the bread-based snack bearing his name. She also had many other male admirers including the Reverend James Hackman, a former soldier and rector of Wiveton in Norfolk. Hackman, ten years her junior, was obsessively jealous of her male friends and decided to follow her to a meeting with another gentleman, Lord Coleraine, at a performance of the comic opera *Love in a Village* by Isaac Bickerstaffe. Dressed in black, he waited in a coffee house until she exited the playhouse. As she was helped up into her coach, he approached with two pistols drawn. He fired the first at her head at point-blank range. The second was reserved for himself, but Hackman failed to cause any serious injury and was arrested. In his pocket was a love letter for Martha Ray. Hackman was convicted of murder at the Old Bailey and hanged at Tyburn on 19 April.

8 April

The trial of Richard Patch in 1806 aroused so
much interest that a royal box was fitted in the
court to cater for their royal highnesses the
Dukes of Cumberland and Sussex, fifth and sixth
sons of George III. Patch was accused of murdering
his benefactor and business partner Isaac Blight,
a ship-breaker, in an attempt to avoid paying a
debt of £1,000. On 23 September 1805, Patch visited
Blight at his home in Rotherhithe, south London.
After a few drinks in the back parlour, he took up
a candle and told the servant he was 'disordered
in his bowels' and needed to go to the privy.
A few moments later, the servant saw the flash of
a pistol. Her master Blight managed to stagger
into the kitchen before collapsing and dying.
The prosecutor, William Garrow, asserted that it
was impossible for anyone else but Patch to have
carried out the murder, but Patch claimed he was on
the toilet when he heard the shot. The jury delib-
erated for ten minutes before finding Patch guilty.
He was hanged three days later on 8 April 1806.

9 April

On 9 April 1747, an 80-year-old man became the last person to be publicly beheaded in Britain. Simon Fraser, 11th Lord Lovat and chief of Clan Fraser, was a traitor, a rapist and a bigamist who had survived countless political intrigues, thanks to his ability to switch sides. Having offered his allegiance to both the Protestant Hanoverians and the Catholic Stuarts, his downfall finally arrived in 1746 after Bonnie Prince Charlie was defeated at the Battle of Culloden in 1746. Lord Lovat, denounced as 'the most detested man in his Country', was captured hiding inside a hollow tree near Loch Morar and carried to London in chains to be tried, convicted and sentenced to death for treason. He was executed with 119 other Jacobites at the Tower of London (Lovat was actually sentenced to be hanged, drawn and quartered but

as a lord was permitted the more noble death of beheading). According to one version of the event, several spectators died when a scaffold collapsed shortly before the execution. Lord Lovat is said to have found this highly amusing even after placing his neck on the block, and so literally laughed his head off.

10 April

Easter Sunday, 1955. A man walks out of a pub to be confronted by a small, striking woman with spectacles and platinum blonde hair. 'Hello David', the woman says. The man ignores her. 'David!' She tries again, this time with a .38 revolver in her hand. He sees the gun, hears a shot. It misses. He runs round his car to escape her. She fires again. A searing pain explodes in his back. He stumbles, falls to the ground. The woman fires again, and again, and again, standing over his dead body. The gun clicks but does not fire. A pause, and then the sixth shot rings out. The bullet bounces off the ground into the hand of a passing 53-year-old banker's wife. There are no bullets left. David Blakely – former public school boy, racing driver, drinker – is dead. It is the end of a turbulent, tragic, abusive relationship with his killer, Ruth Ellis – model, actress, nightclub hostess. At her trial for murder, Ruth is calm, controlled. She tells the court: 'It is obvious when I shot him I intended to kill him.' She is condemned to death. On 13 July she becomes the last woman to be executed in the UK.

11 April

On 11 April 1861, 2-year-old George Burgess was
abducted, stripped of his clothes, lashed with
sticks and drowned in a pool of water in Stockport,
Cheshire. Incredibly, his killers were just 8
years old. Peter Barratt and James Bradley, who
were strangers to the toddler, were seen playing
with George shortly before his disappearance.
One of them was seen hitting the naked boy with
a stick but the pair ran off with the child after
the witness called out: 'What are you doing with
that child undressed?' Barratt and Bradley were
later questioned by police; both admitted putting
George in the water and hitting him with sticks.
'How long did you hit it with that stick?' asked
the officer. 'Until it was dead,' replied Barratt.
They showed little understanding of the serious-
ness of their crime but were committed for trial
for murder (the 'age of criminal responsibility'
was increased from 7 to 8 in 1933 and from 8 to 10
in 1963). On 8 August, the jury convicted them of
the lesser offence of manslaughter. Upon being
sentenced to one month in jail followed by five
years in a reformatory, both boys burst into tears.

12 April

The sensational trial of Adelaide Bartlett for the murder of her husband Edwin began on this day in 1886. One of the main reasons it attracted so much attention from newspapers around the world was Adelaide's unusual marriage – it was claimed that Adelaide had sex with her husband only once to conceive a child and thereafter refused his attentions because of his terribly bad breath. She later took a lover, the Wesleyan minister George Dyson, with her husband's full knowledge and approval. But perhaps the most puzzling aspect of the 'Pimlico Mystery' was how the caustic liquid chloroform ended up in Mr Bartlett's stomach without burning his throat. Was he poisoned by his wife (who had asked Dyson to buy the poison)? Or did he commit suicide in the belief that he was terminally ill? The jury found Adelaide not guilty on 17 April but, unusually, added the explanation: 'Although we think grave suspicion is attached to the prisoner, we do not think there is sufficient evidence to show how or by whom the chloroform was administered.' The spectators in the courtroom burst into applause and Adelaide walked from court a free woman.

13 April

'No one to love her / No one to care /
For the poor starving wife / In secret despair.'

The newspapers called it 'The Penge
Mystery'. On 13 April 1877, Harriet
Staunton, the 36-year-old niece of a
lord and heiress to a £5,000 fortune,
died at a lodging house in the
London suburb of Penge. She weighed
just over 5 stone; her body was
covered in dirt and lice swarmed
through her hair. The doctor
initially gave the cause of death
as 'cerebral disease and apoplexy'
but alerted the police after
Mrs Staunton's brother-in-law told
him of his suspicions about her
25-year-old husband Louis Staunton.
The police investigation revealed
that Mrs Staunton had been kept
hidden away from public view in
a cottage in Cudham, Kent, by her
husband and his family, presumably
so he could claim her inheritance
when she eventually died of starvation. The murder trial ended in the
conviction of Louis Staunton, his
teenage mistress Alice Rhodes, his brother Patrick
and Patrick's wife. All four were sentenced to
death, only to be reprieved after a public protest.
Alice was given a free pardon and married Louis
Staunton after his release from prison in 1897.

14 April

The 'Blackpool Poisoner' Louisa Merrifield revealed
her plans for her elderly employer with the
chilling prediction: 'She's not dead – but she
soon will be.' Within days of starting her job
as a housekeeper, Louisa, a convicted ration
book fraudster, had persuaded 79-year-old Sarah
Ann Ricketts to change her will. So when Ms
Ricketts died on 14 April 1953, Merrifield and
her 71-year-old husband Alfred were due to get
their hands on a £3,000 bungalow. The plot fell
apart when the doctor became suspicious at Louisa
Merrifield's decision to delay reporting the death
until the next morning and the police were tipped
off about Merrifield's boastful premonition. A full
post-mortem revealed that Ms Ricketts had died
from phosphorus poisoning as a result of eating
the rat killer Rodine. The Merrifields were both
arrested and tried for murder but only Louisa
(who bought the poison at a local pharmacy) was
convicted. She was hanged at Strangeways Prison
in Manchester on 18 September. Her husband walked
away with his share of the bungalow.

15 April

The social event of the year 1776 was the trial of Elizabeth Chudleigh, Duchess of Kingston (and former maid of honour for the Princess of Wales) for bigamy. While the American War of Independence raged across the Atlantic, the realm's most fashionable aristocrats put on their finest dresses and fought to secure a seat to watch the case at the makeshift court in Westminster Hall. The writer James Boswell was one of the lucky ticket holders and wrote in his diary that he 'had not known there had been so many fine women in the universe.' At issue were Elizabeth's unions with Augustus Hervey, later Earl of Bristol, in 1746 and the Duke of Kingston in 1769. Elizabeth had been reluctant to divorce Hervey (it would damage her prospects) and claimed their marriage (which had been carried out in secret so she could keep her job at the

royal court) had been declared null and void by the ecclesiastical court. After a week of evidence, Elizabeth was convicted and pleaded the privilege of the peerage, allowing her to walk away with the reduced status of Countess of Bristol and continue her comfortable life in France.

16 April

It began with the theft of a pair of trousers from a pawn shop. The prime suspect was Daniel Good, a coachman working at stables in Roehampton, south London. So PC William Gardner went to question Good and carry out a search. But instead of locating the missing pants, PC Gardner actually uncovered what at first glance was a pig or a goose. The realisation that it was in fact a headless torso was beginning to dawn on him when Good took the opportunity to lock the officer in the stable and escape. The resulting manhunt lasted ten days and led to intense criticism of the Metropolitan Police for its inability to catch the killer. Finally, on 16 April 1842, a former police officer spotted Good working as a bricklayer in Tonbridge, Kent. Good was returned to London to stand trial for murder, the victim having been identified as his common-law wife Jane Jones. He was publicly hanged outside Newgate Prison on 23 May, aged 44. The outcry over the case led to the formation of the specialist Detective Department the same year, initially with only eight members – two inspectors and six sergeants.

17 April

The seventeenth-century highwayman William Bew
seems to have earned his place in the history
books on the strength of his attempts at flattery.
In the account of the 'highwayman's biographer',
Captain Alexander Smith, Bew was prowling the
roads into London with his brother one day when
he spotted 'a very handsome gentlewoman'. Bew
approached in the guise of a love-struck suitor:
'Madam, you, who have the power to infuse love
and fidelity into the hearts of barbarians, have
captivated me, who never was in love before.'
The gentlewoman was at first delighted with the
attention but at length became tired with his
entreaties, and replied: 'You may intimate your
desires, and make tedious discourses, but, in a
word, I shall never love you.' At this point, Bew
dropped his pretence and demanded her valuables
with the parting shot: 'The time will come when
your face will scare you more than a judge doth
a criminal.' Bew's brother was later shot dead
by a gang of thief-takers outside an inn in
Knightsbridge. Bew himself, after an episode of
bungled grave robbing in France, was captured in
Brentford and hanged at Tyburn on 17 April 1689.

18 April

Four young boys were playing in the woods near
Wychbury Hill in Worcestershire in 1943. One of
them climbed an old hollow tree to look for birds'
nests. Peering down through the branches of the
Wych Elm, he saw something wedged in the middle.
It had hair, teeth and skin. It was a rotting
human skull. The boys ran off, spooked. The police
were called.

Who put Bella in the Wych Elm?

Not just a skull – a whole skeleton. The body of
a woman, 5ft tall, aged around 35, dead at least
18 months. No match to missing persons. A few
further clues – taffeta stuffed into the mouth
of the victim, indicating murder; a gold ring
and a few scraps of clothing; the evidence of a
witness who heard screams coming from Hagley
Wood in July 1941. The investigation drew a blank,
the victim remained unidentified, the murder
unsolved. And then graffiti started to appear on
walls in Birmingham and the East Midlands:

Who put Bella in the Wych Elm?

19 April

For three nights running, Ann Marten had the same dream. It was so vivid that she became convinced it was true: her missing stepdaughter Maria was not living in Ipswich, or Great Yarmouth, or the Isle of Wight as had been claimed; she was dead, murdered, shot, stabbed or strangled and buried under the Red Barn in Polstead in Suffolk. So insistent was she that Maria's father Thomas set out for the local landmark with a shovel on 19 April 1828. There, beneath one of the storage bins, he found the shallow grave containing his daughter's decomposed body inside a sack. Around her neck was a green handkerchief belonging to her lover William Corder, the son of local farmer. At his trial, Corder admitted meeting Maria at the Red Barn on the day of her disappearance the previous year. They argued; he walked away. As he left, he heard a gunshot and ran back to find her body. The guilty verdict was no surprise and Corder was hanged at Bury St Edmunds on 11 August. The notorious 'Red Barn Murder' was the sensation of its day and inspired ballads, plays, films and even Staffordshire ceramic figurines depicting the crime.

20 April

The 'Nun of Kent', Elizabeth Barton, became
famous during the reign of Henry VIII for her
divinely inspired visions and prophecies. She was
consulted by 'great men of the realm' and was
said to speak 'so sweetly and heavenly that every
man was ravished with the hearing thereof'. Such
was her reputation that in 1529 she was granted
an audience with Cardinal Wolsey and then the
king himself. Barton told Wolsey that he would
die if he helped Henry VIII divorce Catherine of
Aragon. Brought before the king, Barton repeated
her warning that he would 'die a shameful and
miserable death' within hours of marrying Anne
Boleyn. Henry pressed ahead but the prophecy did
not come true (although Wolsey was executed in
1530). Undeterred, Barton continued to prophesy
doom for the king until she was arrested in 1533
and confessed she had been faking her visions
all along – her miraculous gift was nothing more
than inside information gleaned by monks in the
confessional box. On 20 April, the 'holy maid' was
(unusually for a woman) hanged and decapitated.
Her torso was buried in the cemetery of Greyfriars
in Newgate Street and her parboiled head was
impaled on London Bridge.

21 April

One of the most sensational Victorian murder
cases began on this day in 1876, with the death
of Charles Bravo at a distinctive white mansion
known as The Priory. It was a slow demise – Bravo
had been poisoned with antimony in the form of
tartar emetic (which induces vomiting) two or
three days earlier. The 31-year-old barrister had
the opportunity to tell doctors who was responsible but was either unable or unwilling to do so.
The mystery was compounded by the proliferation
of suspects. Was it his wealthy wife Florence,
her former lover Dr James Gully, the housekeeper
Jane Cox or a bitter former employee? Or did Bravo
poison himself, either accidentally or deliberately? At the first inquest the jury was unable
to decide and returned an open verdict, to the
dismay of the newspaper-reading public. At the
second inquest Florence revealed scandalous
details of her marriage to Bravo, who appears
to have been a violent and sexually aggressive
husband. This time the jury found that he had been
murdered, 'but there is not sufficient evidence to
fix the guilt upon any person or persons'. The case
remains unsolved.

22 April

The 'Garage Mystery' began with the discovery of
a rotting corpse at a lock-up in Southampton in
January 1929. For the next thirteen months, the
twists and turns of the police investigation
gripped the public. The victim was identified as
Vivian Messiter, a 57-year-old oil company agent,
who had been reported missing two months earlier.
Detectives initially believed he had been shot, but
the discovery of an eyebrow hair on a bloodstained
hammer supported the conclusion of pathologist
Sir Bernard Spilsbury that Messiter had been
bludgeoned to death. They issued an appeal to
trace an F.W. Thomas, nicknamed 'The Man with the
Scar', and his girlfriend 'Golden-haired Lil'. When
Thomas, real name William Podmore, was arrested,
police could only prove that he was involved in
defrauding Messiter while working as a canvasser.
But two fellow prison inmates told police that
Podmore had confessed to hitting Vivian Messiter in
a loss of temper ('I went there to steal a car, but
I had no intention of killing the man'). Podmore
was charged with murder on his release from jail
and went on trial at Winchester. The jury found him
guilty and he was hanged on 22 April 1930.

23 April

On St George's Day 1928, two plainclothes police
officers were patrolling Hyde Park in London when
they spotted a well-dressed man and a much younger
woman sitting next to each other on two chairs.
Convinced the couple were behaving 'indecently',
the officers moved in to make an arrest under park
regulations. The man immediately began struggling to escape, protesting: 'I am not the usual
riff-raff. I am a man of substance. For god's
sake let me go.' His name was Sir Leo Money,
a 57-year-old former MP who had served in the
Ministry for Shipping during the First World War.
He appeared in court the following day along with
his companion, 23-year-old 'valve tester' Irene
Savidge, who would later claim that Sir Leo had
only kissed her once in the park, adding: 'it was
just a peck at that.' The case was dismissed by
a magistrate on 2 May and a subsequent inquiry
criticised the excessive five-and-a-half-hour
interrogation of Miss Savidge by police. Tellingly,
in 1933 Sir Leo was caught passionately kissing
another young woman on the train between Dorking
and Ewell in Surrey in 1933. He was fined £2.

24 April

The eighteenth-century 'celebrity prostitute'
Sally Salisbury went on trial on this day in 1724
for stabbing an aristocratic customer. Salisbury,
real name Sally Pridden, had been in the business
since at least the age of 14 and was favoured
by dukes, lords, diplomats, poets and possibly
even the Prince of Wales (soon to be George II).
Her undoing came when she became convinced that
John Finch, the son of an earl, was attempting
to transfer his affections on to her sister by
presenting her with a ticket to the opera. During
a row in the Three Tuns Tavern in Covent Garden
in December 1723, she took up a table knife and
plunged it into the chest of Mr Finch, who reacted
with a startled cry, 'Madam, you have wounded me'.
Salisbury promptly fainted at the sight of blood.
She spent the next two days by his bedside until
he offered his forgiveness and begged her to flee
in case he died. The jury accepted that Salisbury
did not intend to kill Mr Finch but convicted her
of assault. She was imprisoned at Newgate but died
before completing her twelve-month sentence.

25 April

It began with a phone call to the Liverpool
Chess Club. The caller, giving his name as
R.M. Qualtrough, left a message for 52-year-old
insurance agent William Herbert Wallace, asking
him to visit No. 25 Menlove Gardens East at
7.30 p.m. the next day. Wallace did as requested,
but was unable to find the address despite
appealing for help from a local constable.
Returning home, he found his wife Julia battered
to death in the sitting room. The police suspected
that the apparently harmless Wallace had made the
phone call from a box 100 yards from his home,
carried out the murder while wearing a mackintosh,
and immediately caught a tram to his appointment
with seconds to spare. Although it was a highly
circumstantial case, Wallace was found guilty on
25 April 1931 and sentenced to death. The case made
legal history the following month when the Court
of Appeal quashed the conviction on the grounds
of insufficient evidence. Wallace was released and
returned to his job. The murder, which remains
unsolved, was described by Raymond Chandler as
'unbeatable': 'I call it the impossible murder
because Wallace couldn't have done it, and neither
could anyone else.'

26 April

The audacious burglary of King Edward I's wardrobe
at Westminster Abbey reached its climax on this
day in 1303. This was no ordinary wardrobe –
the term referred to the royal treasury
containing an estimated £100,000 worth of gold,
silver and jewels (equal to the annual revenue of
the state at that time). The man responsible was
a bankrupt wool merchant, Richard of Pudlicott,
who confessed to spending three months tunnelling
through the 13ft stone wall of the chapter house
from the churchyard without anyone noticing. After
breaking through into the treasure chamber on
24 April, he waited two days before carrying off
as much loot as possible. Many pieces of gold and
silver were left along the escape route, to be
discovered by passers-by over the following days.
The investigation led to more than 100 arrests,
including Pudlicott, forty-eight monks and a
variety of palace officials suspected of involvement. Six alleged conspirators were hanged in
March 1304 but Pudlicott was not executed until
March 1305. To prevent future attempts on the
treasury, it was transferred to the much more
secure Tower of London.

27 April

The first victim in the unsolved 'Croydon
Poisonings' case died on 27 April 1928. Edmund
Creighton Duff was a 59-years-old retired
colonial official, who developed stomach pains
after returning home from a fishing trip. Then, in
February 1929, Duff's sister-in-law Vera Sidney
died of what the doctor called 'gastric influenza'
after eating soup for supper. Yet it was not until
the following month, after Duff's mother-in-law
Violet Sidney died shortly after claiming she had
been poisoned, that the police were called in to
investigate. The bodies of all three were exhumed
and found to contain arsenic. New inquests were
launched into the deaths and covered extensively
by the national newspapers: the case was now
being described as 'the greatest poison mystery
of modern times'. The coroner highlighted four
main suspects: the housekeeper Mrs Noakes; Violet
Sidney herself; Grace Duff, who stood to gain
from the wills of her husband and sister; and
Grace's brother Thomas Sidney, who kept weedkiller
containing arsenic at his home. The jury returned
murder verdicts in the cases of Mr Duff and Miss
Sidney but left open the possibility of suicide in
the case of Violet Sidney. Nobody was ever charged.

28 April

London, 1870. A detective followed two young women as they took a cab to the Strand Theatre and entered a private box. During the performance they appeared to be drunk and were all too willing to flirt with the men in the stalls below. But it was not their outrageous behaviour that concerned the police – it was the fact that they were not women, but men in women's clothing. Ernest Boulton and Frederick Park, who performed under the names Stella and Fanny, were arrested as they left the theatre and taken to the police station to be inspected for evidence of sexual intercourse. They appeared in the same dresses at Bow Street Magistrates' Court the next day, charged with conspiracy to commit an unnatural offence. Their trial, gleefully reported by the Victorian newspapers (who referred to the pair as the 'He-She Ladies'), began in April 1871 and ended with their acquittal by a jury after the judge criticised the behaviour of the police. Tragically for Boulton, his aristocratic lover Lord Alfred Clinton (former MP for Newark) had died the day after being served with a subpoena for the trial, possibly as a result of suicide.

29 April

In 1942, a Royal Marine stumbled upon a human
hand sticking out of the mud on the army training
ground at Hankley Common in Surrey. The rest
of the body was dug up and a search of the area
recovered a National Insurance card in the name
of 19-year-old Joan Wolfe, who had disappeared two
months earlier. A reconstruction of her skull by
pathologist Keith Simpson revealed that she had
been stabbed with a distinctively shaped knife and
beaten with a tree branch. But who was the killer?
The prime suspect was August Sangret, a French-
Canadian soldier stationed at the nearby army
camp. Joan Wolfe had written to him a few weeks
before her disappearance and appears to have
been carrying his child. The pair had regularly
stayed together at a wigwam built by Sangret in
the woods and the press quickly began calling the
case 'The Wigwam Murder'. One of Sangret's blankets
was stained with what looked like blood and a
knife was discovered in a drain at his shower
block. Sangret maintained his innocence but the
circumstantial evidence was enough to convict.
He was hanged on 29 April 1943, despite the jury's
recommendation of mercy.

30 April

The word 'Luddite' is now used to describe anybody who struggles with new technology. In the early nineteenth century it referred to textile workers who rioted in protest at the introduction of machinery that drove down wages and put people out of work at a time of economic crisis. Outbreaks of machine-smashing and mill burning in Nottinghamshire, Lancashire and Yorkshire led the government to send in the British Army and in April 1812, two croppers were fatally wounded attacking a mill in Liversedge, West Yorkshire. Later that month a group of Luddites assassinated William Horsfall, a hated wool manufacturer, as he rode his horse through Marsden, West Yorkshire. Such was his reputation that, instead of going to help, the local population 'reproached him with having been the oppressor of the poor'. On 30 April, two days after the attack, Horsfall died of blood loss from a musket wound to the groin. The response of the authorities was to haul in dozens of men for questioning. Eventually, in October, a cropper agreed to testify against three young colleagues, George Mellor, William Thorpe and Thomas Smith. All three were convicted of murder and hanged at York Castle on 8 January 1813.

1 May

In 1820, a group calling themselves the Spencean Philanthropists plotted to murder the prime minister, Lord Liverpool and the entire Privy Council. They hoped to capitalise on the recent death of King George III by storming a cabinet dinner armed with guns and grenades, kicking off a radical revolution and establishing their own government. There was one major snag – the man who came up with this cunning plan, George Edwards, was in fact a government agent. And so, on 23 February, the Bow Street Runners raided the group's safe house in Cato Street in west London. Eleven 'Cato Street Conspirators' would stand trial for high treason at the Old Bailey, with two members giving evidence against the others in return for their own freedom. All were sentenced to death but only five were actually hanged,

on 1 May, before being decapitated and held up to the crowd. According to the writer William Thackeray, the crowd shrank back in horror as the first head was displayed, leaned forward in interest for the second, and then laughed as the third was dropped to the floor by the clumsy executioner, causing one of the spectators to cry 'Butterfingers!'

2 May

Who murdered the princes in the Tower? Or were they not murdered at all? It is commonly believed that Richard III (their uncle) ordered the deaths of 12-year-old Edward V (who ruled for just eighty-six days)

and 9-year-old Richard, Duke of York, to prevent them contesting his seizure of the throne. The two princes seem to have vanished in 1483, but their fates are unclear, despite the finding of two skeletons at the Tower of London in 1674. Sir Thomas More, in his biography of Richard III, claimed that the king's trusted servant Sir James Tyrell confessed to the killings during his trial for treason against Henry VII in 1502. According to this version, Tyrell's horse keeper John Dighton and one of the princes' guards, Miles Forest, smothered them in their beds at midnight. Tyrell was unable to say where the bodies were hidden. He was convicted of treason and condemned to death on 2 May 1502 and executed four days later. Tyrell featured as the murderer of the princes in Shakespeare's play *Richard III*:

The tyrannous and bloody deed is done.
The most arch of piteous massacre
That ever yet this land was guilty of.

3 May

The trial of Dr Thomas Smethurst for the murder of
his bigamous wife in 1859 provoked a debate about
his guilt or innocence that seemed to consume
the entire country. It began with the death of
Isabella Bankes at their home in Richmond on
3 May, just two days after she signed her last will
and testament bequeathing her entire estate to
her husband. Arsenic was found in her vomit and
faeces, but little was found in her body itself.
Some experts testified she had been poisoned,
others suggested dysentery and claimed the traces
of poison came from the medicines Ms Bankes was
taking for her condition. The prosecution expert
Dr Alfred Swaine Taylor also admitted that his
tests had been contaminated by his equipment.
When the jury found Dr Smethurst guilty of murder,
many felt that while there was much suspicion,
there was not enough proof. Newspapers (and their
readers' letters) favoured Smethurst's conviction one week and his acquittal the next. After
a Home Office inquiry, Dr Smethurst was granted a
free pardon for the murder and jailed for twelve
months for bigamy. It has since been suggested
that Ms Bankes was suffering from Crohn's disease.

4 May

Richard 'Dick' Turpin, perhaps the most famous highwayman of them all, was executed not for murder or robbery, but for horse theft. The crime that was his undoing was said to have taken place in Welton, East Yorkshire, in 1739, and involved a mare valued at £3 and a foal worth 20 shillings. Unfortunately for Turpin, horse stealing had been a capital offence since the sixteenth century and he was convicted at York Assizes. Turpin greeted the verdict with dismay – he was clearly expecting to be returned to his native Essex, where he was wanted not only for a series of highway robberies on the approaches to London, but also for shooting dead a keeper at Epping Forest on 4 May 1737. Turpin was hanged on 7 April 1739. Many years passed before Turpin became associ-

ated with a 200-mile escape from London to York upon the steed Black Bess, as depicted in the nineteenth-century novel *Rookwood*. This feat was based on the reported adventures of an earlier highwayman, William (or John) Nevison, who famously escaped prison by faking the plague and was nicknamed 'Swift Nick' by Charles II. Nevison was executed at York Castle on 4 May 1684.

5 May

Noble blood did not prevent Earl Ferrers from being
hanged like a common criminal at London's Tyburn on
this day in 1760. The earl, descended from the royal
house of Plantagenet, had murdered the steward of
his family estate in a dispute over the accounts
at his mansion in Staunton Harold, Leicestershire.
Witnesses heard Ferrers shout: 'Down on your other
knee! Your time is come – you must die,' before
the sound of a gunshot. The next morning, after
Mr Johnson's death, Ferrers was seized while
wandering drunkenly across the bowling green armed
with a blunderbuss, two pistols and a dagger. As a
member of the House of Lords, he was entitled to be
tried before his peers rather than a normal jury
and the case was heard in Westminster Hall. Ferrers,
known for his eccentric behaviour, attempted to
plead insanity but was convicted of murder and
sentenced to death. He was taken to the gallows in
his own horse-drawn carriage and was hanged wearing
his white and silver wedding suit. The earl was
then taken to the Royal College of Surgeons to be
dissected and exhibited in public.

6 May

Lord William Russell, the 72-year-old retired MP
and uncle of a future prime minister, was found
murdered in his bed on the morning of 6 May 1840.
All the circumstances appeared to point to a
daring burglary gone wrong – there were marks
of forced entry on the pantry door and the lower
floors at the house in London's Mayfair district
had been ransacked. Further investigation,
however, suggested that the supposed burglary
had been staged and the killer was a member of
the lord's household. Suspicion soon fell on the
victim's Swiss valet Francois Courvoisier after
stolen gold and silverware were found secreted
in one of his rooms. A locket containing the
hair of Lord Russell's dead wife was found in his
pocket. At his trial, Courvoisier tried to blame a
maidservant for the killing but was convicted on
circumstantial evidence. He then confessed that
he cut Lord Russell's throat as the victim slept:
'His lordship was very cross with me and told me
I must quit his service. My character was gone,
and I thought it was the only way I could cover my
faults by murdering him.' Courvoisier was hanged
at Newgate on 6 July 1840.

7 May

The long-winded indictment against Sir Thomas More began with the charge that, on 7 May 1535, he had 'falsely treasonously, and maliciously, in the Tower of London, imagining, wishing and desiring,

against the duty of his allegiance, to deprive the said serene lord our king of a dignity, title, and name of his royal condition'. In short, the former Lord Chancellor and author of *Utopia* had refused to answer the question whether he accepted Henry VIII as Supreme Head on Earth of the English Church. More had replied only: 'I will not meddle with any such matters, for I am fully determined to serve God, and to think upon his passion and my passage out of this world.' At his trial two months later, More successfully argued that his refusal to answer should be regarded in law as consent rather than denial. His fate had already been decided, however. Solicitor-General Richard Rich claimed to have personally heard More deny that the king was Supreme Head of the Church. More was convicted of treason and sentenced to be hanged, drawn and quartered. Henry mercifully downgraded his punishment to plain decapitation and he was beheaded on 6 July 1535.

8 May

In 1753 an 18-year-old maidservant named Elizabeth Canning claimed she had been robbed in the street, kidnapped, threatened with prostitution and imprisoned in a hayloft on a diet of bread and water. At least that was the story she told her mother when she returned home in a filthy and malnourished  condition after disappearing for nearly a month. Elizabeth identified her captors and their home in Enfield Wash, north London, and an Old Bailey jury convicted the gypsy woman Mary Squires of assaulting Canning and stealing her stays (worth 10 shillings). But with Squires facing the death penalty, the doubt-ridden trial judge, Sir Crisp Gascoyne, took the unusual step of launching his own investigation into the case and ordered Canning to be arrested for perjury. This new trial, which lasted a week, divided the nation into supporters of the maid, the 'Canningites', and those of Mary Squires, 'the Egyptians'. On 8 May 1754 the jury returned their verdict: Elizabeth Canning was guilty of perjury. She was sentenced to a month in prison followed by seven years' transportation to the American colonies and she died in Connecticut in 1773. The truth about her disappearance remains a mystery.

9 May

Only a fool or a genius would try to steal the Crown jewels. Captain Blood was neither, but he almost got away with it. At 7 a.m. on 9 May 1671, Blood visited the Tower of London disguised as a parson, or 'Doctor of Divinity', and persuaded the keeper, Talbot Edwards, to open the Jewel House for a private viewing of the solid gold Sovereign's Orb, Sceptre with the Cross and St Edward's Crown, then valued at £100,000. Once inside, Edwards was knocked to the floor with a mallet, stabbed and tied up. Blood, an Irish rogue who fought on both sides of the English Civil War, used the same mallet to flatten the crown so he could hide it under his coat. The orb was stuffed down an accomplice's trousers and the sceptre was sawn in half. Blood then attempted to escape but was captured before he got to the gate. There was a happy ending of sorts: the jewels were recovered, Edwards survived into old age and the crown was repaired (it was used at the coronation of Queen Elizabeth II). As for Blood, he somehow managed to convince King Charles II to spare his life.

10 May

There was a foul smell in the left luggage office
at Charing Cross railway station. It seemed to be
coming from a large trunk and was so unpleasant
that, on 10 May 1927, a suspicious attendant
decided to fetch a police officer. The source of
the noxious odour was quickly revealed to be the
dismembered body of a woman, wrapped in paper and
tied up with string. Her identity was confirmed with
a piece of good detective work: one of the items of
clothing in the trunk was marked P. HOLT, which led
to a Mrs Holt in Chelsea (who was very much alive),
and then to one of her former servants, Minnie
Bonati, who had gone missing. The taxi driver who
carried the luggage led police to the home of John
Robinson, a struggling estate agent, and on 19 May
Robinson was lured to a meeting with his second
wife and arrested. Confronted by the evidence of a
bloodstained match, Robinson told police she had
fallen over at his office and hit her head on a coal
scuttle; he cut her up in a panic, thinking nobody
would believe his story. Robinson was hanged for
murder on 12 August.

11 May

The only assassination of a British prime minister took place on 11 May 1811. Spencer Perceval had been in power for three years and was struggling to deal with economic unrest, a mentally ill

King George III and the continuing war against Napoleon. At 5.15 p.m. he was entering the lobby of the House of Commons when he was confronted by John Bellingham, a bankrupt export trader who blamed the prime minister for his woes. Bellingham took a pistol out from under his coat and shot Perceval in the heart. The prime minister managed to gasp 'Murder' before collapsing to the floor. He died within minutes. Bellingham was arrested in the lobby and stood trial at the Old Bailey on 15 May. In his defence, he admitted shooting Perceval but told jurors he should be acquitted, adding: 'I trust that this serious lesson will operate as a warning to all future ministers.' The judge, Lord Chief Justice Mansfield, burst into tears as he summed up to the jury. It took just fourteen minutes for them to convict Bellingham of murder and he was hanged outside Newgate Prison on 18 May.

12 May

1935: The death of Louisa Baguley, an 87-year-old widow, at a nursing home in Nottingham was unexpected but hardly surprising. That was until her disabled daughter died at the same home four months later and left her estate to the managers of the home, Ronald Sullivan and Nurse Dorothea Waddingham. Louisa's body was exhumed and tests revealed both mother and daughter had died of morphine poisoning. Sullivan was acquitted of murder but Waddingham, aged 36, was convicted and sentenced to death. She was hanged on 16 April 1936 after making the statement: 'Tell my children I am innocent.'

1937: While the rest of Britain was celebrating the coronation of King George VI, an illiterate labourer named Frederick 'Spud' Murphy was strangling a prostitute in the cellar of a furniture store in Islington, north London. It was not his first killing: he had cut the throat of 43-year-old Kathleen Peck in 1929, only to be acquitted of murder by a jury. Murphy did not get away with the murder of Rosina Field, however. Following his conviction, he launched a ten-minute harangue at the judge, jury and police, to no avail. Murphy was hanged on 17 August.

13 May

William York was only 10 years old when he killed
a girl and buried her in a dunghill. It was
13 May 1748 and he was playing with 5-year-old
Susan Mahew at the poorhouse in the parish of Eyke
in Suffolk. There was a row about her wetting the
bed they shared; he slapped her face and she ran
out of the house crying. William followed her with
a knife and cut her wrists to the bone. As she
bled to death, he gathered a bucket of water and
washed her body clean before concealing it in the
muck. William then cleaned his clothes of blood
and sat down for breakfast. The girl's disappearance was soon noticed and a worker spotted
the dunghill had been freshly turned. York was
convicted on his own confession and sentenced to
death, but the execution was repeatedly delayed
because of his age. In 1757, he was pardoned on
condition he joined the navy. The youngest person
to be hanged in Britain is probably John Dean,
who was aged 8 or 9 when he was convicted on
23 February 1629 of burning two barns in Windsor
'with malice, revenge, craft and cunning'.

14 May

Kidnapped, the popular Robert Louis Stevenson
novel about a young Highlander and his struggle to
claim his rightful inheritance, features a real-
life murder which took place on this day in 1752.
The victim was Colin Campbell, known as the 'Red
Fox', who had been appointed to manage the estates
surrendered by the Stewart clan after their defeat
in the Battle of Culloden. Campbell was out riding
near a wood south of Ballachulish in Argyll when he
was shot in the back with two bullets by a sniper.
The Stewarts were immediately suspected, and in
particular Allan Stewart, a veteran of Culloden
who had previously threatened Campbell. When Allan
Stewart escaped arrest, the Campbell clan turned
on James of the Glen, one of the Stewart leaders.
Despite having an alibi for the time of the
shooting, James was convicted as an accessory and
executed on 8 November. His body was left hanging
on a gibbet near the ferry crossing in Ballachulish
for eighteen months as a warning to Jacobites.
It is now agreed that James Stewart was innocent.
The true identity of the killer remains a mystery.

15 May

1800: As the national anthem began playing at the Theatre Royal in Drury Lane, King George III entered the royal box and began to bow to the audience. Moments later a shot rang out, but the lead ball passed harmlessly above the king's head. All eyes turned to the gunman, James Hadfield, who was standing on a seat in the pit with a horse pistol in his hand. Hadfield was seized by the audience (and enthusiastic members of the orchestra) but seemed unflustered: 'it is not over yet – there is a great deal more and worse to be done.' Hadfield, a Chelsea pensioner who had suffered a head wound fighting the French in Flanders six years earlier, insisted that he had deliberately missed the king and was simply tired of life. Further investigation revealed he had fallen under the influence of the millenarianist Bannister Truelock, who claimed to be the Supreme Being. Hadfield was acquitted of high treason on the grounds of insanity after a trial at Westminster Hall and released (as was then the custom). Parliament swiftly passed the Criminal Lunatics Act 1800 to ensure he was arrested and locked up at Bedlam Asylum.

16 May

The 'Yorkshire Witch' Mary Bateman was in reality a thief, a fraudster and a murderer. Her first notable deception involved claiming a hen had laid an egg inscribed with the prediction 'Christ is coming'. Then, in 1806, she was asked to help remove an 'evil wish' from a married woman named Rebecca Perigo in Bramley, Leeds. Over the next year Bateman conned Mrs Perigo and her husband William out of £70 in cash, a goose, a tea caddy, 60 pounds of butter, three bottles of spirits, a new waistcoat, shirts, a gown, 200 eggs, two tablecloths, six pieces of china, three silver spoons, a camp bedstead and a pair of worsted stockings. The following year Bateman provided them with six bags of powder to add to their pudding mixture every day for six days. On the final day, 16 May 1807, both became seriously ill after eating the pudding. Rebecca died in agony while William, who had only eaten a mouthful, survived. It took another year and five months for William to realise that he had been duped and make an official complaint. Bateman was convicted of murder and hanged on 20 March 1809.

17 May

1521: Edward Stafford, 3rd Duke of Buckingham, was executed on Tower Hill for plotting against his cousin Henry VIII. His crime was to ask a fortune-telling monk whether the king would produce a male heir (which would affect his own prospect of succeeding to the throne). Even if the allegation was untrue, Stafford was well aware of the dangers of court politics; when he was 5 years old, his father Henry Stafford was beheaded for leading a rebellion against Richard III in favour of Henry Tudor.

1839: An unexplained murder took place at the home of the magistrate Henry Edgell in Chelsea, south-west London, while he was away on a trip to Kent. The only two people present were William Marchant, an 18-year-old footman, and the junior housemaid Elizabeth Paynton. When the rest of the staff returned, they found themselves locked out. The coachman broke in through the back door and found Miss Paynton lying in a pool of blood, her throat cut with a razor. Of Marchant there was no sign. Two days later the teenager handed himself in to the police and confessed. Marchant pleaded guilty to murder at the Old Bailey and was hanged on 8 July.

18 May

On 18 May 1756 a Scotsman and an Irishman, John
Macleary and Michael Sullivan, were executed for
enlisting an Englishman in the Prussian army.
Their victim, a tailor named William Maxwell,
claimed that two men he met in a pub conned him
into taking a merchant ship to Holland, supposedly
as a servant. He was then sold for 20 guineas to a
Prussian general who tied his hands together and
tossed him in a wagon headed to Pomerania, where
he was to serve as a mercenary for the Prince of
Bevern. A few days later, Maxwell found himself
fighting the Austrians in the opening land battle
of the Seven Years' War at Lobositz. Determined to
escape, Maxwell and John Gleed, another 'recruit'
of Macleary's, absconded while out on a foraging
expedition. They marched 1,000 miles to Ostend
and crossed to Dover before setting out to find
and arrest the men responsible for their hardship.
At their trial at the Old Bailey, Macleary and
Sullivan claimed that no harm was done as the King
of Prussia was now an ally of Britain. They were
both convicted of the crime of 'seducing from
allegiance' and sentenced to death.

19 May

Good Christian people, I have not come here
to preach a sermon; I have come here to die.
For according to the law and by the law I am
judged to die, and therefore I will speak nothing
against it. I am come hither to accuse no man, nor
to speak of that whereof I am accused and condemned
to die, but I pray God save the King and send him
long to reign over you, for a gentler nor a more
merciful prince was there never, and to me he was
ever a good, a gentle, and sovereign lord. And if
any person will meddle of my cause, I require them
to judge the best. And thus I take my leave of the
world and of you all, and I heartily desire you all
to pray for me.

The queen then removed her hood
and placed her dark hair under
a cloth cap before kneeling
down before the executioner's
block at Tower Hill. She was
still praying when the
executioner drew his
sword and swiftly
chopped her head
from her neck with
one blow. So, on
19 May 1536, the
life of Anne Boleyn,
the second wife of
King Henry VIII, came to
an end.

20 May

Drunkenness provides the tedious backdrop to many crimes in British history. One example, which might serve as yet another warning against the temptations of alcohol, concerns two eighteenth-century 'libertines' who found themselves locked up in the Fleet debtors' prison in London. At 3 a.m., having spent the past eleven hours in drink, Nathaniel Parkhurst, the son of respectable parents from Northamptonshire, staggered to the room of his fellow inmate Lewis Pleura, who claimed to be an Italian count, and shouted: 'Damn you, Sir Lewis, pay me four guineas you owe me' before stabbing him twenty times with a rapier. Parkhurst then left, only to return to the mortally injured man's bedside to shout: 'Damn ye, Pleura, are ye not dead yet?' The victim soon complied with Parkhurst's wishes and passed away. At his trial for murder at the Old Bailey Parkhurst claimed insanity, backed by eyewitness accounts of his ridiculous behaviour over the past two years. The jury, aware that drunkenness is no defence, found him guilty and he was sentenced to death. On 20 May 1715, Parkhurst feasted on chicken and a pint of liquor before being taken to Tyburn to be hanged.

21 May

Billy Hill proudly – and probably rightly – boasted of being 'Boss of Britain's Underworld' during the 1950s. His specialities were burglary and robbery rather than murder ('Only mugs do murder', he said, preferring to maim with a knife rather than kill). One of his most successful exploits is said to be the planning of the Eastcastle Street mail robbery in London in 1952. At 4.20 a.m., a postal van carrying more than £236,000 in treasury notes was blocked in by two cars as it drove along Eastcastle Street on its route from Paddington Station to the central depot. The robbers pulled out the driver and his colleagues and drove off with the mail bags. The van was abandoned near Regent's Park, stripped off its valuable cargo. The evidence (including the prior disabling of the alarm siren on the vehicle) suggested an inside job, but nobody was ever caught or convicted. Two men were charged with receiving some of the stolen money but were acquitted following a trial. So successful was the robbery that it earned a mention in the film *The Ladykillers*, released in 1955.

22 May

1722: Highwayman William Burridge was finally
executed at Tyburn at the age of 34 after years
spent playing the system as a prosecution witness
against his fellow criminals. His downfall came
when he was caught riding a stolen bay gelding
valued at £8. In his speech to the baying crowd,
he claimed his parents had been too soft on him as
a child, adding: 'I beg all Parents not to indulge
their Children, for it will bring a good Mind to
Wickedness and a shameful Death.'

1814: Francis Panckhurst woke up to find that
six of his chickens had been stolen during the
night. All that remained were three severed
chicken heads. He followed the trail of blood
to his neighbour's house but saw no sign of the
missing fowl. The culprit, 18-year-old Namon Key,
was already in police custody, having been
caught red-handed with two decapitated chickens.
Mr Panckhurst matched the heads to the bodies and
Key was charged with theft. Key claimed he got the
chickens from his friend James Santy, the son of
Mr Panckhurt's neighbour, but was found guilty and
sentenced to twelve months' imprisonment in the
Clerkenwell House of Correction.

23 May

For three years after his execution on 23 May 1701,
the body of Captain Kidd was left hanging in
chains from a gibbet at Execution Dock in Wapping,
east London, as a warning to all tempted to take
up piracy. Kidd first became known as a priva-
teer in 1689 after he led the mutiny of a ship
later renamed the *Blessed William*. Although his
adventures initially gained the approval of King
William III, by 1698 he had been declared a pirate
after a series of incidents including the killing
of one of his crew, a refusal to comply with the
orders of an officer of the Royal Navy, and the
seizure of an Armenian ship loaded with gold,
silver and silk. Kidd – nicknamed 'The Wizard of
the Seas' – was arrested in Boston in July 1699
and sent back to England to be questioned by
Parliament; according to some reports he appeared
drunk. He was convicted of murder and piracy after
a trial at the High Court of the Admiralty and
sentenced to death. The first attempt to hang him
failed after the rope snapped and he fell to the
ground. The second attempt was successful.

24 May

It is 1725 and the most hated man in London is on his way to the gallows. Huge crowds line the street hurling mud, stones and the foulest curses they can muster as the cart passes.

An even greater throng awaits his execution at the 'Triple Tree' in Tyburn. The best spots have already been reserved. Tickets have been issued. The writer Daniel Defoe is here to report on events. So who is the man they have come to see die? It is Jonathan Wild, 'Thieftaker-General of Great Britain and Ireland', hero-turned villain in the flesh. He was loved once, when the public knew only of his heroic deeds bringing count-less thieves to justice and restoring stolen property to the victims. It was all a sham. Wild orchestrated the same thefts he claimed to be

solving. Wild pocketed the rewards. Wild implicated his rivals in court and sent them to their deaths. He was finally arrested on 15 February for helping one of his men break out of jail. As his empire crumbled around him and his former associates turned against him, he was convicted of stealing 50 yards of lace and sentenced to death.

LC-DIG-ggbain-03860

25 May

On the night of 25 May 1876, the master criminal
Adam Worth (nicknamed 'The Napoleon of Crime')
stole the most talked-about painting in London.
Thomas Gainsborough's portrait of the eighteenth-
century society beauty Georgiana, Duchess
of Devonshire had recently been auctioned at
Christie's for 10,000 guineas after being redis-
covered in the collection of a dead art dealer.
Worth, perhaps besotted with the duchess and her
ivory skin (not to mention her large black hat),
decided to steal it. First, he prepared the ground
by viewing it on show at the gallery of Thomas
Agnew and Sons in Old Bond Street. Then, shortly
before midnight, he returned with two accomplices
to break in through a casement window and cut the
painting from its frame. Worth kept the painting
for the next twenty-five years. It was only in 1901,
after spending four years in a Belgian prison
for a cash-in-transit robbery, that he agreed to
return the painting in exchange for 25,000 dollars.
Worth died the following year and was buried at
Highgate Cemetery. The painting is now part of the
Devonshire Collection at Chatsworth House.

26 May

Farmer's wife Mary Lefley was hanged at Lincoln
Gaol on this day in 1884 for murdering her
60-year-old husband William with a poisoned rice
pudding. She maintained her innocence to the
last and many doubted her conviction because the
source of the arsenic was never found. Perhaps
someone else with a grudge had interfered with
the dish while she was away at the market? Another
eight years passed before the mystery was solved.
According to the deathbed confession of one
of their neighbours (and Mary's former lover),
he bought the arsenic after she told him she
wanted to get her husband 'out of the way'. Mary
then made the pudding and left it in the oven
for her husband at their home in the village of
Wrangle while she went to Boston market to sell
some butter. On her return she found her husband
dying in agony. At trial, Mary suggested that
her husband had either committed suicide or been
poisoned by someone else. She was convicted and
sentenced to death but hoped for a reprieve right
up to the moment the executioner entered her cell.
She went to her death screaming: 'Murder! Murder!'

27 May

The legal right of trial by battle, which since
the Middle Ages had allowed two opposing sides to
settle their differences with a fight to the death,
was finally abolished in 1819 after a notorious
murder case. Abraham Thornton, a builder's son,
was accused of killing a 20-year-old children's
nurse a few hours after meeting her at a dance
in Erdington near Birmingham. The body of Mary
Ashford was found in a flooded sandpit on the
morning of 27 May 1818. Footprints and a trail of
blood at the scene suggested that Mary had been
raped and thrown into the water to drown. Thornton,
confronted with the evidence of blood on his
clothing, admitted having sex with Mary but called
alibi witnesses that made it impossible for him to
have been at the scene at the time of the murder.
The jury found him not guilty. The public outrage
at the verdict encouraged Mary's brother William
Ashford to pursue a private appeal, but Thornton
responded by throwing down a leather gauntlet in
front of him: William had to fight for his life or
drop the case. He chose not to accept the challenge and Thornton walked free.

28 May

1686: The brief career of Paskah Rose as Newgate executioner ended with his own hanging for stealing a man's camblet coat and trying to hide it down his breeches. Rose, a butcher and convicted bigamist, had already been publicly flogged for threatening the sheriff over unpaid wages within days of his appointment. His replacement was his predecessor, the notorious Jack Ketch.

1809: Two members of a gang which specialised in stealing salt were executed at Chester for robbing a local salt works in Odd Rode. The hanging did not proceed smoothly. To the dismay of the crowd (who prefer quick, efficient deaths), the ropes around the necks of William Proudlove and George Glover both snapped under the strain and the criminals were deposited upon the ground unharmed. The condemned men did not appear shocked, but rather disappointed not to be dead already, and were taken back to prison to resume their prayers while stronger ropes were obtained. At 3 p.m. the pair were taken back to the gallows. This time they were successfully 'launched into eternity' (in the words of the *Newgate Calendar*).

29 May

Horatio Bottomley worked his way up from
working-class East End orphan boy to millionaire
businessman with homes in Monaco and Pall Mall.
He founded the *Financial Times* in 1888 and the
John Bull magazine in 1906 and was elected to
the House of Commons as Liberal MP for Hackney
South. Even allegations of fraud and bankruptcy
failed to derail his rise, and on the outbreak
of the First World War, Bottomley cast himself
as 'The Unofficial Recruiting Agent to the British
Empire'. His success at persuading men to fight for
their country saw him elected to Parliament again
in 1918. The house of cards only fell down in 1922
when he was charged with defrauding members of
the public who invested in his 'John Bull Victory
Bond' scheme. On 29 May he was sentenced to seven
years' imprisonment while a crowd of several
hundred waited expectantly outside the Old Bailey.
'These people trusted you, and you robbed them of
£150,000 in ten months,' said the judge. 'The crime
is aggravated by your high position, by the number
and poverty of your victims, by the trust which
they reposed in you.' Bottomley's reputation never
recovered and he died penniless in 1933.

30 May

The official story is that Christopher Marlowe was stabbed to death in a trivial row over a bill at a guest house in Deptford, south London, on this day in 1593. It was a tawdry end for the playwright who is still remembered for describing Helen of Troy as 'the face that launched a thousand ships'. Or was this a cover up for a larger conspiracy involving Queen Elizabeth I herself? Why was Ingram Frizer, the man who plunged a dagger into Marlowe's head, granted a royal pardon on the grounds of self-defence? Was Marlowe a government spy? Or was he killed because of his atheism? And how much was the bill (known as the 'Reckoning') anyway? The only witnesses to the killing were at the very least unreliable and have been described as professional liars with links to the spymaster Francis Walsingham. One theory has it that Marlowe faked his death and continued his career as a playwright under the name of William Shakespeare. The killing is referred to in Shakespeare's *As You Like It* (written around 1600), when a clown says: 'Understanding, it strikes a man more dead than a great reckoning in a little room.'

31 May

At 3 a.m. on 31 May 1810, the Duke of Cumberland,
fifth son of George III, screamed out to his valet
at St James' Palace: 'Neale! Neale! I am murdered!'
Cornelius Neale arrived to discover his master
bleeding from wounds to his head and leg. The duke
claimed he had been attacked in his bed by an
intruder who had apparently long gone. It was
soon noticed that the only servant not roused by
the hue and cry was another valet, Joseph Sellis.
Once the locked door had been broken down, they
discovered Sellis dead in a pool of blood, his
throat cut. Two rival theories emerged: either
Sellis was the intruder and killed himself after
failing to kill the duke, or the duke had murdered
Sellis and set it up to look like suicide.
The jury at the inquest concluded Sellis had
died by his own hand, having heard evidence that
Sellis' slippers were found with a dark lantern
in the Duke's closet. Motives for Sellis' attack
included revenge for the duke making advances
towards his wife, robbery and jealousy over the
duke's favouritism towards Neale (and a possible
homosexual relationship between the two).

1 June

The unsolved Peasenhall Murder case began with the discovery of the body of 22-year-old Rose Harsent at a country cottage in Suffolk. On the morning of Sunday, 1 June 1902, her father William entered the house to find her lying at the bottom of the stairs with her throat cut and her nightdress partially burnt. She was six months pregnant but had kept it secret from everybody, including the Baptist elder who employed her as a servant. There was no murder weapon but there was an unsigned letter arranging a secret meeting at midnight, at a time when the other residents of the village were sheltering from a violent thunderstorm. A broken bottle of paraffin found at the scene was linked to William Gardiner, a married choirmaster at the local Methodist church. Gardiner's wife insisted he had been at home with her at the time of the murder and no blood was found on his clothing. Gardiner walked free after two separate juries failed to reach a unanimous verdict (majority verdicts were not allowed until 1974). The first was split eleven to one in favour of conviction and the second ten to two in favour of acquittal.

2 June

Nine years before the French Revolution began in
Paris with the storming of the Bastille, London
experienced its own uprising. The Gordon Riots
began on this day in 1780 with a march on the
Houses of Parliament by around 50,000 people waving
banners reading 'No Popery' and bearing a petition
demanding the repeal of the Papists Act, which
removed some of the penalties imposed on Catholics
living in England. Their demand was rejected. Over
the next seven days the mob, swelled by the poor,
the unemployed and the disaffected, ransacked
and burned Catholic houses and churches, tore
down Newgate Prison and released the prisoners,
attacked Buckingham Palace, Downing Street,
the Bank of England and Bow Street Police Office,
and even raided a gin distillery which was
rumoured to house a Catholic chapel. On 7 June
the army flooded the streets with orders to fire on
any groups who failed to disperse, although the
government backed away from declaring martial law.
More than 200 protestors were killed before peace
and quiet returned. Dozens were convicted and
hanged. Lord George Gordon, who led the initial
march, was tried for treason but acquitted.

3 June

On 3 June 1885, 13-year-old Eliza Armstrong was sold into prostitution by her mother for £5. She was bought new clothes and underwear and taken to a 'Madame Mourez' to check she was still a virgin before being drugged with chloroform to await her first client. His name was William Thomas Stead, the editor of the *Pall Mall*  *Gazette* and author of a sensational article which was published the following month. 'The Maiden Tribute of Babylon' presented itself as an exposé of 'white slavery' and child prostitution at the heart of the British Empire. It was so shocking to Victorian morals that Parliament swiftly passed the Criminal Law Amendment Act, raising the age of consent from 13 to 16. The scandal also earned Stead a three-month prison sentence for kidnapping and indecent assault after Eliza Armstrong and her mother testified that they believed she was being taken on as a domestic servant. In other words, it was a set-up. Stead's accomplice Rebecca Jarrett (who arranged the deal with Mrs Armstrong) was sentenced to six months' imprisonment and Louisa Mourez six months' hard labour. Twenty-seven years later, Stead drowned with the *Titanic*.

4 June

The murder of architect Francis Rattenbury
in 1935 was one of the sensations of the age.
It sprang from a classic love triangle involving
his 31-year-old wife and his 18-year-old chauffeur. Francis, who had already attracted gossip by
divorcing his first wife to marry his much younger
mistress Alma Pakenham, was bludgeoned over the
head with a croquet mallet in the sitting room of
their home, the intriguingly titled 'Villa Madeira'
in Bournemouth. What followed was a series of
twists worthy of any thriller. Alma admitted
to carrying out the attack, only for the police
to learn that her teenage lover, George Stoner,
had made his own confession to the housekeeper.
Francis died four days later on 28 March and both
were charged with murder. At trial the lovers each
denied involvement, but only Stoner was convicted.
Alma walked away from the Old Bailey to the
boos of those who believed she had put her lover
up to it. Four days later after her acquittal,
on 4 June, Alma stabbed herself six times in
the chest and flung herself into the River Stour.
Stoner was granted a reprieve and served only
seven years in prison.

5 June

In the eighteenth century, boxing was nothing like the sport it is today: these were mainly bare-knuckle fights with few rules, and in some cases contestants employed head-butts, bites and eye-gouges as part of their arsenal. In 1789 the rising star was the future heavyweight champion of England, Daniel Mendoza, who pioneered the technique of ducking and diving rather than simply swapping blows while standing still. His chief rival at this time was Richard Humphries, and the fight between them that year was a topic of conversation, argument and hefty wagers. It also provided the backdrop to a much less glamorous 'prize fight' between two complete strangers that ended fatally for one contender. William Ward, an experienced pugilist, was on his way to see the Mendoza-Humphries match in the village of Stilton when he challenged Edwin Swain, an Enfield blacksmith, to a fight for a guinea. Swain lasted two rounds before announcing he would fight no more and attempted to walk away, at which point Ward landed the fatal punch to the temple. On 5 June, Ward appeared at the Old Bailey charged with murder but was convicted of the lesser offence of manslaughter and jailed for three months.

6 June

What can a beautiful young woman do when she finds
herself locked in marriage to a man she detests?
Why, murder him, of course. Katharine Nairn, 21,
decided to kill her wealthy husband Thomas Ogilvie
with a cup of tea laced with arsenic just four
months after the wedding. He died in agony a few
hours later on 6 June 1765. The ensuing trial at
Edinburgh High Court revealed a scandalous love
affair between Nairn and Mr Ogilvie's younger
brother Patrick, which under the law of that time
amounted to incest. The couple had not exactly
been careful to hide it – it was said that they
'frequently went to bed together without the
precaution of shutting the chamber-door' at the
marital home in East Miln, Forfar, Scotland. Both
Nairn and Patrick Ogilvie, who had sent his lover
the poison, were convicted of murder and sentenced
to death. Ogilvie was executed on 13 November but
Nairn was spared until the following year because
she was pregnant with her lover's child. A few days
before she was due to hang, she escaped in the
guise of a prison officer and fled to Calais. Nairn
was never heard from again.

7 June

On 7 June 1594, the 70-year-old physician-in-chief to Queen Elizabeth I was hanged, drawn and quartered for treason. Rodrigo Lopes - a possible inspiration for Shakespeare's character Shylock in *The Merchant of Venice* - was born in Portugal to Jewish parents who had been forcibly converted to Christianity. He fled to England to avoid the Inquisition, who suspected him of secretly adhering to Jewish faith, and networked his way up to the royal court via the patronage of Elizabeth's favourite Robert Dudley (it was also rumoured his skills in the art of poison were valued by the spymaster-general Francis Walsingham). But Lopes had also made a dangerous enemy - Robert Devereux, the Earl of Essex, who accused him of plotting against the queen as part of a labyrinthine conspiracy involving Spanish double agents, the pretender to the crown of Portugal and a diamond and ruby ring worth £100. Lopes was tortured into confessing he had been offered 50,000 ducats by the King of Spain to poison Elizabeth. He recanted at trial but was convicted and sentenced to death. His last words, jeered by the crowd, were that he loved the queen as much as he loved Jesus Christ.

8 June

Statement issued by the Foreign Office on
8 June 1951:

> Two members of the Foreign Service have been
> missing from their homes since May 25. One is
> Mr. D. D. Maclean, the other Mr. G. F. De M. Burgess.
> All possible inquiries are being made. It is known
> that they went to France a few days ago. Mr Maclean
> had a breakdown a year ago owing to overstrain
> but was believed to have fully recovered. Owing to
> their being absent without leave, both have been
> suspended with effect from June 1.

The disappearance of Donald Maclean (code named
Homer) and Guy Burgess (Hicks) made headlines
around the world. It was only publicly confirmed in
1956 that they had defected to Moscow. Both were
members of the 'Cambridge Five' spy ring recruited
by the Russians while studying at Cambridge
University. They had been tipped off by Kim Philby
(who worked with Burgess at the British Embassy in
Washington DC) that the British and the Americans
were searching for a mole in the Foreign Office and
suspected Maclean. The fourth spy was named as
former MI5 agent Anthony Blunt by Margaret Thatcher
in November 1979. There continues to be speculation
about the fifth spy.

9 June

The case of Albert Milsom and Henry Fowler is
remembered as a classic example of a 'cut-throat
defence' – where a suspect casts the blame on
his co-accused, only to convince a jury of his
own guilt as well. Both men were accused of the
murder of Henry Smith, a wealthy recluse who was
battered to death during a burglary at his home
in Muswell Hill, north London, in February 1896.
Milsom, tied to the scene by a toy lantern he left
behind, insisted Fowler alone was responsible for
the violence. Fowler denied all knowledge of the
killing but Milsom's evidence at the Old Bailey
trial was damning and halfway through the case
Fowler jumped out of his seat and tried to
strangle his co-defendant in the dock. The jury
felt little sympathy for Milsom and found both
men guilty of murder. On the day of execution,
on 9 June 1896, the two men were hanged either
side of a third killer, William Seaman, who had
been sentenced to death for the murders of a pawnbroker and his housekeeper. It was reported that
Seaman's last words were: 'This is the first time
I've ever been a bloody peacemaker.'

10 June

The close relationship between King Edward II (reigned 1307–27) and his right-hand man Piers Gaveston is still debated to this day. Were they homosexual lovers, blood brothers or just good friends? Medieval chroniclers

certainly believed that Edward's fondness for Gaveston was damaging to the realm – Gaveston, the son of a French knight, was showered with money, gifts, huge tracts of land and the title of Earl of Cornwall. Gaveston was even left to run the country while Edward married Isabella of France in 1308. His arrogant, preening behaviour did not endear him to his fellow nobles and he quickly became the most hated man in the country. Parliament demanded Gaveston be exiled and the king reluctantly agreed, only to restore him in 1309. Two years later, Gaveston was exiled again. By now it was clear Edward could not do without his companion and Gaveston was welcomed back within a few months. This time his rival nobles decided to finish the job once and for all. On this day in 1312, Gaveston was captured at the rectory in Deddington, Oxfordshire. Nine days later he was run through with a sword and beheaded on Blacklow Hill in Warwickshire.

11 June

Pirate captain John Gow took so long to die on the gallows on this day in 1725 that his friends pulled on his legs in an attempt to hasten his passing. The rope snapped and Gow had to be hanged all over again. He and his fellow pirates were dumped in the Thames before being covered in black tar and publicly displayed in a gibbet on the riverbank. Gow's career as a pirate began with a mutiny onboard the merchant ship *Caroline* during a journey from Tenerife to Italy. The crew, unhappy about their treatment, food and pay, decided to take over the ship in November 1724. Gow, the second mate, was chosen as their leader and personally dispatched the captain with two pistol shots to the stomach. After throwing the body overboard, the mutineers renamed their vessel *Revenge* and spent the rest of the night drinking. The pirates then set about plundering other merchant ships of their cargoes of fish, wine, oil and weapons before deciding to sail to the Orkney Islands to avoid capture and restock on provisions. Gow was eventually arrested on the Calf of Eday and sentenced to death.

12 June

The 'Chocolate Cream Poisoner' Christiana Edmunds was driven to murder by her obsession for a married doctor called Charles Beard. Her first target was his wife Emily. In September 1780, Edmunds gave Emily a box of sweets poisoned with strychnine. Emily Beard was violently sick but survived and suspicion naturally fell on Edmunds, who claimed that the manufacturer must have been at fault. In a bizarre attempt to prove it, she began planting poisoned chocolate creams in shops across Brighton. More people fell ill. Then, on 12 June 1871, 4-year-old Sidney Barker ate one of the chocolates while on holiday in Brighton and died. At the inquest Edmunds came forward to say that she and her friends had also become ill after eating chocolates from the same shop, J.G. Maynard's. She even wrote anonymous letters to the Barker family, suggesting that they take legal action against the store. Meanwhile, the poisonings continued. On 10 August, Emily Beard and five other Brighton residents received poisoned cakes by courier. Dr Beard went to the police and Edmunds was arrested. She was convicted of murder on 16 January 1872 but was spared the death sentence and died in Broadmoor Asylum in 1907.

13 June

THE MONSTER

The 'London Monster' was the name given to a notorious pricker of female bottoms in the late eighteenth century. Time and time again between 1788 and 1790, he approached an attractive lady in the street and either jabbed her in the buttocks or slashed her clothes. Nobody could stop him, not even the fabled Bow Street Runners. Panic swept the city and women took to wearing copper pans over their backside to guard against attack. And then, on 13 June 1790, he was spotted by one of his victims, Anne Porter, during a Sunday stroll in St James's Park. That was the man, she said, the wretch who slashed her right hip in St James's Street on the queen's birthday and abused her in such foul language she could not bear to repeat it. The suspect, Renwick Williams, was arrested and charged with defacing her silk gown, her silk petticoat, her linen petticoat, a third petticoat, her stays and a shift, worth a total of 45 shillings. Williams claimed to be working for an artificial flower maker on the day of the attack but was convicted of assault and jailed for two years. But was he really the Monster?

14 June

The case of the Rugeley Poisoner, Dr William
Palmer, was so shocking that a new law was passed
to allow him to be tried in London rather than
Staffordshire, on the grounds that it would be
impossible for him to receive a fair trial in his
home county. Local newspapers had not only reported
on the murder of his friend John Parsons Cook
but also on the deaths of four of Palmer's infant
children, his wife, his brother and his mother-in-
law. Cook died at the Talbot Arms in Rugeley in
the early hours of 21 November 1855 after being
repeatedly dosed with strychnine in coffee, brandy
and soup. Dr Palmer interfered with the post-mortem
to conceal evidence of poison but was arrested and
charged with murder. Thanks to the passing of the
Central Criminal Court Act (known as Palmer's Act),

Dr Palmer's case was
transferred to the
Old Bailey. His defence
rested on the fact that
no poison was found in
Mr Cook's body, although
there was plenty of
evidence that Dr Palmer
had obtained strychnine
and was struggling
to pay huge gambling
debts. He was convicted
by the jury and on
14 June 1856 was hanged
at Stafford Prison.

PALMER, THE RUGELEY POISONER.

15 June

The Peasant's Revolt of 1381 effectively ended on this day when its leader Wat Tyler was killed while negotiating with King Richard II. Tyler and his men – perhaps 120,000 of them – had appealed

to the king to free them from their virtual slavery under the feudal system; the right to choose their employer, the right to hunt and fish, the right to buy cheap land. They had run riot through the city of London and burnt down the Savoy Palace. They had executed those they blamed for enforcing the oppressive Poll Tax, including the Archbishop of Canterbury. But they did not want anarchy – their slogan was 'With King Richard and the True Commons'. Playing for time, the king agreed to meet Tyler alone in Smithfield in central London. Tyler must have suspected a trick but was easily provoked into violence by one of the king's men and cut down by the Mayor of London. His head was chopped off and mounted on a pike to be paraded in front of the remaining rebels. The revolt limped on in parts of Essex, Kent, Suffolk and Hertfordshire but the king's forces were now in control. The serfs went back to work.

16 June

On 16 June 1759 the under-sheriff of the
Old Bailey, Arthur Beardmore, was jailed for two
months for contempt of court after he failed to
uphold the sentence passed on one of his friends,
the satirist John Shebbeare. Beard's job was to
ensure that Shebbeare stood on the pillory with
his head and arms in the stocks for a whole hour,
while the crowd pelted him with assorted rubbish.
Instead Shebbeare was allowed to shelter under an
umbrella as the mob cheered in support. As the
judge put it:

> ... no one could possibly doubt that suffering a gross
> offender, an infamous Libeller of the King and
> Government, to stand in triumph, erect upon the
> Pillory, with a servant holding an Umbrella over
> his head, instead of standing with his head in the
> pillory, by way of disgrace and ludibrium, was a
> highly improper and insufficient manner of executing
> this Rule of the Court.

Shebbeare had been convicted of criminal libel for
portraying the king's dead father George I as a
corrupt, tax-hungry German with no concern for the
people of England. In addition to the pillory, he
was fined £5 and imprisoned for three years.

17 June

Colonel Valentine Baker had enjoyed a fine military career in the British Army dating back to before the Crimean War. He was well known as the brother of the Victorian explorer Samuel Baker and counted the Prince of Wales among his friends. And then, on 17 June 1875, the 50-year-old married father of one spotted a 22-year-old woman sitting on her own in a first-class carriage on the train from Portsmouth to London. After regaling her with some polite conversation about the military life and the theatre, he moved beside her and whispered: 'You must kiss me, darling.' As she attempted to fend him off, he repeatedly kissed her on the mouth while running his hand beneath her dress. Eventually she managed to escape his grasp, open the carriage door and edge along the exterior footboard while the train was still moving. Colonel Baker (whose trousers, according to newspaper reports, were 'disarranged') was arrested when they arrived at Esher. He was convicted of indecent assault and sentenced to twelve months' imprisonment by the judge for what was described as a 'libertine outrage'. Dismissed from the army in disgrace, he spent most of the rest of his life in Egypt.

18 June

Fourteen-year-old maidservant Elizabeth Mason decided that murder was the only way to escape a life of household drudgery in London's Covent Garden. In Easter 1712, while on an errand, she bought some rat killer containing arsenic from a druggist's shop. The next morning Mason served her two mistresses with breakfast coffee laced with poison. Jane Scoles, who claimed to be the girl's godmother, fell violently ill and died in agony within twenty-four hours but Mrs Scoles' sister Catherine Cholwell survived. So, two weeks later, the teenager went back to the same shop for more poison to mix into the breakfast gruel. Unfortunately for Mason (who hoped to inherit the sisters' fortune after their deaths), this second murder attempt also failed when Mrs Cholwell spotted the poison lying at the bottom of the bowl and summoned the local apothecary to purge her stomach with oil. The young maid quickly confessed to not only the poisonings but also stealing money from her employer. Asked why she did it, Mason blamed 'the Devil, and her own Pride, and the Hope of living at Ease'. She was hanged at Tyburn on 18 June 1712.

19 June

A day at the races at Royal Ascot, 1832.
King William IV steps forward to acknowledge the
respectful greetings from his loyal subjects.
Below him, a decrepit old man with a wooden leg
clutches two small stones. Belying his advanced
years the pensioner cocks his arm back and lets
the first missile fly. It clatters harmlessly into
the grandstand. He hurls the second; his aim is
true and the stone smacks the king in the middle
of the forehead. William falls back, perhaps
thinking of the story of David and Goliath.
The crowd turns, seizes the culprit, roughs him
up. His name is Dennis Collins, a retired sailor,
at least 70 years old. Collins was bitter about
the loss of his navy pension. 'I had neither
workhouse nor overseer to apply to, and had not
broke my fast for three days,' Collins later told
the court. 'Mere distress drove me to it. I am
exceedingly sorry.' Collins was convicted of
assault with intent to wound the king on 22 August
and sentenced to be hanged, drawn and quartered,
although it was reduced to transportation to
Tasmania for life. He died in 1834.

20 June

On 20 June 1923, a 13-year-old paperboy knocked
on the door of one of his customers in Coatbridge,
Lanarkshire, with a copy of the evening edition.
The boy, John Johnstone, was invited inside the
flat. Moments later, the landlady heard three loud
thumps. He was never seen alive again. The next
morning a curtain-twitcher in Duke Street,
Glasgow, spotted a woman struggling with a heavily
loaded go-cart and watched in dismay as first a
human foot and then a head flopped out of the
bundle of rags. The police arrived as the woman
took the body into a backyard. John Johnstone
had been burnt to the side of the face, battered
over the head, strangled and wrapped in a bed
cover. The woman, 30-year-old Susan Newell, at
first claimed her husband was the killer – but he
had an iron-clad alibi. At trial the key witness
was Newell's 6-year-old daughter, who arrived home
from an errand to collect beer, whisky and wine
to find 'a wee boy dead on the couch'. There was
no eyewitness to the crime but the jury convicted
Newell of murder. On 10 October she became the
last woman to be hanged in Scotland.

21 June

The investigation into the death of army instructor Lieutenant Hubert Chevis from strychnine poisoning took a bizarre turn when his father received a telegram consisting of just three words:

HOORAY HOORAY HOORAY

Chevis had fallen ill after sitting down to a partridge dinner with his wife Frances at their bungalow at Blackdown Camp in Aldershot. He had barely taken a bite when he pronounced the meal inedible and ordered it destroyed by the cook. Chevis died at hospital a few hours later at 1 a.m. on 21 June 1931. Frances, who took only a small bite, recovered. The hooray telegram, which appeared to have been sent from Dublin, arrived on the day of the funeral. After the message was published in a newspaper, Chevis' father received a postcard reading: 'it is a mystery they will never solve. J. Hartigan. Hooray.' The inquest returned an open verdict, leaving a host of unanswered questions. Was it an accident? Or a murder connected to his service in India (where his father was a judge)? Did his wife's ex-husband have anything to do with it? And was the telegram sent by the killer or by someone gloating at Chevis' death?

22 June

Field Marshal Sir Henry Wilson was an obvious target for the IRA in the aftermath of the Irish War of Independence (also known as the Black and Tan War). The Irish-born officer, who had served as military adviser to the prime minister during the First World War, was a vocal supporter of martial law before the introduction of Home Rule and the suppression of the guerrilla campaign led by Michael Collins. Wilson also opposed the ceasefire treaty in July 1921 which created the Irish Free State and described Sinn Féin as 'murderers'. Four months after his election as MP for North Down, he was assassinated outside his home in Belgravia, west London. On 22 June 1922, he was returning from the unveiling of a war memorial at Liverpool Street Station in full ceremonial dress and sword when he was shot six times by two IRA volunteers, Reginald Dunne and Joseph O'Sullivan. He futilely attempted to draw his sword before collapsing on his doorstep. The killers also shot two police officers in their attempt to escape before being captured near the scene. Dunne and O'Sullivan were convicted of murder and hanged at Wandsworth Prison on 10 August 1922.

23 June

On 23 June 1921, 15-year-old Harold Jones was
acquitted by a jury of murdering 8-year-old Freda
Burnell in Abertillery, Wales. The young shopkeeper's assistant, who was the last person to
see Freda alive, returned home in triumph. Then,
seventeen days later, his 11-year-old neighbour
Florence Little went missing. Harold Jones joined
in the search for the child in the streets of the
town. It was only when officers arrived to search
his home that the girl's body was found in his
attic. This time he was unable to blame a mystery
stranger for the murder and confessed to luring
her into his home and cutting her throat, adding
that his motive was 'a desire to kill'. Jones also
admitted murdering Freda Burnell on 5 February
after she visited Mortimer's Corn Stores (where he
was working) on an errand to buy poultry grit for
her father. Her body was found the next morning
on a secluded lane but it was believed the killing
was carried out in a shed behind the shop. Jones
was not executed because of his age (he was not
yet 16 when he was sentenced), but remained in
prison until 1941.

24 June

They call him the 'Flying Dustman',
    he drives a horse and cart
Round every house in Islington,
    in and out he'd dart
'I'm here to take your ashes, ma'am',
    (this service is for free)
And off he went with baskets full,
    (full of coal dust, see)
The dust he'd sell for making bricks,
    or to fertilise the fields
It's a profitable business,
    all the cinder that it yields

But then one morn in 1812,
    as the dustman bears a load,
He's caught by Mr Lacock,
    and detained upon the road
The dustman has no licence,
    for which others do well pay
He's been stopped four times already,
    before this bright June day
The desperate man takes up his fists,
    commits a grave assault
The jury find him guilty,
    as in truth he is at fault.

Charles Fox the Flying Dustman,
    he's headed now for jail
Three months inside his punishment,
    and so concludes our tale.

(The author)

25 June

The eighteenth-century Scottish outlaw Rob Roy
MacGregor was a cattle dealer who embarked on a
bitter feud with a rival landowner after being
forced into bankruptcy. Believing that his estate
had been wrongly seized by the Duke of Montrose,
Rob Roy prevented the tenants from paying their
rent, raided the duke's lands, kidnapped his
property manager and demanded the cancellation of
his debts and an end to the dispute. The ransom
did not materialise and, after twelve months on the
run, Rob Roy surrendered, only to escape two days
later. On 25 June 1717, he issued his 'Declaration
to all true lovers of honour and honesty', claiming
he was the victim of a political conspiracy and
had had been tricked by false promises into giving
himself up. Rob Roy returned to cattle rustling
and grain stealing and the feud continued until
he was pardoned in 1725 after promising his allegiance to the king (having previously supported
the Jacobites). By then Rob Roy was already a
popular hero, partly thanks to Daniel Defoe's book
The Highland Rogue, published in 1723. His life
story was later turned into the classic historical
novel by Sir Walter Scott in 1817.

26 June

He has been called 'Georgian Britain's worst husband': Andrew Robinson Stoney, later MP for Newcastle and High Sheriff of Durham, was a charming lieutenant in the British Army when he persuaded Mary Eleanor Bowes, the Countess of Strathmore, to marry him by pretending to be mortally wounded in a duel. The relationship quickly turned sour. Stoney restricted her social life, kept her under constant observation and subjected her to repeated beatings. He took out insurance policies on her life and in one episode of violence, forced her to sign over the income from her considerable estate. While pregnant with their first child, he bedded the wet nurse. Finally, after eight years, Mary fled their home in London with the help of her trusted servants while he was out at dinner, and filed for divorce. In a desperate bid to prevent the case being heard, Stoney arranged for her to be kidnapped at gunpoint. This time the law finally took notice and Stoney was arrested and charged with falsely conspiring to imprison the countess. On 26 June 1787 he was fined £300, jailed for three years and ordered to find a £20,000 security for his good behaviour for fourteen years.

27 June

1556: Eleven men and two women were burned at the stake for heresy after refusing to recant their Protestant beliefs during the reign of Queen Mary. The 'Stratford Martyrs' had been rounded up from Essex, Hertfordshire and Sussex and were aged between 22 and 50. One of the women was eleven weeks pregnant.

1881: The body of Isaac Gold, a 64-year-old coin dealer, was found shot and stabbed to death in Balcombe Tunnel on the railway line from London to Brighton. Detectives quickly connected the killing to Percy LeFroy Mapleton, an aspiring writer, journalist and confidence trickster who claimed to have been attacked by three robbers in a first-class compartment on the same line but had since disappeared. A manhunt was launched and an artist's impression of the suspect was issued, with the description: 'Age 22, middle height, very thin, sickly appearance, scratches on throat, wounds on head, probably clean shaved, low felt hat, black coat, teeth much discoloured.' Mapleton was arrested within days. While awaiting execution, he confessed to killing Gold and the unsolved murder of Lieutenant Percy Roper at Chatham barracks four months earlier. He was hanged at Lewes on 29 November.

28 June

Police Constable Joseph Grantham became the first British police officer to die in the line of duty on this day in 1830. He was patrolling the area of Somers Town in London when he saw two drunken Irish bricklayers arguing in the street. PC Grantham, whose wife had given birth to twins the previous day, decided to intervene.

He was promptly knocked out with a single punch and cracked his head on the pavement. The attacker responsible for the fatal blow, Michael Duggan, was at first charged with murder but a police surgeon concluded that PC Grantham's death was caused by apoplexy 'brought on by the exertion and excitement of the moment'. Duggan was convicted of assault and jailed for six months. At the time of PC Grantham's death, the Metropolitan Police had only been established for a year. Previously, law enforcement had been carried out by unpaid parish constables appointed by local magistrates, or, from 1753 in London, by the Bow Street Horse Patrol. It was not until 1856 that it became compulsory for police forces to be established in every county and borough across England and Wales.

29 June

The disappearance of an 8-year-old boy in Lincoln
in 1255 added to the notorious 'blood libel' claims.
According to the chronicler Mathew Paris, young
Hugh was abducted by the Jews of the city around
the feast day of the Apostles Peter and Paul
(29 June). He was fattened up with milk for ten
days before being whipped, crowned with thorns,
spat at, mocked as a false prophet, crucified and
lanced in the side in a re-enactment of Christ's
execution. After a failed attempt at divination
using his bowels, his body was dumped in a well at
the house of a Jew named Copin on 29 August. Copin
confessed that Jews from around the country were
invited to the ritual and ninety Jews were arrested
and imprisoned in the Tower of London accused of
involvement. Although most were pardoned and set
free, Copin and eighteen of the wealthiest Jews
of Lincoln were hanged. Hugh became an unofficial
saint and martyr and was name-checked in Geoffrey
Chaucer's *Canterbury Tales*. His death was one of a
number of child murders (including the alledged
killing of William of Norwich in 1144) used to
make false accusations against the Jews during the
Middle Ages.

30 June

On the bright summer morning of 30 June 1860, it
was discovered that a 3-year-old boy had disappeared from his cot at a country house in Road,
Wiltshire. At first, the nursemaid thought Francis
Kent had been taken out by his mother, but by
8 a.m. it was clear that the child was missing
and a search of the house and grounds began.
Just over an hour later, the boy was found dead
in the servants' outside toilet. His throat was
cut. The case quickly became a national sensation and two weeks later, the local magistrates
decided to ask for help from Scotland Yard.
Detective Inspector Jack Whicher concluded that
the killer was the boy's 16-year-old stepsister
Constance Kent but the evidence was not strong
enough for a trial and she was released. Whicher
retired four years later, his reputation damaged
by his failure to solve the case. The following
year, on 25 April 1865, Constance Kent walked
into London's Bow Street Magistrates' Court and
confessed. She was sentenced to death but was
reprieved and spent the next twenty years in
prison. Constance later emigrated to Australia and
died at the age of 100.

1 July

In 1863, a middle-aged married woman named Sarah
Potter was accused of running a sadomasochistic
brothel catering for gentlemen with a taste for
flogging teenage girls. One 15-year-old victim,
Agnes Thompson, told a court how she was stripped
naked, tied to a ladder, gagged with a towel
and whipped with birch rods by Englishmen using
pseudonyms such as 'Sealskin', 'The Count' and
'White Teeth'. When she objected to such treatment,
Potter told her: 'Oh never mind, it is nothing.'
It was only when she was thrown out of the house
after contracting 'a loathsome disease' from one
of the clients that she made her complaint to the
Society for the Protection of Females and Young
Women. Potter was prosecuted by the society for
assaulting Agnes Thompson on 1 July. Another girl,
Ellen Wilton, 17, testified that a moustachioed
gentleman paid £10 for the pleasure of both
whipping her and being whipped. Detectives also
found pornographic slides and sadomasochistic
poetry at Potter's establishments in Soho, Pimlico
and Chelsea. The magistrate sentenced Potter
to six months' hard labour, while her clients
(rumoured to include a duke's nephew) escaped
arrest by fleeing abroad.

2 July

The term 'Teddy Boy' was coined in 1953 after a 17-year-old apprentice engineer was stabbed to death by a gang in south London. Witnesses told police how John Beckley was attacked at a bus stop in Clapham on 2 July that year by young men wearing distinctive suits with long jackets, ties and narrow trousers. The press described this new fashion as Edwardian and referred to the gang as 'The Edwardians' (they were also known as 'the Plough Boys', after the name of a local pub). This was shorted to 'Teddy Boys' for the first time by the *Daily Express* during the trial of two of the suspects for murder at the Old Bailey. The case ended with the conviction of John Davies, a 20-year-old labourer who had been seen wielding a knife during the attack by a bus passenger. Davies insisted he only used his fists and it is now widely believed that he did not inflict the fatal wounds. After spending ninety-two days facing the death penalty, he was granted a reprieve by the Home Secretary. He was released in 1960, after his sister presented new evidence casting doubt on the conviction.

3 July

LC-US262-93417

Queen Victoria survived seven assassination attempts during her long reign and memorably remarked that 'it is worth being shot at to see how much one is loved'. None of them caused serious injury and they seemed only to increase her popularity. The fourth attack took place on this day in 1842 and resulted in the passing of a new Treason Act, which created a lesser offence of 'assaulting the Queen, or of having a firearm or offensive weapon in her presence with intent to injure or alarm her or to cause a breach of the peace'. The would-be assassin was 17-year-old John William Bean, a 4ft-tall hunchback who aimed to follow in the footsteps of two previous mentally unstable assassins, Edward Oxford and John Francis, both of whom were spared the death penalty.

Bean bought an old pistol from a pawnbroker and waited for Victoria to drive past in her carriage. He aimed and pulled the trigger, but it did not fire (and in any case was loaded only with paper and tobacco). Bean was sentenced to eighteen months in prison. He died in 1882, aged 58, after poisoning himself with opium.

4 July

The notorious 'Cleveland Street Scandal' began
to unravel on 4 July 1889 when Charles Swinscow,
a 15-year-old messenger boy, was arrested by
police investigating a theft from the London
Central Telegraph Office. Asked why he had 14
shillings in his pocket (it was much more than
his wages), Swinscow told detectives he had been
paid for working as a rent boy at a homosexual
brothel at No. 19 Cleveland Street in Fitzrovia.
The manager of the brothel, Charles Hammond,
escaped prosecution by emigrating to America,
while 18-year-old Henry Newlove was sentenced
to four months' hard labour for recruiting the
boys, including Swinscow. But the case only
really erupted into full view when Ernest Parke,
a journalist for the *North London Press*, named
two of the brothel's clients as the Earl of Euston
and Lord Arthur Somerset, equerry to the Prince
of Wales (later King Edward VII), and hinted that
a member of the Royal Family was also involved
(the Prince of Wales' son, Albert Victor). Although
the earl admitted having Hammond's calling card
for the brothel (bearing the address under the
phrase 'poses plastiques'), Parke was convicted of
criminal libel and jailed for twelve months.

5 July

1600: The celebrated Scottish beauty Lady Warriston, Jean Livingstoune, was beheaded in Edinburgh for hiring a servant to strangle her husband John Kincaid in his bed. She was only 20 years old. The killer, Robert Weir, evaded capture for four years before being 'broken on the wheel' – a fatal form of torture which involved strapping the condemned man to a circular wooden frame (also known as the Catherine Wheel after the saint and martyr) before breaking his bones with a club.

1919: The body of young maidservant Bella Wright was found lying in a road in Little Stretton near Leicester with a single bullet wound to the head. Former schoolteacher and First World War veteran Ronald Light was acquitted of her murder after a trial, despite accepting that he was with the victim shortly before the shooting and had owned bullets of the same calibre.

1940: War Reserve police officer Jack Avery was stabbed in the thigh after confronting a man writing on a piece of paper near the gun emplacement at London's Hyde Park. The suspect, Frank Cobbett, was convicted of murder but the appeal court reduced it to manslaughter with a sentence of fifteen years in prison.

6 July

Thomas Griffiths Wainewright is now remembered
as a poisoner and a possible serial killer. But
he was never charged, let alone convicted, of
any murder. He styled himself as an artist and
writer; he dressed in flamboyant clothes and
walked with a swagger; he mingled with the
literary figures Thomas de Quincey, Charles Lamb
and William Hazlitt. By 1830 he was living with
his wife, mother-in-law and two sisters-in-law at
Linden House in the London suburb of Hammersmith.
The mother-in-law died suddenly that same year,
and then one of the sisters, Helen Abercromby,
died of a stomach illness after taking out insurance policies worth £12,000. Wainewright was the
beneficiary but the insurance companies refused
to pay out and he fled to France to avoid arrest.
He was widely suspected of poisoning not only his
wife's mother and sister, but also his uncle and a
friend with strychnine. Wainewright only returned
to England in 1837, and was promptly arrested for
forgery relating to his embezzled inheritance
(to the amount of £5,250). He pleaded guilty at the
Old Bailey on 6 July 1837 and was sentenced to
transportation for life to Tasmania. He died ten
years later.

7 July

On 7 July 1862, Jessie McPherson, a young servant girl, was found hacked to death with a meat cleaver in the basement of a house in Sandyford Place, Glasgow. There were two prime suspects. The first, 87-year-old James Fleming, was the father of her wealthy employer John Fleming and had a reputation as a drunken rogue (he had impregnated a previous servant). Mr Fleming claimed he had not seen Miss McPherson all weekend and had made no attempt to investigate her disappearance. The second suspect was Jean McLachlan, a former servant who had pawned cutlery stolen from the house. Blood spots were found on clothing belonging to both suspects and police believed both were capable of inflicting the forty-nine separate blows to the victim. The case divided the country, with many believing McLachlan's claims that old Mr Fleming attacked Jessie when she refused his advances and threatened to tell his son. The crucial evidence that convinced a jury of McLachlan's guilt was a match between her footprint and a photograph taken of a bloody footprint left at the scene. She was convicted of murder but was granted a reprieve from the death sentence. McLachlan was released in 1877.

8 July

Neville Heath was a sadistic ladykiller who seduced his victims by posing as a lieutenant colonel in the Royal Air Force. His first victim, Margery Gardner, was found dead at the Pembridge Court Hotel in Notting Hill Gate in west London, in June 1946. She had been tied up, whipped with a riding crop, bitten and suffocated. Heath, a convicted fraudster, was quickly linked to the murder and fled to Bournemouth, where he booked a room in the name of 'Group Captain Rupert Brook'. Heath met his second victim, Doreen Marshall, while walking on the promenade on 3 July and invited her to dinner. At the end of the night, he offered to walk her back to her hotel. Doreen was never seen alive again but it was not until 8 July that her mutilated body was found in the undergrowth at Branksome Dene Chine. Heath was charged with both murders but stood trial only for the first. He attempted to plead insanity but was convicted and sentenced to death. Shortly before his execution on 16 October, he was offered a shot of whisky. Heath accepted and then paused before saying: 'Make that a double.'

9 July

At 10.10 p.m. on 9 July 1864, two city workers
entered an empty first-class carriage at Hackney
railway station to find blood spattered on the
window and seats. Twenty minutes later, 69-year-old
Thomas Briggs was found fatally injured back down
the track in Bow. He had been beaten about the
head with a blunt object and pushed off the train.
Mr Briggs never regained consciousness and died
just over an hour later, becoming the first person
to be murdered on the railway in Britain. His watch
and gold chain were missing, presumed stolen.
The key to the case was a squashed black hat left
behind in the train compartment by the killer.
Mr Briggs' own top hat was missing. The police
investigation eventually led to Franz Muller,
a German tailor who had left for America on 15 July.
Detective Inspector Richard Tanner gave chase,
intercepting Muller on his arrival in New York.
Muller was carrying Mr Briggs' watch and hat.
He was extradited back to Britain to stand trial
and was convicted after a three-day trial at the
Old Bailey. The execution took place on 14 November
before an estimated crowd of 50,000 people.

10 July

It seemed like an open and shut case. At 2 a.m. on
10 July 1923, three shots rang out at suite No. 41
on the fourth floor of the Savoy Hotel in London.
A porter ran to the scene to see 'Madame' Marie
Margaret Fahmy throw a gun to the floor. 'What
have I done, my dear?' she repeated in French,
over and over again. Slumped against the wall of
the suite with a bullet wound to the head was her
wealthy Egyptian husband, Ali Kamel Fahmy Bey.
At the trial she admitted killing her husband but
claimed she acted in self-defence. Her barrister,
Edward Marshall Hall, skilfully played upon the
prejudices of the jury (and the general public) to
portray the victim as an abusive husband who maintained a harem and forced his women to wear a veil
and indulge his perverted obsession with anal sex.
Even the judge concluded that 'we in this country
put our women on a pedestal: in Egypt they have
not the same views'. On 14 September, Madame Fahmy
was acquitted by a jury at the Old Bailey and
walked free from court.

11 July

The Scottish serial killer Peter Manuel – nicknamed 'The Beast of Birkenshaw' – was hanged
on this day in 1958. He was convicted of seven
murders dating back to September 1956, when
Marion Watt, her daughter Vivienne and her sister
Margaret Brown were found shot dead at their home
in Glasgow. Manuel was investigated but police
were convinced that Marion's husband William had
faked a break-in and murdered his own family, even
though he was on a fishing trip 90 miles away at
the time. Manuel was eventually brought to justice
after the murders of Peter Smart, his wife Doris
and their 10-year-old son Michael at their home
in Uddingston in January 1958. Upon his arrest,
he confessed to murdering not only the Smarts
and the Watts but also a 17-year-old girl who
disappeared on the way to a school dance, even
taking police to the field where he buried her body.
Manuel was also charged with the murder of another
17-year-old girl in January 1956 but the case was
dropped during the trial at Glasgow High Court.
His last words before his execution are said to
have been 'Turn up the radio and I'll go quietly'.

12 July

One of the first cases of police brutality concerned the death of John Peacock Wood in 1833. At 1 a.m. on 12 July that year Mr Wood, a 32-year-old waterman, was drinking a pint of ale with a female friend at the White Hart pub in Shadwell High Street in east London. The police arrived and ordered the pub to be cleared. Witnesses disagreed about what happened next but somehow Mr Wood ended up sprawled on the pavement with a fractured skull. He spent the rest of the night in the cells and died the following afternoon. But did he fall or was he pushed? Or was he, as some claimed, beaten to death? Doctors testified that the fatal injury was caused by a blunt object not dissimilar to a policeman's truncheon but the coroner declared that there was 'not a tittle of evidence that can be relied upon against the police'. The jury accused the coroner of being 'partial' and the coroner retaliated by accusing the jury of 'giving way to their prejudices'. The arguments continued for six days until finally the jury returned a verdict of 'wilful murder against a policeman unknown'. Nobody was ever charged.

13 July

13 July 1959: Guenther Podola – small-time burglar
and wannabe gangster – enters a phone box in
South Kensington. He calls an American woman,
demands £500 for the return of her jewellery;
the jewellery he stole from her home. The call
is traced; Podola is arrested while still on
the phone. Podola breaks free, runs blind;
is cornered in the hallway of a nearby block of
flats by two detectives. Podola bides his time.
One detective leaves to fetch a patrol car while
the other stands guard. Podola seizes his chance;
pulls out a 9mm pistol and shoots Detective
Sergeant Raymond Purdy in the heart. Podola
escapes as Purdy slumps to the floor, dead.

16 July 1959: Podola is traced to a hotel room in
nearby Queen's Gate and arrested.

10 September 1959: Podola appears at the Old Bailey.
He claims he is unfit to stand trial; says he has
amnesia – the result of a beating at the hands of
the police. His claims are rejected.

25 September: Podola is convicted of murder after
a two-day trial and sentenced to death.

5 November 1959: Podola is executed; the last person
to be hanged for the murder of a police officer.

14 July

THE MURDER OF MISS HOLLAND BY DOUGAL.

The serial seducer Samuel Herbert Dougal got away with murder for four years until his execution on this day in 1903. Dougal, a retired army clerk, shot his 56-year-old lover Camille Holland in the head on 19 May 1899 and buried her in a ditch near their home at Moat Farm in Saffron Walden. He then invited his wife down to stay with him, gave her the victim's clothing and jewellery and set about plundering Ms Holland's assets, emptying her bank accounts, selling her shares and taking over the property. As Dougal enjoyed the fruits of his crimes, he became the focus of local gossip due to a string of affairs and his fondness for giving cycling lessons to naked girls in the meadow. Eventually, in March 1903, the police managed to gather enough evidence to charge him with forgery of Ms Holland's signature. The investigation then turned to finding her body. For more than a month officers searched the area, digging up land and draining the moat, to the voyeuristic delight of thousands of sightseers drawn to the scene of 'The Moat Farm Mystery'. Finally on 27 April they made the grim discovery, sealing Dougal's fate.

15 July

Serial killer John Reginald Halliday Christie was executed at Pentonville Prison on 15 July 1953. Christie, an impotent former soldier and special constable, had confessed to murdering his wife Ethel and six other women over the past ten years while living at the infamous (and no longer standing) address of No. 10 Rillington Place in Notting Hill, west London. Christie could have been stopped in 1949 when the bodies of his lodgers, 20-year-old Beryl Evans and her 13-month-old daughter Geraldine, were discovered in the wash-house in the backyard. Unaware that two more bodies were waiting to be found, detectives became convinced that Beryl's husband Timothy Evans was responsible. Evans was convicted of the child's murder and hanged on 9 March 1950, thanks partially to Christie's evidence at the Old Bailey. It was another three years (and four more victims) before the truth emerged. In March 1953, Christie moved out of No. 10 and the new tenant discovered three dead bodies in an alcove. The manhunt lasted ten days before Christie was arrested while wandering along the Thames Embankment in Putney. In his pocket was an old newspaper clipping referring to the criminal proceedings against his former lodger Timothy Evans.

16 July

It was called the 'Switch of the Century'.
On 16 July 1953, punters at Bath racecourse watched
as 10–1 outsider Francasal romped home to win the
Spa Selling Plate by two lengths. Normally this
unexpected victory might have been put down to the
gods, but suspicions were raised after it emerged
the phone line connecting outside bookmakers to
the course had been cut shortly before the race,
meaning those setting the odds were not informed
that heavy bets had been placed on a horse which
had never won a single race (and only once finished
in the top six). The police were called in to
investigate and within days it was discovered that
Francasal (bought for £820) had been replaced by
the similar-looking but faster 2-year-old colt
named Santa Amaro (bought for £2,000). The deception is said to have earned the plotters, led by
bookmaker Henry Kateley and professional gambler
Maurice Williams, at least £60,000. It also earned
them a trial at the Old Bailey for conspiracy
to defraud. In March 1954 Kateley was jailed for
three years, Williams and turf accountant Gomer
Charles were sentenced to two years and bloodstock
dealer Victor Dill received nine months.

17 July

The 'Brighton Trunk Murders' case began in 1934
with a horrific discovery at Brighton railway
station. On 17 June, a cloakroom attendant noticed
a foul smell and called in the police. Inside
one of the pieces of luggage were a headless
torso and two arms wrapped in paper. The next
day, the legs were found in another trunk at
King's Cross station. The victim was aged around
25 and was pregnant at the time of her death.
Detectives trawled missing person records and
began house-to-house enquiries without luck until,
on 15 July, they visited the home of Tony Mancini
at Kemp Street in Brighton and found the body
of another dead woman inside a trunk. She was
quickly identified as Mancini's lover Violet Kaye,
a 42-year-old dancer and waitress. Two days later,
on 17 July, Mancini was arrested and charged with
murder. At trial, Mancini was found not guilty
after claiming that he had found his lover dead in
their flat and put her in the trunk out of panic.
Detectives never solved the murder of the first
trunk victim, who was referred to in some
newspapers as 'The Girl with the Pretty Feet'.

18 July

Frank Russell, the 2nd Earl Russell, probably
hoped to be remembered either as the first
person to be issued with a car number plate
(A1, in 1903), the first peer to join the Labour
Party, or grandson of a former prime minister
and brother of the philosopher Bertrand Russell.
But in scandal-hungry Edwardian England, he was
known as the 'Wicked Earl' who stood trial at the
House of Lords for bigamy. On this day in 1901, he
pleaded guilty to the charge after a curiously
ceremonial proceeding that struck some observers
as 'quaint' or 'medieval'. It was presided over by
the Lord High Chancellor sitting on a dais above
ten judges surrounded on either side by more than
200 peers dressed in bright red robes, ermine and
gold lace. By contrast, Earl Russell wore a grey
suit and red tie. After an attempt to dismiss
the case on the grounds that he had obtained a
divorce in America, Russell pleaded guilty and was
given a lenient sentence of three months in jail.
He served his sentence in a relatively comfortable
apartment (stocked with his own choice of food and
wine) at Holloway Prison in north London.

19 July

In 1822 the British newspapers shuddered with combined horror and delight at the scandalous arrest of a bishop for what was described as 'an abominable offence'. On 19 July Percy Jocelyn, the Anglican Bishop of Clogher, was spotted 'in a situation' with John Moverley, a private in the Grenadier Guards, in a back room of the White Lion pub in St James's, Westminster. According to some reports, members of the public were so incensed at his behaviour that he was lucky to escape with only a severe beating. The following day Jocelyn, ironically a member of the Society for Suppression of Vice, managed to obtain bail in the sum of £1,000 at the magistrates' court and fled the country, never to be seen again. Inspired by his example, the soldier also jumped bail. Jocelyn failed to turn up for his case before the Metropolitan Court of Armagh in October and was deprived of the bishopric. It has been suggested that the scandal led indirectly to the suicide of the Foreign Secretary Viscount Castlereagh, who claimed he was being blackmailed 'for the same crime as the Bishop of Clogher'. On 12 August, Castlereagh cut his own throat.

20 July

In 1318, a mysterious one-eared stranger appeared in Oxford and insisted that he was the rightful heir to the English throne. The story told by John of Powderham was that he had been replaced by a carter's son after being mauled by a sow in his royal cradle: Edward II was therefore an imposter – a fact that could be proved in armed combat. It was an unlikely tale but Edward II was so hated by his countrymen and possessed so few of his father's virtues (in addition to an un-royal fondness for roofing houses), that word quickly spread across the country. Under pressure from his queen, Isabella, Edward had John brought before him at Northampton. 'Welcome, my brother,' he derisively greeted the challenger. 'Thou art no brother of mine,' John replied, 'but falsely thou claimest the kingdom for thyself.' The king was not amused. On 20 July, John was delivered from Northampton Gaol to be sentenced to be dragged to the gallows, hanged and burned. John, who was in reality a tanner's son from Exeter, now confessed: an evil spirit had offered him the throne if he travelled to Oxford accompanied by a dog, a cock and a tomcat.

21 July

The seventeenth-century hangman Jack Ketch became
notorious for the gruesomely cack-handed way he
carried out executions. One of his victims was
William, Lord Russell, on this day in 1683. Russell
had been convicted of treason for supporting the
so-called 'Rye House Plot' against King Charles II
and his Roman Catholic brother James II, who was
next in line to the throne. The sentence was death
by being hanged, drawn and quartered, but after
persistent pleas for mercy from his wife, the
punishment was reduced to simple beheading. Hoping
for a quick and painless death, Russell bribed
Jack Ketch 10 guineas to do a professional job.
Ketch proceeded to botch it spectacularly (perhaps
deliberately?); the first blow embedded itself in
Russell's shoulder, the second chopped off his ear
and the third only superficially wounded his neck.
Russell is said to have shouted: 'You dog!' as
Ketch continued to try, and fail, to finish the job.
In the end, Ketch had to sever Russell's head with
a saw. The executioner later published a sort of
apology for his performance in which he complained
that he was put off his swing because Lord Russell
had not 'disposed himself as was most suitable'.

22 July

On 22 July 1910,
the captain of the
SS *Montrose* sent a
wireless telegram to
Liverpool as his ship
steamed across the
Atlantic towards Canada.
It read as follows:

LC-DIG-ggbain-08612

Have strong suspicions that Crippen London cellar
murderer and accomplice are amongst saloon passen-
gers moustache taken off growing beard accomplice
dressed as boy voice manner and build undoubtedly a
girl both travelling as Mr and Master Robinson.

The message quickly reached Chief Inspector Walter
Dew of the Metropolitan Police and nine days later,
with the help of a quicker vessel, both Mr and
Master Robinson were under arrest. They were
in fact the most wanted criminals in Britain –
the homeopathic 'Dr' Hawley Harvey Crippen and his
mistress Ethel Le Neve. Crippen was accused of the
murder of his wife Cora, a flamboyant music hall
singer performing under the name Belle Elmore,
who had last been seen alive five months earlier.
On 13 July police discovered human remains, hair
curlers and women's clothing (but no bones) in
the cellar at the couple's home at No. 39 Hilldrop
Crescent in Upper Holloway, north London.
Dr Crippen, the first criminal to be caught using
a wireless telegram, was hanged on 23 November at
Pentonville Prison.

23 July

It was a fine summer's morning in 1943 and
Archibald Brown was enjoying his daily outing in
his bathchair in Rayleigh, Essex. The 47 year old,
dressed in his pyjamas and dressing gown, had
been left paralysed after a motorbike accident
and relied on his private nurse Doris Mitchell
to take him about town. They were about a mile
into their journey when the bathchair suddenly
exploded, scattering pieces of the unfortunate
Mr Brown over the neighbouring gardens (his left
leg was later recovered from the upper branches of
a tree). Miraculously, nurse Mitchell escaped with
minor injuries and was able to continue her career.
The ensuing murder investigation revealed that
someone had placed a British-made No. 75 Hawkins
anti-tank grenade under the cushion. Suspicion
soon fell on Mr Brown's 19-year-old son Eric, who
had been seen emerging from the air-raid shelter
where the bathchair was kept. Eric later confessed,
telling police: 'I decided that the only real way
in which my mother could lead a normal life and my
father to be released from his sufferings was for
him to die mercifully.' He was tried at Chelmsford
on 4 November and found 'guilty but insane'.

24 July

The dubious honour of being the only Archbishop
of Canterbury to kill a man goes to George Abbott,
who held the post from 1611-33 and was one of the
translators of the King James Bible. The occasion
was a stag-hunt organised by the diplomat
Lord Zouche on his estate in Bramshall, Hampshire,
on Tuesday, 24 July 1621. Armed with a crossbow,
the archbishop was aiming for a deer but somehow
managed to hit gamekeeper Peter Hawkins with
his bolt instead. Hawkins soon bled to death
and Abbott was overcome by guilt and depression.
In penance, he fasted one day every month for the
rest of his life. While everybody accepted it was
a tragic accident, King James I was pressured into
setting up a commission to investigate whether
the archbishop should be prosecuted and removed
from his post. The commission narrowly decided
not to take any action and Abbott was formally
pardoned by the king. He went on to perform the
coronation of King Charles I in 1626 and died
in 1633. A statue of him stands in his home town
of Guildford.

25 July

The legal dispute over whether drunkenness was
a defence to a murder charge went all the way to
the House of Lords in the case of Arthur Beard in
1919. Beard had raped and strangled 13-year-old
Ivy Lydia Wood at Hyde in Cheshire (now Greater
Manchester) on 25 July that year. At his trial,
the judge directed the jury that Beard could only
be convicted of the lesser offence of manslaughter
if he was so drunk that he did not know what he
was doing. Beard was convicted of murder but
the Court of Appeal overturned the verdict and
changed the sentence to twenty years' imprisonment
on the grounds that the judge had used the wrong
legal test. The attorney general appealed and the
House of Lords reversed this decision, ruling that
Beard must have had the necessary intent because
of the conviction for rape. Beard was not executed,
however, as the Home Secretary had already
announced that the death sentence would not be
carried out. He spent the next seventeen years
behind bars before being released in 1937.

26 July

The suspected serial killer Dr John Bodkin
Adams was accused – and famously acquitted – of
murdering one of his patients in 1957. The motive,
according to the prosecution, was greed; Dr Adams
had made a habit of benefitting from the wills
of his dead patients since the 1930s and was
described as 'the wealthiest GP in England'. One of
them, 81-year-old widow Edith Morrell, left the
doctor her Rolls-Royce Silver Ghost and a chest
of Georgian silver cutlery before her death in
1950, a few hours after a large morphine injec-
tion. Six years later, the local police received a
tip-off about the unexpected death of 50-year-old
Gertrude Hullett, known as 'the Grande Dame of
Eastbourne'. She too had left Dr Adams her Rolls-
Royce. The exhaustive investigation highlighted
163 suspicious deaths over the previous ten year
period, but Dr Adams was only prosecuted for the
murder of Mrs Morrell (which many thought the
weakest case). The jury found him not guilty
after a seventeen-day trial, then the longest
murder trial in English history. Three months
later, on 26 July 1957, Dr Adams was fined £2,400 for
forging prescriptions and making false statements
on cremation forms.

27 July

The first woman to be executed for witchcraft in Britain was a 64-year-old widow with a white cat named Satan. Mother Agnes Waterhouse first tested Satan's powers by willing him to kill one of her own hogs at her home in Hatfield Peverell. Then she used him to take revenge on anyone who was not to her liking: Satan killed Father Kersey's hogs, Widow Goody's cow and a neighbour's geese; he ruined their brewing and spoiled their butter. Each time Satan carried out her wishes, she rewarded him with a drop of blood pricked from her own hand or face. At least, that was what she told the judges at her examination in Chelmsford in 1566. On 27 July that year, she appeared before Queen Elizabeth's attorney Sir Gilbert Gerard and confessed to using witchcraft to kill a man named William Fynee, murdering her late husband and turning the cat into a toad. She denied letting the cat suck her blood but the jailer lifted up her head covering to reveal spots on her nose and face. Two days later, after confessing she had been a witch for twenty-five years, she was hanged.

28 July

1540: Thomas Cromwell, chief minister to Henry VIII, architect of the Dissolution of the Monasteries and all-round master of manipulation, was beheaded on this day for treason, heresy and corruption. His mistake was to encourage the king to marry his fourth wife, Anne of Cleves. Henry was not impressed with his new bride and never consummated the union. At this moment of weakness, Cromwell's many enemies pounced. He was arrested at a meeting of the Privy Council and sent to the Tower of London. There was no trial; Cromwell was sentenced to death by a Bill of Attainder passed in the House of Lords and his head was impaled on a spike on London Bridge.

1865: Edward Pritchard, the magnificently bearded doctor-turned-poisoner, was hanged for the murders of his wife and mother-in-law at their home in Sauchiehall Street, Glasgow. Their deaths were not at first thought suspicious (thanks to Pritchard's status) but an anonymous letter led to the bodies being exhumed: traces of antimony, aconite and opium were found. Pritchard had concealed the drugs in their food and drink (tapioca, cheese, 'egg flip', porter, wine and beer). His motive was thought to be money and his affair with a 15-year-old maid.

29 July

The bizarre case of Adolf Beck proved the unreli-
ability of witness identification evidence and led
to the creation of the Court of Appeal in 1907.
Beck's tragic story began on 16 December 1895,
when he was mistaken for a charming grey-haired
swindler using the name Lord Wilton de Willoughby.
To his dismay, Beck was identified by a series
of single ladies who had all fallen victim to
the same moustachioed con man. Despite several
discrepancies (Beck did not have a scar on the
right side of his neck and did not use American
slang), he was convicted and sentenced to seven
years in prison. Beck was released in 1901 but
three years later, was again accused of swindling
five more women. On the basis of their identification of him as the con man he was convicted by a
jury – but this time even the judge was beginning
to have doubts. Ten days later the real crook,
Wilhelm Meyer (alias John Smith), was arrested
for pulling exactly the same scam on an actress
and the truth was exposed. Beck was granted a
free pardon by King Edward VII on 29 July 1904
and rewarded with £5,000 in compensation for
his ordeal.

30 July

Highwayman Jerry Abershaw, who haunted the
approaches to London from Kingston and Wimbledon,
was notorious for his cavalier attitude to execution. On 30 July 1795, he was being taken by
coach to Croydon to stand trial for the murder
of a constable trying to arrest him at a pub in
Southwark. As they convoy passed the gallows
on Kennington Common, Abershaw leaned out of
the window and asked his captors: 'Do you think
I will be TWISTED on that pretty spot by the
next Saturday?' Abershaw would in fact be hanged
there on Monday, 3 August after being convicted
of murder and shooting with intent to murder.
As the judge placed the black cap on his head
and pronounced the sentence of death, Abershaw
insolently put on his own hat and pulled up his
breeches before flinging curses across the court.
While in his cell awaiting the day of reckoning,
he used cherries to draw cartoons of himself
holding up a carriage at gunpoint while shouting:
'Damn your eyes, stop!' Even with the noose around
his neck, Abershaw laughed and joked with the
crowd, posing with his waistcoat unbuttoned and a
flower in his mouth.

31 July

HAIL! Hi'roglyphick State Machin,
Contriv'd to Punish Fancy in:
Men that are Men, in thee can feel no Pain,
And all thy Insignificants Disdain.

Daniel Defoe, 'Hymn to the Pillory' (1703)

On 31 July 1703, Daniel Defoe spent the last of
his three days in the pillory as punishment for
'seditious libel' by publishing the satirical
anti-establishment leaflet *The Shortest Way with
Dissenters*. This would normally involve being
placed in the stocks for an allotted period while
the gathered crowd flung insults, mud, rotten eggs
and dead animals. In Defoe's case (according to
questionable legend), the crowd in Fleet Street
cheered, drank a toast to his health and threw
flowers at his feet. He was then locked up at
Newgate Prison for more than three months until
his fine and a large surety for his good behaviour
were paid. Following his release, with his brick
and tile-making business in ruins, Defoe wrote the
poem 'Hymn to the Pillory' and his journalistic
account of the Great Storm of 1703. He continued
to write political pamphlets but is best known for
the book *Robinson Crusoe* (1719), now regarded as
one of the first novels in English.

1 August

The Riot Act, which came into force on
1 August 1715, was intended to clamp down on
public unrest following a series of 'rebellious
riots and tumults'. It gave officials the power to
arrest anyone who did not disperse within an hour
of the reading of a proclamation:

> Our Sovereign Lord the King chargeth and comman-
> deth all persons, being assembled, immediately to
> disperse themselves, and peaceably to depart to
> their habitations, or to their lawful business,
> upon the pains contained in the act made in the
> first year of King George, for preventing tumults
> and riotous assemblies. God Save the King.

The act applied if twelve or more people were
gathered in one place and stated that the rioters
could be killed, maimed or hurt with impunity.
It was most notoriously used before the Massacre
of St George's Fields in 1768 and the Peterloo
Massacre of 1819. The Act was repealed in 1973 but
the phrase 'to read the riot act' is still used to
indicate the issuing of a warning or reprimand.

2 August

On 2 August 1830, Captain William Moir was
hanged for shooting dead a fisherman trespassing
on his land near Stanford-Le-Hope in Essex.
The 34-year-old retired soldier was a towering
figure of respectability, and not merely because he
was over 6ft tall – he was descended from Robert
the Bruce and was the cousin of the Lord Advocate
of Scotland. Moir had served seventeen years in
the British Army in France, Spain and America
before shunning the fashionable circuit in London
to buy the 400-acre Shellhaven Farm, blessed
with rivers teeming with the best-quality fish.
His only weakness was an inordinate hatred
of trespassers. So when he spotted a fisherman
named Malcolm setting up his nets in the river
and traipsing across his land with a basket of
potatoes, and having ordered the said Malcolm to
leave only to receive a torrent of abuse, Captain
Moir lost his temper, pulled out his pistol
and fired. The fisherman was hit in the arm but
developed lockjaw and died a few days later. Moir
argued that he was driven to act because his lands
were surrounded by desperate criminals, but was
convicted of murder after a trial at Chelmsford.

3 August

Sir Roger Casement was hanged in London on this day in 1916 after attempting to win German support for a rebellion in Ireland. On the outbreak of the First World War, his sympathy for the cause of Irish Republicanism led him to travel to Berlin to seek an informal alliance. He also attempted to form an 'Irish Brigade' from the Irish prisoners of war captured at the front, without much success.

LC-DIG-ggbain-19597

Then, in early 1916, the Germans agreed to assist the planned 'Easter Rising' by transporting 20,000 rifles and ten machine guns to Ireland. Casement followed in a submarine, but both he and the arms shipment were intercepted on 21 April. Among his belongings were the famous 'Black Diaries', which exposed Casement as a promiscuous homosexual (although it is now believed they were forged). Casement was charged with treason and imprisoned at the Tower of London. Three days later, the Easter Rising broke out. Following his conviction on 29 June, Casement was stripped of his knighthood and sentenced to death. He was executed at Pentonville Prison despite appeals for a reprieve from the writers Arthur Conan Doyle and George Bernard Shaw.

4 August

Goat Fell, a peak on the Scottish isle of Arran,
was the setting for an intriguing murder mystery
in the late nineteenth century. When the body of
English holidaymaker Edwin Rose was discovered
buried beneath a pile of rocks in a gully below the
mountain on this day in 1889, it was suspected he
had been beaten to death and then robbed. The most
likely culprit was his climbing partner John Watson
Laurie, who had been seen climbing the mountain
with Rose on 15 July, only to descend alone. Laurie
went on the run to Liverpool but was eventually
arrested near Hamilton on 3 September. After
a failed attempt to kill himself, he admitted:
'I robbed the man – but I did not murder him.'
The subsequent trial at Edinburgh High Court
attracted so much interest that queues formed at
the entrance to the public gallery. Although no
blood was found on his clothing – suggesting that
Mr Rose had not been bludgeoned to death – Laurie
was convicted of murder and sentenced to death.
He was granted a reprieve and died at Perth
Criminal Asylum in 1930. Laurie maintained his
innocence to the end. So did Edwin Rose fall or was
he pushed?

5 August

The last person to be executed at the Tower of
London was not a king or a queen but a German
spy in the middle of the Second World War.
Josef Jakobs parachuted into England in the early
hours of 1 February 1941 but broke his right leg
in the attempt and had to fire his pistol to summon
help from two farm workers walking past a field
in Ramsey, Huntingdonshire. Jakobs was carrying
a code (which he had ripped up), a wireless
transmitter, a map indicating the position of
RAF Upwood and £498 in cash. He was convicted
of treason on 5 August 1941 after a secret court
martial in London and sentenced to death. Jakobs,
a former dentist, salesman and black marketeer,
admitting being a member of German intelligence
but claimed he wanted to help fight the Nazis and
asked to be locked up until the end of the war.
His request was refused and he was killed by firing
squad ten days later at an old .22 rifle range in
the grounds of the Tower. Jakobs was buried in
an unmarked grave at St Mary's Roman Catholic
Cemetery in Kensal Green.

6 August

The eighteenth-century murderer Eugene Aram owes his infamy more to Victorian poets, novelists and dramatists than his actual crime. Aram was hanged in York on this day in 1759 for the murder of his friend Daniel Clark some fourteen years earlier. Clark, a shoemaker, disappeared along with £200 of silver and other borrowed goods the night before his wedding in February 1745 and was never seen again. Aram was suspected but never charged – until a skeleton was unearthed in a field outside Knaresborough in Yorkshire and a new investigation was launched. This resulted in Aram's friend Richard Houseman revealing that these bones could not belong to Clark, because Aram had buried Clark at St Robert's Cave. Sure enough, a skeleton was found at the exact spot indicated.

Houseman gave evidence for the Crown to save his own skin and Aram was convicted of murder. This humble schoolteacher might otherwise have been forgotten had it not been for a series of romanti-cised accounts of his life which portrayed him as a tragic figure tormented by his own genius, including Thomas Hood's *The Dream of Eugene Aram* and Bulwer Lytton's *Eugene Aram*.

7 August

The trial of Florence Maybrick
for poisoning her husband
with arsenic was a Victorian
sensation on both sides of the
Atlantic. Florence, who was born
in Alabama in the United States,
got engaged to James Maybrick
eight days after meeting him
on board a ship to England
during a holiday with her mother.
After their marriage they set up
a home in Aigburth, Liverpool,
and by 1889 they had a son and a
daughter and were well known on
the social scene. Underneath the
surface, however, the marriage
was failing, both husband and
wife were having affairs and
they had built up heavy debts.
In April that year Florence
bought flypaper containing arsenic, supposedly for
a facial beauty treatment. Her husband fell ill
later that month and died on 11 May and Florence
was charged with murder after the poison was
detected in his body (although at a low level).
She was convicted and sentenced to death on
7 August, but the Home Secretary bowed to public
pressure and spared her from execution. She spent
fourteen years in prison before moving back to
America. In 1992 the so-called 'Maybrick Diaries'
emerged, suggesting that James Maybrick was also
Jack the Ripper.

Mʀ MAYBRICK

Mʳˢ MAYBRICK

8 August

On 8 August 1951, a 9-year-old girl called Cicely Batstone met 21-year-old John Straffen at a cinema in Bath. Straffen, who had a mental age of 10, persuaded her to take a bus out of the city centre and then strangled her in a meadow. The body was found the next morning. On his arrest Straffen confessed to killing not only Cicely but also 5-year-old Brenda Goddard, who was found strangled in a copse yards away from her home. Straffen was charged with both murders but was found unfit to stand trial and sent to Broadmoor. Six months later, on 29 April 1952, Straffen escaped by climbing over the 10ft wall. Within two hours he had found his third victim, 5-year-old Linda Bowyer. By the time her body was found the next morning, Straffen had already been recaptured. Detectives were still unaware of the latest murder when he told them: 'I did not kill the little girl on the bicycle.' This time Straffen stood trial and was convicted and sentenced to death. He was reprieved a few days before the planned execution and spent the next fifty-five years in jail until his death in 2007.

9 August

Nineteen-year-old Herbert Mills thought he had
committed the perfect crime. The only problem,
in his eyes, was that nobody knew about it. So, on
9 August 1951, he telephoned the *News of the World*
to offer them an exclusive story: he had discovered a dead body while picking raspberries in
Sherwood Vale, Nottingham. Mills took officers to
the spot and, sure enough, there was 47-year-old
Mabel Tattershaw, later described by prosecutors
as 'a woman of small significance, unattrac-
tive and very poor'. She had been strangled and
battered to death. The investigation into the
murder was still in its early stages when Mills,
apparently desperate for some kind of credit,
gave a statement to the same paper: 'I had always
considered the possibility of the perfect crime,
murder. Here was my opportunity. I have been most
successful. No motive – no clue. Why, if I had
not reported finding the body I should not have
been connected in any way whatsoever. I am quite
proud of my achievement.' Mills admitted killing
her on 3 August after meeting her in a cinema the
previous day. He attempted to withdraw his confession at trial but was convicted and hanged on
11 December.

10 August

The last person to suffer gibbeting – hanging in chains after death – was executed on this day in 1832. It was a punishment designed to deter other criminals but by the nineteenth century, public opinion was slowly turning against such barbarous customs, not least because local residents thought it objectionable to have a rotting corpse dangling in public view near their homes, even if they were the vilest of murderers. In this case James Cook, a 21-year-old bookbinder, had battered businessman John Paas to death on 30 May to avoid paying a debt. Cook then set about destroying the body by burning it in the hearth at his workshop in Leicester. He might have got away with it had his neighbours not started asking difficult questions about the meat sizzling on his fire. And why were two human thighs and a lower leg concealed in his chimney? Are these pieces of scorched bones in the ashes? Crucially, an invoice signed by the victim was lying on the table. Analysis of the skewed handwriting suggested Mr Paas was hit with a bookbinders' hammer as he drew his initial 'P'. Cook confessed and was condemned to death.

11 August

London's Mayfair, home of the rich and famous,
is now perhaps best known as the most expensive
property in the Monopoly board game. In the first
years of the eighteenth century, the 'May Fair'
was a notorious haunt of prize-fighters, prostitutes, puppet shows and pickpockets. So much
so that Queen Anne felt it necessary to issue a
proclamation calling for its suppression. A squad
of local constables sent in to clear the area
found themselves confronted by a mob armed with
brickbats and swords. One of the gang, a prize-
fighter named Thomas Cook, stabbed a constable in
the stomach during the melee. The constable died
four days later and Cook fled to Ireland. There
he might have remained, had it not been for his
tendency to boast about his exploits in public
houses. Cook was arrested and sent back to London
to be convicted of murder and sentenced to death.
The execution was scheduled for 21 July 1703 but
Cook was granted a reprieve before he got halfway
to the gallows at Tyburn. It was only temporary,
however; Cook, a self-confessed 'Prophane and
Lewd Wretch', was executed on 11 August.

12 August

On 12 August 1926, an Old Etonian, his young wife
and her sportsman lover sat down for a champagne
supper to sort out their differences. The husband,
Francis 'Alfonso' Smith, proposed a deal: his wife,
Mrs Kathleen Smith, would see neither of them for
three months. Mrs Smith and her lover John Derham,
an international rink hockey player, suggested
politely that only Mr Smith should go away for the
three months. The argument was still going when
they returned to Mrs Smith's home, 'Stella Maris',
in Whitstable, Kent. 'I'm not going to have this
lover of yours sleeping in my house,' said Smith.
All three retired to the drawing room. The next
moment, a shot was fired from Mr Smith's pistol and
witnesses saw Mr Derham stagger out of the house,
clutching a bullet wound to his stomach. He died
the next day. Mr Smith claimed that he never
touched the trigger and suggested the gun went off
accidentally when Mr Derham grabbed it. Mrs Smith,
the only other witness, never revealed her side
of the story. The jury found Mr Smith not guilty
of murder and he was jailed for only twelve months
for possessing the gun.

13 August

George Joseph Smith earned his nickname of
'The Brides in the Bath Murderer' after drowning
three of his wives in order to steal their money.
His crimes were exposed after the death of
Margaret Lofty (who believed her new husband was
called John Lloyd) at a lodging house in Islington,
north London, on 17 December 1914. The inquest
verdict was accidental death but a report of the
tragedy in the *News of the World* was spotted by the
father of another woman, Alice Burnham, who had
also drowned in the bath in Blackpool the previous
year – five weeks after marrying George Smith.
Detectives confirmed Lloyd and Smith were the
same person and exhumed the body of Miss Burnham.
In February 1915, they were tipped off about the
death of Bessie Mundy in Herne Bay in almost iden-
tical circumstances. Smith was charged with murder.
At the Old Bailey trial, the pathologist Bernard
Spilsbury suggested he had drowned his wives by
suddenly yanking them up by the feet as they took
a bath. The case was circumstantial (there were no
eyewitnesses) but he was convicted and hanged at
Maidstone Gaol on Friday, 13 August 1915.

14 August

Twenty-year-old Ann Whale first attempted to murder her husband by adding roasted spiders to his beer. When this method failed, her friend and housemate Sarah Pledge kindly offered to go and find a more reliable poison – arsenic. Suitably equipped, Ann mixed some of the rat killer into Mr James Whale's pudding while he was tending their baby at their home in Horsham, Sussex. He died in agony the next day. Suspicion naturally fell upon the two women closest to the victim, as Whale was rumoured to be in line to inherit the sum of £60 and Mrs Pledge had recently fallen out with her friend's husband. The examination of the body confirmed foul play and they were charged with murder. Both confessed to police in the hope of escaping the noose. Both were convicted of murder and sentenced to death. On 14 August 1752 Pledge was hanged, while Whale was first strangled and then burnt on the stake (murdering a husband at this time was seen as petty treason and so warranted a more severe punishment – although the strangulation before burning was seen as a merciful act).

15 August

The Maid of Buttermere, Mary Robinson, was a
famous beauty of the Lake District who became
tangled up in the shady dealings of a fraudster
known as 'The Keswick Imposter'. Mary's youthful
charms were first noticed in 1792, when the author
of a popular guide book rapturously described her
as 'the reigning lily of the valley' (although he
called her Sally of Buttermere, perhaps to protect
her from unwanted attention). Ten years later,
aged 24, Mary was seduced by an overweight but
handsome gentleman in his 40s who claimed to be
Colonel Alexander Hope, an MP and brother of the
Earl of Hopetoun. Their marriage on 2 October 1802
was reported in a London newspaper by the poet
Samuel Taylor Coleridge. Within days Colonel Hope
was unmasked as John Hatfield, a bigamist and a
bankrupt who had swindled large sums of money
from businessmen in Keswick. Hatfield went on the
run, passing through Ravenglass and Chester before
being arrested in Swansea. He was put on trial
in Cumberland on 15 August 1803 and convicted
of forgery. Hatfield was executed in Carlisle
on 3 September. Mary Robinson was later given
a mention in William Wordsworth's posthumously
published poem 'The Prelude'.

16 August

1264: King Henry III issued a pardon for Inetta de Balsham, convicted of harbouring thieves, after she survived being hanged from 9 p.m. until sunrise the following morning.

1819: More than 60,000 men, women and children packed into St Peter's Field in Manchester to hear calls for political reform and express their discontent at the poverty and unem-

ployment blighting the country. The authorities, fearing the potential for violence and insurrection, gathered a force of 600 Hussars, several hundred soldiers, two artillery guns, and around 350 members of the local volunteer force known as the Yeomanry. Shortly before 2 p.m., around 120 cavalry received the order from the local magistrates to arrest the speakers at the meeting, including the radical politician Henry Hunt. In the panic and confusion that followed as many as fifteen people were crushed, battered or hacked to death and hundreds more injured. The carnage was quickly dubbed 'The Peterloo Massacre', an ironic nod to the famous British victory against the French just four years earlier. Hunt was tried for sedition in March 1820 and sentenced to thirty months' imprisonment. The magistrates were thanked by the Prince Regent for their 'preservation of peace'.

17 August

Murder weapons come in all shapes and sizes. In the case of Joseph Hastings, the deadly item was his own 'Unicorn's Horn'. On 17 August 1730, he decided to show off his horn (which was in fact the tusk of a narwhal) while playing skittles with friends in Holborn, central London. It was a valuable item, and Hastings was heard to say that he had 'bid more for that item than any man in the ground had in his pocket'. It had even attracted a bid from the wealthy collector Sir Hans Sloane. One of the local residents, John Williams, cheekily offered him 3 pence for it and was promptly branded a 'son of a bitch'. A fight broke out. Williams was seen to jab Hastings in the stomach and head with the horn before kicking him repeatedly as he lay on the ground. A bruised and battered Hastings managed to stagger home to his wife that night, but died of his injuries eleven days later on the 28th. Williams was charged with murder but was acquitted after claiming he had only pushed the man away in self-defence.

18 August

One of the most famous witch trials in English history took place in Lancashire in 1612 and ended with the execution of eight women and two men. The Pendle Witches – who included four members of the same family – were accused of crimes ranging from turning beer sour to child murder. Chief among them was Elizabeth Device, who suffered from a deformity that made one eye point upwards and the other downwards. Device appeared at Lancaster Assizes on 18 August, accused of killing three men by witchcraft. The key witness was Elizabeth's own 9-year-old daughter Jennet Device. When Jennet stood up to give evidence, Elizabeth cursed and 'cryed out against the child in such fearefull manner' that she broke down in tears and asked the judge to take her mother out of court. Only then did Jennet reveal that her mother had requested help from a spirit called Ball, in the form of a brown dog, to kill each of the three men. Elizabeth Device, along with her son James and older daughter Allizon, was found guilty and sentenced to death by Sir Edward Bromley. On 20 August, they were hanged at Gallows Hill.

19 August

Leopold Harris was a professional arsonist.
His lucrative business involved creating fake
companies, taking out insurance and then setting
fire to the warehouses and shops holding the
stock. Harris could then claim back huge sums of
money from Lloyds and other underwriters using
forged inventories. The 'Great Fire Conspiracy'
made at least £270,000 before the police arrested
Harris and his gang – although by then he had
spent most of his profits gambling on the Stock
Exchange. At the Old Bailey trial, it emerged that
the plot began to unravel when one of the gang
tried to recruit a new member. The approach was
passed on to former intelligence agent at Lloyds,
who took the information to a solicitor, William
Charles Crocker. Over the following weeks and
months, Crocker gathered evidence about dozens of
fires, including one at a silk company in London's
Oxford Street, which made more than £20,000.
In each case Harris, a 34-year-old insurance
assessor, acted for the business, making the claim
without revealing that it was in fact his own
company. On 19 August 1933, Harris was sentenced
to fourteen years' imprisonment. Fifteen other
men, including Harris' brother, were also jailed.

20 August

In 1911, the first successful appeal against a
murder conviction led to the condemned man
walking free. Charles Ellsom, a 22-year-old
labourer, had been sentenced to death for killing
his 19-year-old lover Rose Render, who was
found collapsed on the doorstep of a house in
Clerkenwell, central London, in the early hours
of 20 August 1911. The key witness, former soldier
John Fletcher, claimed that Ellsom showed him a
bloodstained knife and confessed: 'I have killed
Rosie. She drove me to it.' He admitted stabbing
Rose after she refused to go back home with him
and told him: 'I like my Italian boys best.' This
account was supported by a neighbour, who heard a
woman scream: 'Don't Charlie, don't,' during the
attack. Ellsom was convicted at the Old Bailey but
applied for his case to be considered by the Court
of Appeal, established just three years earlier.
In his historic judgement, Mr Justice Darling
ruled that the conviction should be quashed
because the trial judge had misdirected the jury
about the evidence of the witness – John Fletcher.
At that time the court did not have the power to
order a retrial and Ellsom was released.

21 August

It is 1887 and an umbrella-stick salesman called
Israel Lipski is awaiting execution for the
murder of a young married woman in her room in
Whitechapel, east London. The facts of the case
are bizarre: Miriam Angel, the 22-year-old wife of
a Polish boot rivetter, was found lying half-naked
on her bed after her neighbours kicked down her
locked door. She had been poisoned. Lipski, who
lived in the same building, was discovered unconscious underneath the bed next to an empty bottle
of aqua fortis (nitric acid). When Lipski recovered,
he told police that two workmen forced it into
his mouth, demanded his gold chain and told him:
'If you don't give it to us you will be as dead
as the woman.' Although Lipski was convicted of
murder and sentenced to death, many are convinced
he is innocent and should be granted a reprieve;
the issue is even raised in Parliament. It is only
on 21 August 1887, the day before his hanging, that
Lipski confesses he was trying to steal money from
Mrs Angel's room: 'I will not die with a lie on my
lips. I alone was guilty of the murder.'

22 August

Reverend Thomas Hunter was executed on this day in 1700 for killing two of his pupils after they caught him having sex with a young maid. The boys revealed what they had seen to their father, a wealthy merchant who employed Hunter as a chaplain. The maid was sacked over the scandal but Hunter kept his job by making a fulsome apology. All seemed settled. Then, one afternoon, Hunter took the boys on a walk in a field of wild flowers and butterflies half a mile from Edinburgh Castle, reprimanded them for telling their father about what they had seen, bent them over his knee and cut their throats. The foul deed was witnessed by a gentleman walking on Castle Hill and Hunter was captured as he attempted to drown himself in the river. He pleaded guilty and was hanged at the scene of the murders. His right hand was cut off, impaled on the murder weapon and mounted above his body on a gibbet. Hunter's last words were to renounce his faith: 'There is no God – if there is I hold him in defiance.'

23 August

The execution of Scottish freedom fighter
Sir William Wallace is marked by a plaque near
London's Smithfield Market. It was on this day in
1305 that Wallace was dragged naked by a horse
from the Tower of London and hanged, his genitals
hacked off and his bowels pulled out and burnt.
His head was cut off and exhibited on a pike on
London Bridge. His body was cut into quarters
and dispatched to Newcastle, Berkwick-upon-Tweed,
Stirling and Perth. The plaque inscription states
that he 'fought dauntlessly in defence of the
country's liberty and independence in the face of
fearful odds and great hardship'. His most famous
victory, memorably depicted in the Hollywood
epic *Braveheart*, was at the Battle of Stirling
Bridge in 1297. Wallace was defeated at Falkirk in
1298 but evaded capture until 1305, when he was
betrayed by a Scottish knight loyal to the English
King Edward I. Wallace was put on trial for
treason at Westminster Hall and is said to have
replied: 'I cannot be a traitor, for I owe him
no allegiance. He is not my Sovereign; he never
received my homage; and whilst life is in this
persecuted body, he never shall receive it.'

24 August

It is a summer's day in 1908. Caroline Luard,
wife of a respected retired soldier, Justice of
the Peace and school governor, is standing on
the veranda of a secluded summer house in woods
near Ightham in Kent. At around 3.15 p.m., she is
clubbed to the ground and shot twice in the head
at point-blank range. Her rings and purse are
stolen. Two hours later, her husband Major-General
Charles Luard raises the alarm after finding
her body. He says he last saw her at 3 p.m., but
many suspect he is responsible and he receives a
series of letters accusing him of the murder. Fast
forward three weeks to 18 September. Major-General
Luard eats his breakfast, writes a letter to his
son ('I have gone to join her') and walks to the
railway at Teston before jumping in front of the
9.08 a.m. train to Tonbridge. Was this a confession, or the last act of a grieving husband? No
one knows for sure – the 'Seal Chart Murder' case
was never solved and the only suspect charged
had a cast-iron alibi (he was locked up at the
workhouse). The case files were later destroyed by
Kent Police.

25 August

The Bloody Assizes began on this day in 1685.
By the time they had finished, more than 1,400
people had been dealt with, either by imprisonment, death or transportation. Their crime was
to have joined the Monmouth Rebellion (otherwise
known as the West Country Rebellion) against the
Catholic king James II. Its leader was the Duke
of Monmouth, James Scott (the illegitimate son of
James' brother Charles II), who led a ragtag band
of Protestant supporters from Lyme Regis towards
Bristol before being defeated by the professionally
trained Royalist forces at the Battle of Sedgmoor
in Somerset. Monmouth was beheaded on 15 July and
the king decided to make an example of anyone
who helped the rebels, including twenty-seven
schoolgirls ('The Maids of Taunton') who presented
Monmouth with a banner of support. The trials,
presided over by Lord Chief Justice George
Jeffreys, began at Winchester, where Lady Alice
Lisle was convicted of harbouring fugitives and
beheaded, and ended at Wells on 23 September. More
than 300 rebels were tried at Dorchester, and 500
at Taunton Castle. Many confessed and pleaded for
mercy. It is thought around 200 of the total were
executed by being hanged, drawn and quartered.

26 August

In 1873, the confidence of the City of London was shaken by a brazen attempt by four American con men to steal £100,000 from the Bank of England. It was only foiled because the dates had been left out on two of the forged bills of exchange. Staff contacted the man named on the bill and quickly realised they had been duped. Although one of the gang, Edwin Noyes, was arrested on his return to the bank, the other three men managed to evade detectives for several weeks, despite the rewards on offer. George Macdonell was captured in New York, Austin Bidwell was traced to Havana and Bidwell's brother George, the mastermind of the scheme, was captured in Edinburgh the following month. Leading up to the trial, there were allegations that bribes had been offered to warders at Newgate Prison by a third Bidwell brother but the rumoured jailbreak never took place. On 26 August, all four were convicted at the Old Bailey and sentenced to life imprisonment. The judge said: 'It should be well known that those who commit crimes which only persons of education sometimes commit will be sure to meet with a very heavy punishment.'

27 August

1645: Eighteen witches were hanged at Bury St Edmunds after being accused by the self-proclaimed 'Witchfinder General', Matthew Hopkins. The vicar's son was famous for testing his suspects by throwing them into water (all those who floated to the surface were proved to be witches) or depriving them of sleep to force them to confess. One of his 'witches' was an 80-year-old church minister who confessed to

MATTHEW HOPKINS.

brewing storms to wreck ships, while another said the devil appeared to her in the form of a black bee or a shaggy red dog and tempted her to kill her own infant children. Legend has it that the Witchfinder General died two years later, after being subjected to his own dunking.

1660: Two books written by the poet John Milton (most famous for *Paradise Lost*) were burned by the hangman after the Restoration. Both *Iconoclast*, which was written a few months after the execution of Charles I in 1649, and *Defence of the People of England* supported the Parliamentarians against those who mourned the death of the king. Milton had gone into hiding, fearing for his life, but was pardoned under the Act of Oblivion on 29 August.

28 August

By day William 'Deacon' Brodie was a respected member of the Edinburgh Town Council, noted for his large eyebrows, fancy attire and dandified swagger. By night he was a housebreaker

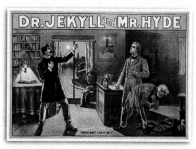

LC-USZC4-8267

and a thief, using his inside knowledge as a carpenter to target the most lucrative houses and offices. This secret double life helped him to maintain two mistresses, five children and a gambling habit until 1786, when some of his gang were arrested after a raid on an Excise Office at the heart of Edinburgh. One of them decided to get a better deal for himself by naming Brodie as the mastermind behind the series of audacious break-ins across the city. Brodie attempted to flee to the United States via Amsterdam but was captured and tried for theft. On 28 August 1788, he was convicted by the jury and sentenced to death. Brodie was hanged at the Tolbooth, on gallows he had helped to design, on 1 October. In the nine-teenth century, his 'double life' was dramatised by Robert Louis Stevenson and may have provided the inspiration for Stevenson's novel *Dr Jekyll and Mr Hyde*.

29 August

On 29 August 1948, 68-year-old widow Nancy Chadwick was found dead in the street in Rawtenstall, Lancashire. The telltale imprints of a hammer on her skull indicated that she had been murdered. Detectives soon found a suspect in 42-year-old Margaret Allen, who had for many years struggled to establish her identity as a transsexual man (she wore male clothing, took on traditionally male jobs, and called herself Bill). Allen boasted she had been the last person to see Mrs Chadwick and when officers went to her home near the murder scene, they found bloodstains in her hallway and cellar and the victim's hair on her clothing. Confronted with the evidence, Allen confessed that she had carried out the killing 'on the spur of the moment' after Mrs Chadwick knocked on her door the previous night. 'I was in a funny mood,' she added. Allen denied murder on the basis that she was insane at the time of the killing, but was convicted nevertheless. There was little public sympathy for her plight (a petition to save her from the death sentence attracted only 162 signatures) and Allen was hanged at Strangeways Prison in Manchester on 12 January 1949.

30 August

In 1894, Alfred Monson sued Madame Tussauds for
defamation after they exhibited a waxwork of him
wielding a gun at the entrance to their Chamber of
Horrors*. This, he claimed, clearly implied that
he was guilty of murder. The victim of the murder
in question was young Cecil Hambrough, who was
shot in the head during a hunting expedition
with Monson (his tutor) on the Ardlamont estate
in Argyll, Scotland, on 10 August 1893. Monson
claimed that Cecil must have shot himself
accidentally but it soon emerged that Monson had
taken out a £20,000 life insurance policy on his
young protégé just three days earlier. Monson was
charged with murder on 30 August; the trial lasted
ten days and featured testimony from Dr Joseph
Bell (the inspiration for Sherlock Holmes) and
his assistant Dr Watson. It ended in the jury
returning the verdict 'not proven'. The following
year, Monson won the case against Madame Tussauds
(thereby establishing the principle of libel
by innuendo) and was awarded the paltry sum of
1 farthing in damages.

*Monson's dummy was placed in a room with Napoleon
and the murderess Florence Maybrick.

31 August

Jack Sheppard, a humble apprentice carpenter-turned-robber, achieved folk hero status by the age of 22 with a series of daring escapes from prison. The first two, at St Giles' Roundhouse and New Prison Clerkenwell in central London, involved the old trick of knotting bed sheets together to climb down from an insecure window or roof. His exploits

earned him the attention of 'Thief-taker General' Jonathan Wild, and he was imprisoned at Newgate for theft. Sheppard escaped within hours of receiving the order for his execution on the evening of 31 August 1724. After filing down one of the spikes above the door of the condemned cell, he squeezed his limber frame through the gap and walked off in the company of two female accomplices. Sheppard enjoyed a month on the run before being arrested and taken to the dreaded 'Castle' at Newgate. Sheppard picked his cuffs, removed his chains, climbed up the chimney, broke through six barred doors into the chapel and scampered across the rooftops to freedom. He was captured two weeks later and on 16 November was hanged at Tyburn before an estimated crowd of 200,000 people. This time there was no escape.

1 September

One of the most important cases in English criminal law began on this day in 1670. William Penn and William Mead were two Quakers accused of 'unlawful assembly' after preaching to a crowd of around 300 people in central London. The judge at the Old Bailey took an instant dislike to the pair after they failed to take off their hats in court. He became even more frustrated when the jury refused to convict them of the charge, offering only the verdict that they were 'guilty of speaking to an assembly'. The jury were rewarded by being locked up overnight without food or water. 'I say you shall bring in another verdict or you shall starve,' added the judge. After two days, the jury found Penn and Mead not guilty. The judge promptly ordered their imprisonment until they paid a fine of 40 marks (roughly £26). One of them, Edward Bushel, refused to pay and sought a writ of habeas corpus. Bushel's case, as it became known, led to the landmark ruling that a jury could not be punished solely on the basis of their verdict.

2 September

The Restoration actor Cardell Goodman was
famous – not for his performances on stage but
his scandalous love affair with Barbara, Duchess
of Cleveland. Being the toy boy lover of the
former mistress of King Charles II had its
advantages – the position came with a fancy job
title (Gentleman of the Horse), a handsome wage,
a lavish lifestyle and plenty of sex (the duchess
was renowned for her skills in the bedroom).
So flagrant was their behaviour in public that
people in high places began to try and engineer
his downfall. He was arrested on suspicion of
highway robbery, only for the grand jury to return
verdict of 'ignoramus' on 2 September 1684 and
set him free (perhaps because the witnesses had
been bribed). The following month he was accused
of plotting to poison two of the duchess' sons
with King Charles II – Henry, Duke of Grafton,
and George, Duke of Northumberland. He was found
guilty of high misdemeanour and spent two months
in Marshalsea Prison in south London until the
duchess persuaded the dying King Charles to let
him out. He was officially pardoned by the new
King James II in October 1685.

3 September

The word 'holocaust' was used to describe the mass
murder of England's Jews after the coronation of
Richard I (Richard the Lionheart) at Westminster
on this day in 1189. Richard, then aged 31,
had barred Jews and women from the ceremony
(during which holy oil was poured over his head as
he knelt before the altar in shirt and breeches
and gold-embroidered sandals). When a small group
of Jewish leaders approached the abbey to offer
him presents, they were stripped and flogged.
Rumours spread that the king had ordered all
Jews to be killed; Jews were whipped, robbed and
forcibly baptised and their homes were burnt to
the ground. The anti-Semitic chronicler, Richard of
Devizes, recorded that 'a sacrifice of the Jews to
their father the devil was commenced in the city
of London, and so long was the duration of this
famous mystery, that the holocaust could scarcely
be accomplished the ensuing day'. The violence
threatened to spread across the whole country,
until the king ordered that the ringleaders of the
massacre should be arrested and hanged. Richard
went on to lead the Third Crusade in the Holy Land,
although he failed to recapture Jerusalem.

4 September

1685: Ann Scot, a 40-year-old Irish widow, was executed for stealing a mantua worth £2 from a shop in London.

1724: At Tyburn, two 27-year-old men were hanged: Joseph Ward for robbing two women of their gold jewellery in Kentish Town, north-west London; and Anthony Upton for breaking into a house and stealing ten iron bars worth £5.

1839: Farmhand Charles Wakeley, 29, was executed at Ilchester for the murder of a 16-year-old maid after she rejected his advances while they milked the cows in Worle, Somerset.

1844: Pub landlord Joel Fisher, a 55-year-old veteran of the Battle of Waterloo, was hanged outside Taunton Prison for battering his wife with an iron bar and cutting her throat.

1925: Wannabe gangster Lawrence Fowler, 25, was hanged at Armley Gaol in Leeds for murdering a former boxer, William Francis Plommer, in a revenge attack in the street. Lawrence was seen to hit the victim with a poker and shout: 'Let's do him in.' His brother Wilfred had been hanged the previous day.

5 September

In the early eighteenth century, bigamy was a
serious felony carrying a potential death sentence,
although most offenders were burnt or branded on
the hand. On 5 September 1719, Catherine Jones was
facing just such a punishment at the Old Bailey
when she unveiled a novel defence – her second
husband Constantine Booth was not a man at all.
He was in fact 'a Monster, a Hermaphrodite, and had
been shown as such at Southwark Fair, Smithfield,
and several other Places'. Jones even called this
'Monster' to testify to the fact before the jury.
Another witness told the court that 'it' had been
brought up a girl (and dressed as such, and taught
how to sew) until the age of 12, at which point
'he turn'd Man and went to sea'. According to the
Proceedings of the Old Bailey, the evidence showed
that 'the woman was more predominant in her than
the man'. Jones was found not guilty.

6 September

The British serial killer John George Haigh thought he could get away with murder by dissolving the bodies of his victims in concentrated sulphuric acid. His first victim, amusement park owner Donald William McSwan, went missing on this day in 1944. Haigh later claimed he battered McSwan over the head with a table leg or a pipe, slit his throat and drank his blood from a mug (an account which led newspapers to

label him a 'Vampire'). The liquefied remains were poured down the drain. Haigh then killed McSwan's parents in the same basement in Gloucester Road in Kensington, south-west London, in July 1945 and set about plundering their assets. Seven months later, Haigh murdered Dr Archibald Henderson and his wife Rose at his workshop in Crawley, West Sussex. He was finally arrested after killing his sixth and final victim, 69-year-old widow Olive Durand-Deacon. Police searched his workshop and discovered a drum full of sludge containing human body fat, gallstones, human bone fragments and a set of dentures. Haigh confessed to the murders of all six victims (and three more unidentified people) and was hanged at Wandsworth Prison on 10 August 1949.

7 September

On this day in 1736 John Porteous, the hated
Captain of the City Guard in Edinburgh, was
dragged into the main square and lynched in a
fearsome display of mob justice. The story of his
downfall began on 14 April that year, when a riot
erupted at the public hanging of three smugglers.
Porteous ordered his troops to fire on the crowd
(and may even have taken a shot or two himself).
Six were killed, many more were injured. Such
was the outrage that Porteous was charged and
convicted of murder, to the astonishment of the
British Government. He was awaiting execution when
rumours spread that he might be granted a reprieve;
the establishment protecting their own. A new mob
formed. The Tolbooth jail was overrun; Porteous
was taken from his cell and dragged to the
Grassmarket. There he was strung up from a dyer's
pole before being cut down and stripped of his
clothes. He was then strung up a second time and
beaten and burnt, only to be cut down and beaten
some more. Porteous was finally hanged until dead.

8 September

The mysterious death of Amy Robsart, wife of Queen
Elizabeth's favourite Robert Dudley, continues
to divide historians. Was it murder, accident
or bizarre suicide? On 8 September 1560, the
28-year-old noblewoman was found dead at the
foot of the stairs at her home in Cumnor Place,
Oxfordshire. She had suffered a broken neck and
two wounds to her head (one of which was described
as being 'of the depth of two thumbs'). It caused
an immediate sensation across Europe because
of rumours that the queen would marry Dudley,
her Master of the Horse, if his wife ever died.
For some reason Amy had sent away her servants
that morning, perhaps suggesting a planned suicide,
but the inquest concluded that she fell down the
stairs accidentally. Rivals spread rumours that
Dudley and the queen engineered the death to clear
the way for their marriage, even though the scandal
seriously damaged her reputation and made any
wedding virtually impossible. It has been claimed
that Amy's bones were weakened due to breast
cancer, making an accident more likely. Other
theories name William Cecil, the queen's Principal
Secretary, or Dudley's retainer Sir Richard Verney
as potential murder suspects.

9 September

The bodies of Mr and Mrs Steinberg and their four children were found at their home on the morning of 9 September 1834. John Steinberg was lying on the kitchen floor with his throat cut. Upstairs in the main bedroom, the woman believed to be his wife, Ellen Lefevre, and her 8-month-old baby son had been almost decapitated. On the second floor 2-year-old Ellen, 4-year-old John and 5-year-old Henry were also lying dead with similarly horrific injuries. Yet all the doors were locked and there were no signs of a robbery. All the evidence pointed to the killer being the father, John, a 45-year-old whip maker. On the kitchen table lay a blank piece of paper, a suicide note yet to be written. Witnesses at the inquest spoke of his 'almost insane' appearance a few days earlier when he complained about his ruined business. The jury returned a verdict of *felo de se* (meaning 'felon of himself') and he was buried in a pauper's grave after his skull was smashed in with an iron mallet. The 'house of horrors' in Pentonville, north London, meanwhile, was turned into a museum featuring a knife and blood-spattered waxwork dummies.

10 September

The Scottish highwayman Sawny Douglas went to the gallows on this day in 1664 carrying a copy of the ballad *Chevy Chase* rather than a prayer book. It describes a fourteenth-century battle between a Scottish earl and an English hunting party on the wrong side of the border (whereas Douglas, ironically, carried out his own raids in England). One version of the ballad includes the verses:

Of fifteen hundred Englishmen
   went home but fifty-three
The rest were slain in Chevy Chase
   under the greenwood tree
Next day did many widows come,
   their husbands to bewail;
They washed their wounds in brinish tears,
   but all would not prevail.
Their bodies bathed in purple gore,
   they bore with them away;
They kissed their dead a thousand times
   when they were clad in clay.

Douglas, the son of a tanner from Galloway, had fought for the Parliamentary forces during the English Civil War but turned to highway robbery after the Restoration. His victims included the Mayor of Thornbury in Gloucestershire (loot £18) and the Duchess of Albemarle (loot £200+).
His reign ended when he was captured trying to rob the Earl of Sandwich, who delivered him to Newgate Prison.

11 September

The British secret agent Krystyna Skarbek (aka
Christine Granville) had survived missions in
Nazi-occupied Poland, Hungary, and Egypt. She had
escaped the clutches of the Gestapo, smuggled
guns to Allied forces and parachuted into France
to work with the Resistance. Her exploits had
earned her British citizenship, an OBE and the
French Croix de Guerre. But on 15 June 1952, then
aged 44 and working as a stewardess on an ocean
liner, she was stabbed to death on the stairs of
the Shelbourne Hotel in Kensington. Her killer was
Dennis Muldowney, an obsessed former colleague.
Muldowney later confessed: 'She told me she did
not want anything to do with me and was off to
the Continent and would see me in two years' time.
I took the knife from the sheath which I had
in my hip pocket and stabbed her in the chest.'
The sentencing hearing on 11 September lasted just
three minutes. Muldowney, aged 41, was hanged on
30 September 1952. Krystyna is said to have been
the inspiration for the character Vesper Lynd in
Ian Fleming's first James Bond novel *Casino Royale*,
which was published the following year.

12 September

Thirteen years before leading the ill-fated
Charge of the Light Brigade during the Crimean
War, the 7th Earl of Cardigan, James Brudenell,
stood trial for attempted murder. The story begins
with Cardigan ordering the arrest of an officer
of the 11th Hussars who dared to breach mess
hall etiquette by placing a wine bottle on the
table. When Captain Harvey Tuckett wrote a letter
to the *Morning Chronicle* criticising Cardigan
over the 'black-bottle affair', he was challenged
to a duel. It took place at Wimbledon Common on
12 September 1840 and ended with Captain Tuckett
being injured in the leg on the second exchange of
shots. By the eighteenth century, duelling was no
longer tolerated by the courts and both Cardigan
and his second were charged. Cardigan demanded the
right of trial by his peers at Westminster and was
acquitted on the farcical legal technicality that
the evidence related to a Harvey Tuckett (who did
not give evidence) but the indictment referred
to the victim as Harvey Garnett Phipps Tuckett.
His second was cleared of wounding on the same
grounds at the Old Bailey and newspapers commented
there was 'one law for the rich and another for
the poor'.

13 September

The Times, Monday, 13 September 1875

On Saturday night the Southwark police were informed by a young man that there was something very suspicious in a four-wheeled cab which had come over London-bridge. The vehicle contained apparently only a man and woman, and the police on stopping it found a human body in a very decomposed state and mutilated in a shocking manner, being sawn asunder in such a way that parts of it might be disposed of separately.

The body in the cab was later identified as Harriet Louisa Lane, who had gone missing twelve months earlier. The man driving the cab was her married lover, Henry Wainwright, who had killed her on 11 September 1874 and buried her under the floor of his brush shop at No. 215 Whitechapel Road in east London. Exactly a year later, he decided to move the body after money troubles forced him to close his business. Wainwright was caught with the dismembered body when one of his former employees tipped off the police after opening up one of the parcels to discover a human head. Wainwright was hanged for murder on 21 December 1875.

"THE CAB—THERE—AHEAD! STOP IT!"

14 September

ELIZABETH BROWNRIGG IN HER CELL.

How did Elizabeth Brownrigg become one of the most infamous murderers of the eighteenth century? The mother of sixteen appears to have had an impeccable career as a midwife and carer at her local parish workhouse. Then, in 1765, she began taking in poor orphan girls as apprentice servants at her home in Fetter Lane, central London. One girl ran away after being laid across two chairs and whipped for minor misbehaviour. Another was beaten, locked in the closet under the stairs and deprived of all but bread and water. The most barbarous treatment was meted out to 15-year-old Mary Clifford, who was suspended naked from a hook while she was beaten with a belt buckle and a broom or chained to the yard door and forced to scour copper. Mary's ordeal only ended when her mother-in-law alerted a parish overseer after being refused permission to see the child. When Mary was taken to hospital, she was covered in bruises and festering sores. Mary died four days later and Elizabeth Brownrigg, her husband James and son John were charged with murder. Only Elizabeth was convicted. She was hanged before a baying mob at Tyburn on 14 September 1767.

15 September

The murder of poet Sir Thomas Overbury in 1613 has
been described as 'one of the most sensational
crimes in English history'. Overbury was an influential figure in the court of King James I until
he openly objected to the affair between king's
favourite Robert Carr and Frances Howard, Countess
of Essex (Overbury even wrote the poem 'His Wife'
in an attempt to dissuade Carr from marriage).
The Howard family, intent on gaining more power
in government, began engineering Overbury's
downfall. In April 1613, he was imprisoned at the
Tower of London for refusing the king's offer of
a job as Ambassador to Russia. When he died five
months later on 15 September, it was said to be
from natural causes. Two years passed before an
investigation into persistent rumours of foul
play revealed the truth: Overbury had been slowly
poisoned with copper sulphate by a gaoler at
the Tower. Frances Howard and Robert Carr were
sentenced to death for their part in the plot
after being prosecuted for murder by the attorney
general, the philosopher Francis Bacon. Both
Howard and Carr were pardoned by the king. Four
others, including the gaoler were hanged.

16 September

The painter Walter Sickert named his series of four paintings *The Camden Town Murder* after the case of Phyllis Dimmock, a 23-year-old servant who was found lying naked on her bed with her throat cut in 1907. Her room had been ransacked. The inquest on 16 September that year heard that she was probably asleep when she was murdered. The killer had wiped his hands on a petticoat before leaving with a watch, a cigarette case and two rings from her finger. Adjourning the hearing, the coroner speculated that Miss Dimmock had returned to her previous occupation as a prostitute and 'had been tempted to go out and bring home a visitor – a proceeding which had been fatal to her'. The police investigation led to Robert Wood, who was seen with the victim at a pub on the night of the killing. Another witness claimed to have spotted him leaving the scene at 4.40 a.m. on the basis of the 'jerk' of his shoulders. But both his father and his stepbrother confirmed Wood's claim that he arrived home by midnight and the evidence of Wood's colleagues destroyed the prosecution claims of a peculiar gait. Wood was acquitted.

17 September

On 17 September 1945, a 27-year-old private in the British army named Theodore Schurch was court martialled for spying for the enemy during the Second World War. Schurch, the cockney child of an English mother and a Swiss father, had been a member of the British Union of Fascists before signing up to the Royal Army Service Corps. In 1942, he was captured by the Germans at Torbruk and agreed to work for German and Italian intelligence agencies by providing them with information he learnt from fellow prisoners of war. One of them was the commander of the SAS, Colonel David Stirling, who had been warned about the existence of a 'stool pigeon' while being held with Schurch (then using the identity of 'Captain John Richards') at a cavalry barracks in Rome. In 1945 he was arrested and returned to London to face a court martial on nine charges under the Treachery Act and one of desertion. In his statement he said: 'I quite realise, from what I have done in these past years, the consequences and I am quite willing to face them.' He was hanged at Pentonville Prison on 4 January 1946.

18 September

The court martial of ten of the sailors involved in the Mutiny on the *Bounty* ended on this day in 1792. More than three years had passed since Fletcher Christian led a rebellion against the ship's captain William Bligh (who was accused of harshly treating his men) and set Bligh and eighteen of the crew adrift on a 23ft boat before sailing back to the pleasures of Tahiti. It took two years for Bligh to make it back to Britain and report the loss of the *Bounty*. A second crew was sent out to recapture the ship and bring back the mutineers. Fourteen were seized at Tahiti, but four died when the ship ran aground. Of the ten remaining mutineers, six were convicted but only three were hanged – Thomas Burkett, John Millward and Thomas Ellison – on board the HMS *Brunswick* (they were not 'dropped' from a gallows but instead strung up and slowly strangled). As for Christian, he and eight other crewmen avoided discovery by settling on Pitcairn Island with a group of captured women. Christian was murdered in 1793 and only one of the original crew remained when the island was visited by a trading ship in 1808.

19 September

On 19 September 1712, William Johnson and his partner in crime, Jane Housden, were hanged outside the Old Bailey for a murder they had committed in that same court just nine days earlier. Johnson was a butcher-turned-horse-thief and had broken out of Newgate Prison to avoid being transported to America. Instead of making himself scarce, he confidently returned to the Old Bailey to see Housden, who was facing trial for counterfeiting coins. Johnson was spotted and a warrant was issued for his arrest. When a prison officer, Richard Spurling, arrived to take him into custody, Johnson decided to fight rather than go quietly. During the struggle he pulled out two pocket pistols and shot Mr Spurling in the chest in front of dozens of witnesses at the court. Housden meanwhile delivered savage kicks to anyone attempting to prevent his escape. Both were convicted after a trial at the Old Bailey and sentenced to death. Neither confessed their sins when questioned by the Ordinary of Newgate but when it came to their execution, both 'mightily cry'd to God for Mercy'. They were hanged

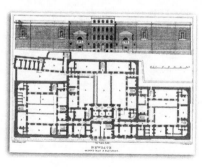

on a gibbet specially erected within sight of the Old Bailey. Johnson's body was then publicly displayed in chains in Holloway.

265

20 September

The 'Tuckshop Mystery' began when 12-year-old
Ellen Marvell visited a sweet store in Ramsgate
in 1930 to buy blancmange powder for her mother.
Owner Margery Wren, who was in her 80s, answered
the door with blood dripping from a nasty head
wound. The girl fetched her parents, and the
elderly woman was taken to hospital. Margery
later gave a series of contradictory statements to
doctors, friends, police and the local magistrate.
'You will never catch him, he has escaped,' she
explained, after describing a man with a red face,
moustache and glaring eyes. 'I do not wish him to
suffer. He must bear his sin.' There was no sign of
any attempt to ransack the sweetshop but Scotland
Yard detectives ruled out the possibility that
she had simply fallen over due to the severe head
wounds and evidence of an attempted strangulation. Margery had told many of her customers that
she kept large sums of money and owned twelve
houses, despite living in poverty. It was even
rumoured locally that she was a descendant of the
architect Sir Christopher Wren. She died five days
later without revealing the true identity of her
attacker and the case remains unsolved.

21 September

Legend has it that King Edward II died a humiliatingly painful death by having a red hot poker inserted up his backside, or as one medieval chronicler put it, 'a hoote broche putte thro the secret place posteriale' (the point being that his body would show no outward sign of injury). This murder, carried out on the order of his queen Isabella of France and her lover, the English nobleman Roger Mortimer, is said to have taken place at Berkeley Castle in Gloucestershire on 21 September 1327. But many historians believe the tale is either an exaggeration or a complete invention. Early accounts of events claim that the king died of natural causes or was strangled or suffocated. It has even been suggested that Edward II escaped the castle before the assassins arrived and lived the rest of his life as a hermit. Whatever the truth, Mortimer and Isabella ruled as regent until Edward III turned 18 and seized power. Isabella was spared by her son but Mortimer was charged with treason and hanged at Tyburn in London on 29 November 1330.

22 September

Brother and sister Charles and Mary Lamb achieved fame and recognition in the early nineteenth century as the authors of a children's book based on Shakespeare's plays. They mixed with writers, poets and artists and formed a literary circle involving William Wordsworth and Samuel Taylor Coleridge. But how many of their readers knew that Mary was a killer? On 22 September 1796, worn down by the stress of looking after her elderly parents, Mary took a kitchen knife and stabbed her 60-year-old mother Elizabeth Lamb in the chest. Charles arrived back at the family home at No. 7 Little Queen Street in central London just moments later and disarmed his 32-year-old sister. The killing was reported in the newspapers but there was no court case – the inquest returned a verdict of lunacy. Mary was at first kept at the Fisher House asylum in Islington, but spent the rest of her life living with her brother Charles in what they called 'a sort of double singleness'. Mary outlived her brother by ten years. In 1847 she was buried next to Charles in Edmonton, north London.

23 September

On the morning of 23 September 1900, the body
of a young woman was found on the beach at Great
Yarmouth by a 14-year-old boy heading out for a
swim. She had been strangled with a bootlace.
The town was gripped by reports of the murder
and it was not long before a local boarding house
owner recognised the victim as one of her guests,
a 'Mrs Hood'. It was several weeks before she was
properly identified, with the help of a laundry
mark on her clothing, as Mary Jane Bennett.
Detectives soon arrested her estranged husband
Herbert Bennett and found Mary's missing gold
chain at his lodgings. This key piece of evidence
was enough to convince a jury that he killed his
wife so he could marry his lover, a 21-year-old
parlour maid. Bennett, who claimed shift records
proved he was at work at the time of the murder,
was hanged at Norwich Prison on 21 March 1901.
The twist in the tale came eleven years later when
another young woman, 18-year-old Dora Gray, was
found strangled with a bootlace on the same beach.
Was it a coincidence, a copycat murder or was
Herbert Bennett innocent all along?

24 September

The seventeenth-century highwayman Captain James Hind is most famous for attempting to rob Oliver Cromwell soon after the execution of King Charles I. Hind and his accomplice Thomas Allen stopped Cromwell's coach on the journey between Huntingdon and London, only to be confronted and overpowered by seven armed guards. Allen was captured but Hind managed to  escape, driving his horse so hard that it died of exhaustion. Undeterred, Hind continued to target Parliamentarians, including the preacher Hugh Peters, who was forced to hand over thirty pieces of gold and his cloak, and judge John Bradshaw, who had presided over the trial of the king. According to the account in the *Newgate Calendar*, Hind told Bradshaw: 'I fear neither you nor any king-killing son of a whore alive. Though I spare thy life as a regicide, be assured that, unless thou deliverest thy money immediately, thou shalt die for thy obstinacy.' Hind was eventually arrested and condemned to death for high treason. He was hanged, drawn and quartered, aged 34, on 24 September 1652, and his severed head was placed upon the gate at the end of the old bridge across the River Severn.

25 September

Nineteenth-century con woman Madame Rachel made
her fortune selling worthless beauty products
at inflated prices. Customers were lured to her
Bond Street store by the promise of remaining
'beautiful for ever' and a host of luxurious-
sounding products such as Magnetic Rock Dew for
Removing Wrinkles and Royal Arabian Face Cream.
Madame Rachel (real name Sarah Rachel Russell)
also had a sideline in extorting money from her
most gullible patrons: in 1868 she was put on
trial accused of defrauding a colonel's widow,
Mary Tucker Borradaile, out of £1,400 by claiming
that a certain Lord Ranelagh was in love with her
and was interested in marriage. It was only when
Ms Borradaile's money ran out that she discovered
it was a sham. Madame Rachel was convicted of
fraud on 25 September that year and sentenced
to five years' imprisonment. 'You pillaged her of
everything she had,' said the judge. Ten years
later, Madame Rachel was jailed again for conning
a stockbroker's wife out of £200 for treatment to
an 'eruption' on her face, having told the victim
that if she did not pay up she would be disfigured
for life. Madame Rachel died in jail in 1880.

26 September

The popular highway robber 'Sixteen-String Jack' was finally brought to justice after he held up a coach on this day in 1774. Noted for his arrogance, his way with women and his foppish style of dress (including the sixteen strings on his breeches), Rann was only 24 years old but was already a veteran of the courts and loved to play to the public gallery. In the twelve months before his execution, he was acquitted of highway robbery twice at the Old Bailey and was confident he could do it again. But the testimony of his final victim was not so easily dismissed: Dr William Bell, chaplain to Princess Amelia, daughter of King George II, told the jury that he was riding home to Gunnersbury when Sixteen-String Jack rode up and demanded: 'Your money, or I will blow your brains out.' Rann was arrested later the same day after Dr Bell's stolen silver and tortoiseshell watch was offered to a pawnbroker. At his trial, Rann appeared unconcerned and flaunted a new pea-green waistcoat in court. 'I know no more of it than a child does unborn,' he declared. The jury found him guilty and he was hanged on 7 December.

27 September

Of all the hoaxes staged throughout history, the story of Mary Toft, 'The Rabbit-Woman of Godalming', ranks as the strangest. It began on 27 September 1727, when Mary first gave birth to what appeared to be pieces of dead animal. Over the next three months she delivered seventeen 'praeter-natural' rabbits and several doctors, including the king's surgeon, Nathaniel St Andre, professed themselves believers. Mary quickly became a tourist attraction and national sensation, albeit one that put people off their food (it is said that rabbit and hare temporarily disappeared from the dinner table). The extraordinary tale was also illustrated by the satirical cartoonist William Hogarth, who depicted Mary lying on a bed next to a litter of mostly intact bunny rabbits. In reality, the animals were all 'born' dead and in pieces – limbs, internal organs and on one occasion a whole skull. Once supplied with the rabbit parts by her relatives, Mary's talent was in

 mimicking the exertions of labour and contorting her stomach so that it seemed as if the bunnies were jumping and kicking inside her womb. Finally, on 7 December, under threat of surgical investigation, Mary confessed and spent the next four months in prison.

28 September

The socialist politician Victor Grayson mysteriously disappeared on this day in 1920 after
exposing corruption at the heart of government. Earlier in the year, at a public meeting
in Liverpool, Grayson had accused Liberal Prime
Minister David Lloyd George of selling honours,
ranging in price from £10,000 for a knighthood
to £40,000 to a baronetcy. He also threatened to
name the 'monocled dandy' behind the scandal,
an apparent reference to the fixer (and possible
MI5 spy) Maundy Gregory. The circumstances of his
disappearance remain unclear. Witnesses claimed
to have seen him walk out of the Georgian restaurant in the Strand after receiving a message that
his luggage had been delivered to the wrong hotel.
For years afterwards there were repeated sightings
of him across the world, yet he never responded to
appeals from his family or claimed his war pension.
It has been suggested Gregory was responsible for
his murder, but his body has never been found.
Gregory was eventually caught trying to offer a
peerage for £12,000 and on 16 February 1933 was
jailed for two months. He remains the only person
to be convicted under the Honours (Prevention of
Abuses) Act 1925.

29 September

On 29 September 1935, a woman walking the hills of Dumfriesshire in Scotland called police after stumbling across dozens of parcels of rotting human body parts. The sheer number of pieces (two heads, two upper bodies and shoulder blades, seventeen limb portions and forty-three pieces of soft tissue) made identification difficult but the key to the case proved to be the newspaper used to wrap them up. The killer had used the 15 September edition of the *Sunday Graphic*, distributed in Lancaster and Morecambe. Detectives realised that two women from that area had gone missing: Isabella Kerr and her housemaid Mary Rogerson. Their identification, using what were then cutting-edge forensic techniques, helped seal the fate of the prime suspect, Isabella's common-law husband Dr Buck Ruxton. The Indian-born GP was convicted of Isabella's murder and hanged at Strangeways Prison on 12 May 1936. In his confession, published by the *News of the World* in return for £3,000, he stated: 'I killed Mrs Ruxton in a fit of temper because I thought she had been with a man. I was mad at the time. Mary Rogerson was present at the time. I had to kill her.'

30 September

The conquest of Wales by King Edward I in 1283
finally brought an end to its independence. It also
saw the demise of Dafydd ap Gruffydd, who was
effectively the last free ruler of the country
(although his elder brother is known as Llewelyn
the Last, having signed the Treaty of Aberconwy
with Edward in 1277). Dafydd began the final
attempt to resist the English king in Easter 1282
by attacking Hawarden Castle, but the struggle
took a turn for the worse when Llewelyn was killed
in battle at Builth Wells in December. Dafydd,
assuming the title of Prince of Wales, held out
another six months before being found hiding in
a bog with his youngest son. Dafydd was taken
to Shrewsbury and, on 30 September 1283, was
condemned to death for common-law treason for
plotting the king's death (the Treason Act did not
become law until 1351). A few days later the prince
was dragged through the town by a horse, hanged
until unconscious, disembowelled and forced to
watch his guts being burnt in front of him before
being cut into four pieces and fed to the dogs.
His sons spent the rest of their lives in prison
at Bristol Castle.

1 October

In 1876, a credulous London public was wowed by the feats of acclaimed American medium Henry Slade. At his séances (entry fee 20 shillings), spirits were invited to leave mysterious chalk messages on writing-slates, play the tune 'Home Sweet Home' on the accordion, make tapping noises and levitate objects in front of the dazzled spectators. It was a lucrative business, until a certain Professor Ray Lankester accused him of fraud in a letter to *The Times* and launched a criminal prosecution. The trial, at Bow Street Magistrates' Court, took place on 1 October 1876. Slade was supported by statements from the naturalist Alfred Russel Wallace and other respectable witnesses who were convinced by his performances, while the prosecution relied on the evidence of magician John Nevil Maskelyne. Slade was convicted under the Vagrancy Act of 1824 (which banned deceiving people by use of palmistry 'or otherwise') and sentenced to three months' imprisonment with hard labour. The conviction was later quashed on a technicality and Slade continued his performances in Europe and Australia before returning to America, where he was again exposed as a fraud after being caught writing messages on the slate with his foot.

2 October

At the height of the Jack the Ripper murders,
the detectives of Scotland Yard were humbled by
another unsolved case right on their doorstep.
On this day in 1888, builders working on the new
Metropolitan Police headquarters at Whitehall
reported finding a headless and limbless torso in
the basement. It was matched to a right arm found
three weeks earlier on the north shore of the
Thames near Chelsea. Then, on 16 October, a journalist's dog unearthed the left leg and left arm
on the opposite side of the basement to the torso.
The case was dubbed the 'Whitehall Mystery' and
the newspapers naturally raised the possibility it
might be linked to the Ripper. The victim – said
to be a young woman in her 20s – was never identified but doctors believed she could have died
several weeks earlier and then been dismembered.
But why leave the body at the future site of New
Scotland Yard? Was someone taunting the police?
The mystery remains to this day.

3 October

Edith Thompson and her husband Percy Thompson
were making their way home from the theatre on
3 October 1922 when a man stepped out, knocked
Edith to the ground and stabbed Percy to death.
At the police station Edith revealed she knew the
killer – it was 20-year-old Frederick Bywaters,
the couple's former friend and lodger. Upon his
arrest, officers discovered a stash of love letters
from Edith Thompson which referred to previous
attempts to kill Percy and an apparent appeal to
'do something desperate'. Percy had discovered the
affair and thrown Bywaters out of the house – was
his murder a desperate attempt to get him out
of the way? At trial, Bywaters insisted Edith
was innocent and the killing was unplanned and
carried out in a loss of temper. The circumstantial evidence was enough to persuade the jury that
Edith knew of the plan and both were convicted of
murder. Despite public appeals and a 1-million-
strong petition against the death sentence,
they were hanged simultaneously at 9 a.m. on
9 January 1923 (Edith Thompson at Holloway Prison
and Bywaters at nearby Pentonville).

4 October

In 1936, fascism was on the rise across Europe.
Adolf Hitler, the leader of Nazi Germany, had
stripped German Jews of their citizenship,
reoccupied the Rhineland and staged the Olympic
Games in Berlin. Mussolini had conquered
Abyssinia. The Spanish Civil War was underway.
Even in England, the former Tory MP Oswald Mosley
was exploiting significant support for his British
Union of Fascists with its sinister red and
blue lightning-bolt flag. To celebrate the fourth
anniversary of its formation, 3,000 uniformed
'blackshirts' gathered near the Tower of London to
march into east London on 4 October. But if they
had expected free passage, they were to be denied
by tens (if not hundreds) of thousands of 'anti-
fascists' including Jews, communists and ordinary
workers blocking the route. Between the two
sides stood perhaps 6,000 police officers tasked
with clearing the crowds to allow the marchers
through. The result was the Battle of Cable Street.
The police charged with their batons drawn, only
to be pushed back with sticks, stones, fists and
feet. Mosley was advised to call off the march
and the fascists retreated, their influence on
the wane. It was a symbolic victory that was soon
overshadowed by the Second World War.

5 October

While many condemned men confessed their sins upon the gallows, the Reverend Peter Vine was staggeringly unrepentant. Vine, the 35-year-old vicar of Hartland in Devon, had not only raped an 11-year-old girl he was supposed to be tutoring but also shot dead the man who attempted to arrest him for the crime. On 5 October 1744, dressed in a morning suit, he mounted the ladder at the site known as Heavy-Tree-Gallows, and made a final speech: 'Loving people,' he began, 'I see here are numbers of you assembled to see me depart this sinful Life, in shame, and as I am a dying Parson no doubt but you expect to hear something of the Fame for which I suffer.' Vine then proceeded to insist he was not guilty of raping the child and was justified in shooting the parish constable's assistant in self-defence 'because he never told me his business when he came to take me.' Vine also claimed he fled the scene of the rape 'on account of my father's ill state of health'. After a few prayers and the singing of a Psalm, Vine went to his death with the words: 'Lord Jesus, receive my Spirit.'

6 October

The Jacobean playwright and actor Ben Jonson appeared at the Old Bailey accused of manslaughter on this day in 1598. His comedy *Every Man in His Humour* had only just made its debut at the Curtain Theatre in Shoreditch when he plunged his rapier into the side of a former actor, Gabriel Spencer, in nearby Hogsden Fields on 22 September. Jonson pleaded guilty, despite telling friends that Spencer – 'whose sword was ten inches longer' – challenged him to a duel. He was locked up in Newgate Prison to await sentencing but was soon released after making use of an archaic legal loophole known as Benefit of Clergy (only abolished in 1823). This involved dressing up as a member of the clergy (including tonsured hair) and reciting Psalm 51 (otherwise known as the neck-verse because it could save the condemned man's neck):

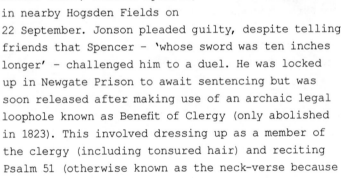

> Have mercy upon me, O God, after Thy great goodness
> According to the multitude of Thy mercies do away
>   mine offences.
> Wash me throughly from my wickedness: and cleanse
>   me from my sin.
> For I acknowledge my faults: and my sin is ever
>   before me.

Jonson's punishment was to be branded on his left thumb.

7 October

In 1946, George Orwell wrote an essay about
the general feeling of newspaper readers that
'you never seem to get a good murder nowadays'.
The example he used – in comparison to great cases
like Dr Crippen and Jack the Ripper – was called
the Cleft Chin Murder, which he complained had 'no
depth of feeling in it'. On 7 October 1944, a man
with a cleft chin and ink-stained fingers was found
shot dead in a ditch in Staines, Middlesex. He was
34-year-old taxi driver George Heath. His killers
were a wannabe Bonnie and Clyde, named Karl Hulten
and Elizabeth Jones. The couple had only met a few
days earlier (Hulten was a US army deserter and
Jones was an 18-year-old waitress), but had already
run over and killed a cyclist and battered a hitch-
hiker unconscious. After flagging down Mr Heath in
Hammersmith, the couple directed him down the A4
before shooting him in the back and stealing £8
from his pockets. At their trial, they blamed each
other and were convicted of murder. Hulten was
hanged on 8 March 1945 but Jones was spared the
death sentence and was released nine years later.

8 October

The Reverend John Selby Watson had led an
impeccable life as a clergyman, grammar school
headmaster and scholar. Then, on 8 October 1871,
aged 67, he battered his wife Anne to death with
the butt of a pistol and hid her body in a locked
room at their home in Stockwell, south London.
When the maid noticed a dark red stain on the
library carpet, Watson explained that he had spilt
a decanter of port wine and that Anne had 'gone
away to the country' for the week. Three days
later, he wrote out a confession and attempted to
poison himself with Prussic acid. The note, left
for the doctor on a dressing table, read: 'In a
fit of fury I have killed my wife. Often and often
I have endeavoured to restrain myself, but my
rage overcame me, and I struck her down. Her body
will be found in the little room off the library.'
Put on trial at the Old Bailey, Watson claimed
he was insane at the time of the killing but was
convicted of murder and sentenced to death. He was
reprieved by the Home Secretary and died in prison
in 1884.

9 October

Aspiring novelist Reginald Buckfield might have got
away with murder had he not written a story based
on the crime. On the night of 9 October 1943 he
stabbed 34-year-old Ellen Symes to death as she
walked home with her 4-year-old son in a pushchair
down Brompton Farm Road in Strood. The boy was
left unharmed and was able to tell police that the
killer was a soldier. Buckfield, an army deserter
who continued to wear his uniform (along with
a strange grin which earned him the nickname
'Smiler'), was spotted in the area the next day.
He was arrested but there was nothing to link
him to the attack – until he handed detectives a
manuscript titled 'The Mystery of Brompton Road'.
Buckfield claimed it was merely his theory of how
the murder was committed but the story appeared
to demonstrate intimate knowledge of Ellen Symes'
daily routine – information that few people other
than the killer would know. It also featured a
character called 'Smiler', described as 'a true
Bluebeard' and 'no sort of man a girl would
go crazy for'. He was convicted of murder but
escaped the death sentence after doctors certified
him insane.

10 October

On the evening of 10 October 1949, a wealthy businessman and his wife returned home from visiting their daughter and her newborn son. Less than half an hour later, Leopold and Esther Goodman were found battered to death in their dining room. There were no other signs of a disturbance and the bloodstained murder weapon, an aluminium television aerial, was lying in the sink in the scullery. But if it was not a burglary, who had the motive? The police quickly focused on the Goodmans' son-in-law Daniel Raven, a 23-year-old advertising agent, after he admitted to an officer that he did not get on with either Mr or Mrs Goodman. A search of Raven's home 500 yards away revealed a bloodstained suit, which had been thrown into the coke boiler. The blood was of the same AB type as the victims. Other bloodstains were found in Raven's car and on his shoes. At his trial, Raven explained he had stumbled upon the murder scene but fled in terror without calling the police. It was also suggested Mr Goodman may have been killed for 'squealing' to police about a counterfeiting operation. Raven was convicted of murder and hanged on 6 January 1950.

11 October

Private William Taylor of the 57th Foot Regiment
was hanged on this day in 1869 for shooting dead
a corporal who forced him to do extra drill.
His downfall began when he decided to skip barracks
in search of a good time, only to get so drunk
on brandy that he was unable to walk back to the
camp in Devonport until the next day. Taylor was
sentenced to extra drill for seven days. On the
third day, Taylor made the mistake of bringing
the wrong knapsack to the parade ground. After
completing the drill, Corporal Arthur Skullin said
he would report Taylor for even more punishment.
The corporal then dismissed the men and walked
towards his room in the barracks. Taylor followed
for 30 paces before suddenly raising his rifle to
his shoulder and shooting Skullin in the head.
The corporal was killed instantly. At his trial
at the Old Bailey in London, Taylor's barrister
argued he should be found not guilty by reason of
insanity; both his father and grandmother were mad
and he had previously attempted to drown himself.
The jury took just five minutes to find him guilty of
murder and Taylor was executed inside Exeter Prison.

12 October

One-eyed teenage murderer Michael Queripel
confessed after being confronted with a single
damning piece of evidence left at the scene – his
bloodstained palm print. The police investigation
began with the discovery of the battered body of
46-year-old Elizabeth Currell at the 17th hole of
Potters Bar golf course in Hertfordshire on the
morning of 30 April 1955. The only clue was the
bloody mark left on the murder weapon, a metal
tee marker. With no other leads, police were
forced to attempt the mammoth task of taking palm
prints from every one of the 18,000 men living
in Potters Bar – including those who had moved
away to Eritrea, Australia, Chile and California.
By 3 July they had reached palm print number 4,605 –
17-year-old Queripel, an office worker at Potters
Bar Council. It was another six weeks before their
experts got round to examining it and confirmed a
match. Queripel, a grammar school boy who spent
his wages on classical records and (according to
his mother) seemed uninterested in girls, pleaded
guilty to the murder during a five-minute hearing
at the Old Bailey on 16 October 1955. As he was too
young to face the death penalty, he was detained
indefinitely.

13 October

Women's Social and Political Union
VOTES FOR WOMEN
Men & Women
HELP THE SUFFRAGETTES
To RUSH THE HOUSE OF COMMONS
ON TUESDAY EVENING, 13th October, 1908 at 7:30

This handbill advertised one of thousands of actions carried out by the Suffragettes from 1905 until the outbreak of the First World War. Police took the reference to 'rush' to be an incitement to breach the peace and issued a summons for the arrest of the organisers – Emmeline Pankhurst, her daughter Christabel and Flora Drummond. The three women handed themselves in shortly before the meeting to await trial the next day. Meanwhile, thousands of demonstrators gathered near Parliament Square, which had been cordoned off by 5,000 police officers. One woman managed to enter the floor of the House at the height of the struggle and twenty-four women were arrested. Ten people were taken to hospital. At trial Christabel argued that the 'rush' did not imply any violence

LC-DIG-ggbain-15348

and simply meant to hurry as if trying to catch a train. All three women were convicted and given the choice of being bound over to keep the peace for a year or spend three months in Holloway Prison. They chose prison.

14 October

The scandalous case of the drunken servant who
attempted to ravish the society beauty was hot
gossip in 1721. On 14 October that year, Griselda
Murray, a former maid-in-waiting to Queen Caroline
and the wife of a military officer, was staying the
night at her father's house in London. At around
4 a.m. she was woken by Arthur Gray entering her
room with a drawn sword in one hand and a pistol
in the other. When she challenged him, he replied:
'Madam, I mean to ravish you, for I have enter-
tained a violent passion for you a long time.
But, as there is so great a difference between
your fortune and mine, I despair of enjoying my
wishes by any means but force.' Murray spent the
next forty-five minutes attempting to dissuade him
before Gray attempted to pull away her bedclothes.
The resourceful Murray pushed him against the
wall, grabbed the pistol and pressed the alarm
bell. At his trial, Gray claimed that he went to
the room to investigate a strange noise – leading
some to suggest Murray had been entertaining a
lover that night. Gray was sentenced to death but
was pardoned after his victim intervened.

15 October

Eighteen theatregoers died on this day in 1805
at London's Sadler's Wells after the traditional
call to arms of 'Fight! Fight!' was fatally
misunderstood as 'Fire!' In a desperate attempt
to escape the imagined inferno, hundreds of
panicked spectators rushed the stage, ran pell-
mell for the exits, smashed their way through
the orchestra and flung themselves from the
gallery into the pit below. Most of the victims
suffocated to death in the crush. They included
a 17-year-old girl who died in the arms of her
mother and a wheelwright who was separated from
his wife and daughter. The youngest was only 9
years old. Dozens of other members of the audience
suffered broken bones or other serious injury.
The blame for the tragedy fell upon Elizabeth
Luker, the woman who shouted 'Fight! Fight!' as
her drunken friends insulted audience members who
dared to disapprove of their loutish behaviour.
Luker was imprisoned for fourteen days after being
convicted of rioting. Her associates, John Pierce
and Vincent Pierce, were jailed for six months and
four months respectively.

16 October

The 'Oxford Martyrs', Hugh Latimer and Nicholas
Ridley, were burned at the stake for their
Protestant beliefs on this day in 1555. Latimer,
former Bishop of Worcester and chaplain to
Edward VI, was a popular figure of the English
Reformation and an obvious target for persecution
under the reign of the Catholic 'Bloody' Queen
Mary. Ridley, the Bishop of London, had been a
supporter of Lady Jane Grey's brief reign until
Mary seized the throne in 1553. In April 1554,
Latimer and Ridley were examined for heresy in
Oxford alongside another leading figure of the
Reformation, Thomas Cranmer, the Archbishop of
Canterbury, but their executions did not take
place for another eighteen months. According
to Foxe's *Book of Martyrs*, as the fire took hold,
Latimer told Ridley: 'Be of good comfort, Master
Ridley, and play the man. We shall this day
light such a candle, by God's grace, in England,
as I trust shall never be put out.' Cranmer was
executed five months later in March 1556. Their
martyrdom followed earlier examples such as Anne
Askew, a Protestant woman who was tortured on the
rack at the Tower of London before being burned
alive on 16 July 1546.

17 October

On this day in 1678, the 56-year-old magistrate
Sir Edmund Berry Godfrey was found impaled on
his own sword in a ditch on Primrose Hill, north
London. The motive did not appear to be robbery –
he still had his money and rings – and examination
of the body suggested he had been strangled
several days earlier before being moved to the
scene (Sir Edmund had gone missing on 12 October).
A £500 reward was offered but the investigation raises more questions than answers. Was he
murdered to cover up the so-called 'Popish Plot'
alleged by Titus Oates? It was this theory that
led to three Catholic men named Green, Berry
and Hill being convicted on dubious evidence and
hanged on Primrose Hill (which became popularly
known as Greenberry Hill). Or was he killed by
Oates' supporters to cover up the fact the Popish
Plot was a fraud? Or was it nothing to do with the
Catholic plot and everything to do with Godfrey's
feud with a man he had previously prosecuted for
murder, Philip Herbert, the Earl of Pembroke?
Others believe Sir Edmund could have committed
suicide by impaling himself on his sword or strangling himself.

18 October

The highway robber Henry Simms earned the
nickname 'Gentleman Harry' for his refined style
of dress and educated eloquence. He began his
career as a postilion rider driving Hackney
coaches for the rich, but was soon distracted by
a life of extravagant whoring and idle depravity.
To fund it he took to crime, holding up travellers on the roads out of London before spending
his winnings on the gambling tables or the ladies
of Covent Garden. In 1745, Simms was convicted of
stealing seven wigs from a shop in the Haymarket
and sentenced to transportation to the American
colonies. No sooner had he arrived in Maryland
than he escaped and sailed back to England to
take up where he left off. On 18 October 1746, he
robbed a man riding a pony near Hoddesden Green
in Hertfordshire, a crime that would earn him
a death sentence eight months later. Simms was
pursued north through Barnet and St Albans before
being captured as he slept on the floor of an
inn in Hockliffe in Bedfordshire. He attempted
to win a pardon by claiming knowledge of a plot
to kill King George II but was hanged, aged 30,
on 17 June 1747.

19 October

The qualities that marked Elizabeth Gaunt out
as a good Christian would also lead indirectly
to her conviction for treason on this day in
1685. Her crime was to take pity on James Burton,
an outlaw accused of taking part in the 'Rye House
plot' to assassinate King Charles II two years
earlier. Though she was only a humble shopkeeper,
Elizabeth offered him food and lodging and even
lent him her savings so he could flee to Amsterdam.
Yet when Burton was captured after the failed
Monmouth rebellion against Charles' brother
James II (who became king in February 1685),
he returned the favour by testifying against her
in return for a pardon. Elizabeth Gaunt was shown
no mercy by judge or jury and was sentenced to
death. On 23 October she was dragged to Tyburn
on a hurdle and chained to a stake surrounded by
piles of wood, straw and reeds. Elizabeth calmly
held up the Bible and declared that she assisted
Burton 'in obedience with the contents of this
book'. She was then burnt alive. Many of the spectators were so affected by her calm, even cheerful,
acceptance of martyrdom that they wept.

20 October

Nurse Catherine Wilson was executed on this day
in 1862 for murdering one of her patients with
poisonous colchicum, a common treatment for gout.
It is believed she killed at least six others so
she could benefit from their wills. Wilson may also
have poisoned her husband using the same method.
Her criminal career came to an end after she gave
an elderly woman a drink containing sulphuric
acid while working as a live-in nurse in Kirkby,
Cumbria. Fortunately, the intended victim spat it
out before it could cause fatal injuries. Wilson,
then aged 40, was arrested and charged with
attempted murder but was acquitted after claiming
it was a simple mistake. She was released, only to
be rearrested by police investigating the deaths
of seven other patients. In September 1862 Wilson
was tried at the Old Bailey for just one, that of
Maria Soames in London in 1858, and was convicted
and condemned to death. After the sentence was
carried out in public in front of Newgate Prison,
one newspaper reported that Wilson 'met a doom as
righteous as human law ever inflicted on a criminal
whose deeds quite equal the atrocities of any
malefactor on record'.

21 October

The now-unfashionable term 'spiv' was commonly
used to describe dodgy dealers and small-time
crooks. Car salesman Stanley Setty fit the bill so
perfectly that he became known around post-war
London as 'Stan the Spiv'. Then, in the autumn
of 1949, Stan, who always dealt in cash, suddenly
vanished. Seventeen days later, on 21 October, his
headless and legless torso, wrapped in carpet felt,
was found in the Essex marshes near Tillingham.
The police investigation eventually led to the
victim's business partner, Brian Donald Hume.
Bloodstains were found at his flat but Hume claimed
that three mysterious gangsters named Green, Max
and The Boy killed Setty and ordered him to get rid
of the body. Hume dutifully dumped the torso out
of a light aircraft he hired at Elstree Airfield.
At trial the jury was unable to reach a verdict
and Hume was acquitted of murder, only to be
jailed for twelve years for disposing of the body.
After his release, knowing that he could not be
tried again for murder under the double jeopardy
laws, Hume admitted stabbing Setty to death with
a decorative German SS dagger. The reason for the
killing? Setty had kicked out at Hume's pet terrier.

22 October

Nineteen-year-old Maud Marsh first met her killer
when she answered an advertisement for a barmaid
at a local tavern in Borough, south London. Two
months later, they were married. Then the beatings
began. A few months later she started to suffer
pains in her stomach, vomiting and diarrhoea.
Then, on 22 October 1902, she died. Tests revealed
a huge dose of the poison antimony in her internal
organs. Her husband, the handsome, moustachioed
pub landlord George Chapman, was the prime
suspect. Sure enough, examination of Chapman's
two deceased wives Mary Spink and Bessie Taylor
revealed the same poison. Chapman was convicted
of the murder of Maud Marsh after a trial at
the Old Bailey and was hanged on 7 April 1903.
Although then known as the 'Borough Poisoner',
Chapman – who was born in Poland with the name
Severin Klosowski – is now remembered as a
potential suspect in the Jack the Ripper murders.
Coincidentally or not, Klosowski is thought to
have been working as a barber in Whitechapel at
the time of the killings and one of his surviving
common-law wives in the 1890s had the same name as
Ripper victim Annie Chapman.

23 October

From the *Manchester Guardian*, 23 October 1943

I AM KING OF POLAND - Defendant's Alleged Statement

Count Geoffrey Wladyslaw Vaile Potocki, of Montalk,
describing himself as Wladyslaw the Fifth, King
of Poland, said, 'I call upon God to punish you.
Heil Hitler!' in court at Epsom yesterday after
having been sentenced to two months' hard labour
for a blackout offence at Half Moon Cottage,
Little Bookham. Dressed in a reddish-brown velvet
suit, scarlet wool socks, red sandals and natural
coloured wool gloves, he wore his long brown
hair fastened at the back with a clip. His green-
sheathed sword lay on the police table. It was
alleged that when spoken to about the light he
replied: 'Your laws and your courts have nothing
to do with the King of Poland,' and added that he
would like to see the Germans overrun Britain.

Potocki, who was born in New Zealand, was an
eccentric poet who was prosecuted for obscene
libel on 8 February 1932 after arranging to
print a manuscript entitled 'Lament for Sir John
Penis'. He was sentenced to six months in prison.
The judge told jurors that 'a man must not say he
was a poet and be filthy. He had to obey the law
just the same as ordinary citizens.'

24 October

The highwayman Tom Rowland is said to have had an ingenious method for avoiding capture – he carried out his robberies disguised as a woman. His ruse worked for eighteen years until he was finally arrested after stealing 1,000 yards of bonelace worth £1,200 from William Bird, a merchant travelling through Hounslow Heath, in July 1690. Rowland, a bricklayer by trade, was then aged 40 and showed no signs of being concerned by his impending trial and execution. He denied both the theft of the lace and the robbery of another merchant of £84 but was convicted and sentenced to death. On his last morning alive he lounged about the Press Yard, where prisoners were allowed to see their loved ones through a grate before being taken off to the gallows. According to the *Newgate Calendar*, Rowland was visited by a common woman and 'had the unparalleled audaciousness to act carnally with her, and gloried in the sin as he was going to execution'. Rowland refused to confess his crimes and was hanged at Tyburn on 24 October.

25 October

The 10th Earl of Eglinton in Scotland did not like poachers. So when he heard about two men crossing his estate in Ardrossan with their guns, he decided to investigate. Close to the shore he found Mungo Campbell, an excise officer he had caught shooting at a hare a year earlier, and demanded the trespasser's weapon. Campbell refused and pointed the muzzle at the nobleman as he backed away, only to trip on a stone. The earl darted forward, Campbell fired; the earl fell down with a mortal wound to his side. Eglinton, a close friend of the author James Boswell, died in the early hours of 25 October 1769. Campbell was convicted of murder by a majority of nine to six and sentenced to death. The execution was scheduled for 11 April 1770 at Edinburgh's Grassmarket but Campbell managed to hang himself with a scarf in his cell the day after the verdict. His friends arranged for him to be buried rather than dissected, but the corpse was dug up by a local mob who felt cheated at the lack of a public hanging. Campbell was eventually buried at sea to prevent further abuse.

26 October

'Wilful murder by person or persons unknown'

On 26 October 1857, an inquest jury returned their
verdict on the case which became known as the
'Thames Carpet Bag Mystery'. The bag in question
had been found three weeks earlier on one of the
abutments of Waterloo Bridge in London by a group
of workmen. Hoping to find treasure inside, they
forced the lock, only to find some old clothing and
a pile of bones. Human bones. When reassembled,
they appeared to be (according to one newspaper
account) 'the mangled and mutilated remains of
the body of a gentleman who had evidently been
most barbarously murdered'. Rips in the clothing
suggested he had been repeatedly stabbed and the
bones showed evidence of being boiled. But who
was the victim? The only clues were the clothing
and the carpet bag itself, which bore a pattern
of roses, forget-me-nots and leaves and the number
48 on the handle. The tollkeeper on the bridge
remembered seeing an old woman carrying a large
bag through the turnstiles the previous night but
she was never traced. Or was it a man in disguise?
The solution remained out of reach and the case
was never solved.

27 October

In the aftermath of the Great Fire of London of 1666, a simple-minded French watchmaker called Robert Hubert made a confession. He first admitted he had started the terrible  inferno in Westminster but changed his story when it was pointed out that the blaze did not reach that district. In this second version he was a Popist conspirator who threw a firebomb through the window of Thomas Farriner's bakery in Pudding Lane. There was no such window but Farriner was insistent that he had doused his ovens and the only explanation was arson. Hubert was put on trial at the Old Bailey and convicted on his own account, even though it appears that few people actually believed it (albeit three members of the Farriner family were on the jury). Hubert was hanged at Tyburn on 27 October 1666 and it was reported that a crowd of vengeful Londoners tore the body apart before it could be delivered for dissection. The following year it was discovered that Hubert only arrived in London by ship two days after the fire started. Hubert was nothing more than a convenient scapegoat for the catastrophe that destroyed vast swathes of the city.

28 October

Styllou Christofi, a grey-haired grandmother who spoke little English, was hanged a year before Ruth Ellis but attracted none of the sympathy and media attention granted to the glamorous blonde. Christofi, like Ellis, was a murderer; but her victim was her innocent daughter-in-law rather than an abusive lover. Fearing that she was going to be forced out of the house and sent back to her native Cyprus, she battered 34-year-old Hella Christofi over the head with a pan, strangled her with a scarf, dragged her body into the yard of their home in Hampstead, north London, and set fire to it with paraffin. In the early hours of the morning, Styllou alerted the fire brigade and told police that she had discovered the burning body of her son's wife after being woken by male voices in the house. Tellingly, the victim's wedding ring was found wrapped in a piece of paper in her room. She was arrested, charged and put on trial at the Old Bailey. After her conviction on 28 October, three psychiatrists found no reason for a reprieve on the grounds of mental illness and Christofi was hanged at Holloway Prison on 15 December 1954.

29 October

The explorer Sir Walter Raleigh is one of the greatest figures in British history. So how did he end up kneeling before an executioner's block on this day in 1618? Raleigh had ingratiated himself into the court of Queen Elizabeth I (supposedly by laying his cloak upon a puddle at her feet), and was knighted in 1585. The queen granted him the right to explore Virginia in America but his attempts

LC-USZ62-2951

to establish the Roanoke colony ended in failure (the settlers disappeared without trace) and he is now remembered (wrongly) for bringing tobacco and potatoes back to Britain. In 1592, he was locked up at the Tower of London for secretly marrying one of the queen's ladies-in-waiting but he was soon restored to royal favour. His downfall came when Elizabeth died in 1603 and he was suspected of plotting against the new king, James I. Raleigh was returned to the Tower of London (where he wrote the first volume of his *History of the World*) before being released in 1616. He was finally beheaded after launching an unauthorised attack on the Spanish during his second attempt to find the fabled El Dorado or City of Gold in modern-day Venezuela.

30 October

Hereford Journal, 30 October 1818

> At the last Leominster Quarter Sessions a Bill of
> Indictment was found against a man for a misde-
> meanour, in selling his wife on the 18th ult. in the
> public market of that town for 2s. 6d.

The practice of 'wife selling' in England is
thought to have begun in the seventeenth century
and was not generally viewed as illegal. It was
not until the nineteenth century that atti-
tudes changed. In May 1881, after a newspaper
reported the prosecution of a man for selling his
wife for a quart of beer in Sheffield, the Home
Secretary Sir William Harcourt was asked in the
House of Commons to correct the popular belief
that 'the sale of wives is a legitimate question'.
The Home Secretary replied:

> I find nothing in this affair, except the casual
> utterance of a drunken ruffian in search of an
> excuse for his own immorality. To say that an
> impression is prevailing that incidents of this kind
> are legitimate transactions is, in my opinion, at
> once a waste of time and an insult to the common
> sense of the House. Everyone knows that no such
> practice exists.

31 October

Some people just never learn. Elizabeth Price was a burglar who specialised in breaking into barristers' handsomely furnished chambers in London's Inns of Court. The first time she was caught, in 1701, she was let off with a whipping. The second (a serge bedspread in 1702) earned her a branding on the cheek, a permanent mark of her sins that nevertheless did not discourage her from pursuing her criminal career. A further whipping followed in 1703. The following year Price was sentenced to death after stealing eight gold rings, a mirror, a beaver hat, a black coat, a nightgown and a collection of legal books, only to be granted a pardon from the queen on condition she do a year and a day of hard labour at Clerkenwell Prison. Not put off by the narrowness of her escape, Price stole a sackful of silverware in 1708. She was branded on the hand and sent to the workhouse. Finally, in January 1712, Price was caught removing a handbasket full of china from yet another chambers and sentenced to death. The hanging was delayed for nine months so that Price could give birth and took place at Tyburn on 31 October.

1 November

The Gorse Hall Murder in Cheshire remains
unsolved after two men were acquitted in separate
trials. On 1 November 1909 the wealthy mill
owner, George Storrs, was at home with his wife,
niece and the cook when a man burst into the
kitchen with a gun. A desperate struggle ensued
between the intruder and Mr Storrs, during which
Mrs Storrs grabbed the gun and rang a bell to
alarm the local police. Two constables arrived
a few minutes later to find Mr Storrs dying from
fifteen stab wounds. He insisted he could not
identify his killer, although his wife identified
Cornelius Howard, a known burglar and a relation
of Mr Storrs. At the trial, it emerged that Howard
was at a pub in Huddersfield on the night of the
murder and he was acquitted. Several months
later, Mark Wilde was tried for the murder after
he used a knife to attack a couple walking near
Gorse Hall. This prosecution also failed after
Wilde's barrister made the obvious point that the
key witnesses had previously identified Howard.
A number of other suspects have been suggested but
the motive for the murder remains just as obscure.

2 November

On 2 November 1952 two teenage burglars, Derek
Bentley and Christopher Craig, were spotted
clambering on to the roof of the Barlow and Parker
confectionery warehouse in Croydon. The police
arrived at around 9.30 p.m. Detective Sergeant
Frederick Fairfax was the first to confront the
pair and managed to grab hold of Bentley, who
(it was alleged) shouted: 'Let him have it, Chris.'
Craig opened fire with a Colt .455 revolver, hitting
DS Fairfax in the shoulder, but the officer refused
to let them escape. Craig fired again. This time
PC Sidney Miles was hit in the head, killing
him instantly. When the boys went on trial at
the Old Bailey, it was argued that Bentley had
encouraged Craig to fire at the police. Both were
convicted of murder but Craig was spared the death
penalty because he was only 16. Bentley, who was
19, was hanged on 28 January 1953 despite concerns
over his low intelligence and epilepsy, and a
petition signed by 200 MPs calling for a reprieve.
The long campaign to secure a pardon for Bentley
was finally successful in 1993 and five years later,
the conviction was quashed on the basis that the
original trial was unfair.

3 November

LADY CHATTERLEY IS INNOCENT –
NINE MEN and THREE WOMEN give their verdict on:
FOUR-LETTER WORDS !*?! ?!*X X!*?

Daily Mirror

It's a sell-out for the innocent Lady C

Daily Express

7 days to Lady C – PENGUINS READY FOR 500,000

Daily Mail

UNEXPURGATED EDITION CAN NOW BE PUBLISHED –
JURY ABSENT FOR THREE HOURS

The Times

These newspaper headlines on 3 November 1960
reported the decision that D.H. Lawrence's novel
Lady Chatterley's Lover could be published in
its full form in Britain for the first time.
The obscenity trial had begun at the Old Bailey
on 20 October. Each of the jurors was given a full
copy of the book to read in the jury room until
they had all finished. Witnesses for the defence
began giving evidence on 28 October, including the
Bishop of Woolwich, the novelist E.M. Forster and
a 21-year-old former convent schoolgirl who read
the book when she was 17. On 2 November the jury,
after deliberating for three hours, found Penguin
Books not guilty. The publishers immediately
began shipping out thousands of paperbacks priced
at 3 shillings and sixpence, along with placards
reading: 'Now YOU can read it.'

4 November

It was meant to be a pleasant day out. Farmer
William Thomas, his wife Alice and their neighbour Sarah Ann Hearn drove to Bude in Cornwall
and stopped off at a cafe to order tea and
cakes. Mrs Hearn, who was grieving the loss of
her sister four months earlier, brought out some
home-made tinned-salmon sandwiches for them all
to share. Two hours later, as they drove back
home to Lewannick, Mrs Thomas was violently sick.
Her doctor thought it must be food poisoning but
the illness got progressively worse until she
died in hospital on 4 November 1930. Mrs Hearn
quickly left town after sending a note to
Mr Thomas reading: 'I am innocent, innocent, but
she is dead and it was my lunch she ate. I cannot
stay.' Further investigation revealed that both
Mrs Thomas and Mrs Hearn's sister Lydia Everard
had been poisoned with arsenic. Hearn was arrested
and charged – but what was the motive? At Hearn's
trial the judge mentioned the 'ludicrously inad-
equate' theory that Hearn had tired of caring
for her sister and wanted to become the new
Mrs Thomas. The jury acquitted her of both charges
of murder and she walked free from court.

5 November

All Guido Fawkes had to do was light the fuse leading to the thirty-six barrels of gunpowder hidden in a cellar under the House of Lords, flee across the Thames and then sit back and watch the massive explosion claim the life of King James I during the State Opening of Parliament. Then, if all went to plan, a Catholic monarch could be restored to the throne. Of course, all did not go to plan and the king, tipped off by an anonymous warning letter to a Catholic peer, ordered the cellar to be searched. Fawkes was found guarding the gunpowder in the early hours of 5 November 1605. Initially defiant, he gave up the names of his twelve co-conspirators after three days of torture and stood trial for high treason on 27 January 1606. Four days later he was dragged from the Tower of London to Old Palace Yard in Westminster to be hanged, castrated, disembowelled and cut into four pieces while still alive. Having watched three others suffer this painful mutilation, Fawkes decided to jump to his death from the scaffold before the noose could be placed around his neck.

6 November

Eleven German spies were executed in the Tower of
London during the First World War. None of them
were particularly good at their job. Take Carl
Hans Lody, aka Charles A. Inglis, a lieutenant in
the German Naval Reserve who arrived in Edinburgh
three weeks after Britain entered the conflict.
Lody had the advantage of an American passport
and fluent English, but was untrained in the art of
espionage. His very first telegram to his handler
in Stockholm was coded ('must cancel. Johnson
very ill. Lost four days. Shall eav [sic] shortly.
Charles') but was intercepted by MI5. Bizarrely,
his later messages were written in plain German.
One of them repeated a false rumour that Russian
troops had been sent to Scotland but others gave
accurate military intelligence. Lody travelled to
Ireland via the port of Liverpool (gathering information as he went) but was arrested at his hotel
in Killarney on 2 October 1914. His real identity
was uncovered, thanks to a tailor's ticket in his
jacket. Lody was returned to London to stand trial
for 'war-treason' and was convicted on 2 November,
having admitted being a spy. His execution –
the first of the war – took place four days later.

7 November

1783: Highway robber John Austin became the last
person to be hanged at London's 'Tyburn Tree'
(in the vicinity of what is now Marble Arch).
The condemned man's traditional procession from
Newgate Prison through the city streets to the
gallows was scrapped and replaced with a 'more
striking and efficacious' execution on a temporary
scaffold outside the gaol itself. This new system
remained in place until 1868, when the public
hangings were banned.

1817: The 'Nottingham Captain' Jeremiah Brandreth
was hanged and beheaded for high treason for
attempting to lead a working-class rebellion
known as the Pentrich Rising. Brandreth, who had
fallen under the influence of the government agent
provocateur 'Oliver the Spy', believed that his
march on the city was part of a nationwide revolution. In the event he only mustered around 300 men
(despite promising 100 guineas, meat, bread and
ale) and was quickly captured. On the gallows at
Derby one of his co-conspirators, William Turner,
shouted: 'This is all Oliver and the Government.'
Brandreth, Turner and fellow rebel Isaac Ludlum
were then hanged and beheaded in front of a
shrieking crowd.

8 November

The 'gentleman highwayman' James MacLaine wrote
a letter of apology to one of his aristocratic
victims after a robbery on this day in 1749. Horace
Walpole, son of the first British prime minister,
was travelling by coach through Hyde Park when
he was confronted by MacLaine and his accomplice
William Plunkett. During the struggle a pistol was
fired, scorching Walpole's face. Two days later,
Walpole received a note assuring him that it was
entirely accidental. 'Tho' we are Reduced by the
misfortunes of the world and obliged to have
Recourse to this method of getting money,' wrote
MacLaine, 'we have Humanity Enough not to take
any bodys life where there is Not a Nessecety
for it.' MacLaine then offered to return Walpole's
stolen watch in return for 40 guineas (twice the
amount of the reward offered in the newspaper).
MacLaine, the son of a Presbyterian minister, was
finally arrested in July 1750 when he tried to pawn
a stolen lace waistcoat. At his trial he withdrew
an earlier confession and tried to cast the blame
on Plunkett, but was convicted and hanged on
3 October 1750. Plunkett was never tried and may
have emigrated to America.

9 November

Father and Mother, they have passed away
Sister and brother, now lay beneath the clay
But while life does remain to cheer me, I'll retain
This small violet I plucked from mother's grave

In the early hours of 9 November 1888, the residents of Miller's Court in Whitechapel heard a young woman singing this mournful song from her lodgings. They recognised the voice – it was Mary Jane Kelly, a 25-year-old prostitute who was known by several, perhaps contradictory, nicknames: 'Ginger', 'Fair Emma' and 'Black Mary'. Neighbours remembered a cry of 'Murder!' at around 4 a.m., but it was not until around 10.45 p.m. that her mutilated body was found arranged upon her bed and the bedside table. This, surely, was the latest in a series of horrific attacks by the serial killer

'Jack the Ripper' (a name first used in a letter published in the *Daily Telegraph* on 1 October). Mary Kelly is now thought to be the fifth and final Ripper victim, but at the time many believed this was the seventh murder in a series which began with Emma Smith in April and may have continued until 1891. Who was Jack the Ripper? We will never know for sure.

10 November

Colonel Francis Charteris earned the nickname
'The Rape-Master General' after attacking his
servant maid on this day in 1729. Charteris was
a notorious rake who had become rich through
gambling, moneylending and speculation. His victim,
Anne Bond, was a 'virtuous and religious young
woman' who had initially been unaware of his true
identity. She was poking the fire in his parlour
when he threw her to the couch, gagged her with
his cap and proceeded to 'ravish and carnally know'
her (in the words of the indictment) before beating
her with a horsewhip when she vowed to take him
to court. Charteris then ordered the clerk of the
kitchen to throw her out of the house, claiming
she had robbed him of 30 guineas. Miss Bond was
not deterred from prosecution and Charteris was
arrested and chained at Newgate Prison before his
trial at the Old Bailey on 25 February 1730. Despite
his attempts to denigrate the character of his
victim, he was convicted and condemned to death –
only to be pardoned by the king. When Charteris
died of natural causes two years later, the London
mob took their opportunity to express their hatred
by flinging dead cats on his grave.

11 November

The eighteenth-century equivalent of the National
Lottery was run by the state to raise money
for great building works and other good causes.
Naturally, it was open to fraud. In one case
a Lottery Office clerk, Abraham Deval, decided
to make his own fortune by filling in blank
tickets, forging the signatures of the Lottery
Commissioners and selling them on to unwitting customers. He was brought to trial at the
Old Bailey on two indictments relating to two
separate certificates. After being acquitted of the
first, the 30-year-old Deval is said to have stuck
out his tongue and suggested the second indictment would go the same way. The jury disagreed and
convicted him of forging a ticket which he sold to
a man in a London coffee shop for £7 and 9 shillings. Deval was sentenced to death but insisted
to the end that he had merely copied a genuine
ticket that had been accidentally torn in half.
On 11 November 1723 he was hanged at Tyburn along
with the highwayman Joseph Blake, alias Blueskin,
and a 16-year-old black servant boy named Julian
who set fire to the home of his mistress to cover
up his theft of 20 guineas.

12 November

On 12 November 1690, a burglar broke into Great
St Bartholomew's Priory in London and stole the
Communion silverware and as many velvet cloths
and cushions as he could carry. It was one of
many sacrilegious acts in the criminal career
of highwayman Jack Collet, who is said to have
preyed upon unwary travellers while disguised as
a bishop. God appears not to have punished him
for such impertinence; indeed, when he lost his
habit in a game of dice, he had the good fortune
to hold up the coach of the Bishop of Winchester
in Surrey. Collet took not only the bishop's purse
but also his robes. Reunited with his disguise,
he continued his profession for several years until
he was caught trying to fence the loot stolen
from the priory. Collet was convicted of 'felony,
burglary and sacrilege' and sentenced to death.
Before his execution at Tyburn on 17 July 1691,
the 32-year-old confessed not only to the burglary
but also that he had 'profaned the Sabbath, had
been excessive in drinking, and assisting others
in carrying on their wicked Practices'.

13 November

Charles Dickens, author and journalist, had come to see the public hanging of a husband and wife side by side on the same scaffold. He was not alone – there were perhaps 30,000 people there shouting and screeching, laughing and joking as Frederick and Marie Manning were strung up outside

MARIA MANNING.

Horsemonger Lane Gaol in Southwark, south London. This was their punishment for the murder of Patrick O'Connor, a wealthy moneylender who came to dinner and ended up buried under their kitchen floor. But Dickens' attention was focused not so much on the Mannings as the baying mob, as he wrote in a letter to *The Times* later that day, 13 November 1849:

> I believe that a sight so inconceivably awful as the wickedness and levity of the immense crowd collected at that execution this morning could be imagined by no man, and could be presented in no heathen land under the sun … I stand astounded and appalled by the wickedness it exhibits. I do not believe that any community can prosper where such a scene of horror and demoralization … is presented at the very doors of good citizens, and is passed by, unknown or forgotten.

14 November

In 1927 the creator of
Sherlock Holmes, Sir Arthur
Conan Doyle, led a campaign
to get a pardon for a
convicted murderer. Eighteen
years earlier, Oscar
Slater had been convicted
(by majority verdict of
nine to six) of battering
82-year-old Marion Gilchrist
to death at her home in
Glasgow. Slater was spared
the death sentence after

20,000 people signed a petition but faced spending
the rest of his life in prison. Doyle believed
that the killer had been known to Ms Gilchrist
and in 1912 wrote an essay highlighting concerns
about witness identification and the determina-
tion of police to concentrate on a suspect with
no link to the victim. Doyle declared that he
was 'morally certain that justice was not done'.
Following the publication of a new book on the
case in 1927, Doyle wrote to leading politicians
and offered £1,000 of his own money towards the
legal fees for an appeal. Eventually the Secretary
of State for Scotland authorised Slater's release
and he was freed on 14 November 1927. His conviction was quashed the following year and he was
awarded £6,000 in compensation. His death in
1948 attracted the headline 'Reprieved Murderer.
Friend of A. Conan Doyle.'

15 November

The last words of Thomas
Neill Cream before the
noose tightened round
his neck were probably
calculated to taunt
the authorities. Like
Jack the Ripper, he had

DR. NEILL CREAM'S PILL CASE.
(Black Museum.)

murdered a series of prostitutes in nineteenth-
century London – but his modus operandi was poison
rather than the knife. Cream, who qualified as a
surgeon in Edinburgh, is thought to have claimed
his first victim in Canada in 1877 (his wife
Flora, whose death was certified as consumption).
Two years later, his lover was found dead from
chloroform poisoning in an alleyway behind his
practice in Ontario. Cream fled to Chicago, only to
be convicted of the murder of the husband of his
mistress in 1881. He was released ten years later
and travelled to England. Between October 1891
and April 1892, he poisoned four prostitutes with
strychnine before his suspicious behaviour led
police to his door. Cream, whether out of greed
or a desire to revel in his crimes, wrote blackmail letters to prominent people, threatening to
expose them as the killer and offered to name the
'Lambeth Poisoner' for a £300,000 reward. He was
convicted of murder and hanged on 15 November 1892.

16 November

The 'Mystery of the Silent House of Llanginning'
was solved on this day in 1953 when two bodies
were found buried in a shallow grave in Pendine,
Carmarthenshire. Farmer John Harries, 63, and his
wife Phoebe, 54, had suddenly disappeared a
month earlier, leaving their home empty and their
animals untended. Their friends and neighbours
became increasingly suspicious despite claims by
25-year-old Thomas Harries, a distant cousin, that
the couple were on holiday for two weeks. When
they failed to show up, Scotland Yard were called
in and by 13 November, more than 400 people were
involved in the search for the couple across 100
square miles between Llanginning and the coast.
The bodies were eventually found at Cadno Farm.
Both Mr and Mrs Harries had been beaten to death
with a hammer. Later that same day, Thomas Harries
was charged with murder. At his trial, it emerged
that Thomas Harries was struggling with a £300
overdraft and had attempted to pay in a forged
cheque for £909 from the victim John Harries.
The jury took an hour and a half to find him guilty
of murder and he was executed at Swansea Prison on
28 April 1954.

17 November

In 1600, the retainers of King James VI of Scotland
were waiting around outside Gowrie House in Perth
when they heard a cry from the turret window:
'Treason!' The king's men rushed up to find their
monarch struggling with Alexander Ruthven, brother
of the Earl of Gowrie, and swiftly dispatched
him with their swords. The Earl of Gowrie was
also slain when he arrived at the scene moments
later. This was the so-called 'Gowrie Conspiracy',
an attempt to kidnap or even kill the king in
revenge for the execution of their father in 1584.
At least, that was the official story: many believed
that the brothers were killed as part of a plot
concocted by the king to get rid of his closest
rivals. Whatever the truth, the brothers' bodies
were preserved and taken to Edinburgh to be placed
on trial. On Monday, 17 November 1600 they were
carried to the Mercat Cross to be hanged, disembowelled and dismembered. Their heads were fixed on
top of the Tolbooth Prison and the remaining parts
of their bodies were publicly displayed in Perth,
Dundee and Stirling. Three years later, James VI of
Scotland became James I of England.

18 November

The astrologer Roger Bolingbroke was executed for
treasonable witchcraft on this day in 1441 for
predicting the death of King Henry VI. He was one
of three scholars consulted by the wife of the
Duke of Gloucester, who was next in line to the
throne. Together they drew up a horoscope which
forecast the king would be struck down by a mortal
illness that summer. Henry ordered an investigation and Bolingbroke was arrested along with
the Duchess of Gloucester, her physician Thomas
Southwell, her chaplain John Home and Margery
Jourdemayne, who was known as 'The Witch of Eye
Next Westminster'. The duchess claimed she had
consulted the witch purely for a potion to help
her fall pregnant, but was convicted and sentenced
to life imprisonment. On 18 November Bolingbroke
was dragged to Tyburn and hanged, drawn and
quartered. The witch was burnt at the stake.
Shakespeare later adapted the tale for his play
Henry VI part 2, featuring Bolingbroke performing
a ceremony to raise the devil Asnath:

BOLINGBROKE: First of the king, what shall of
                     him become?
ASNATH: The duke yet lives that Henry shall
                     depose; But him outlive, and die a
                     violent death.

19 November

On 19 November 1943, a sack containing the naked
body of a woman was spotted in the River Lea
in Luton by two sewer workers. The victim was
aged around 35 and had been strangled, but the
killer had taken care to obscure her identity by
removing her jewellery and false teeth and muti-
lating her face. Her fingerprints did not match
any existing police records. Detectives recre-
ated her face and published photographs in the
newspapers; dentists were asked if she matched
any of their patients; rubbish tips were scoured.
Finally, in February 1944, a dog sniffed out a
woman's coat that led to a Mrs Caroline Manton of
Regent Street, Luton. Detectives questioned her
husband Horace, a former boxer and fire service
lorry driver, but he claimed his wife had run away
to London. Not satisfied with this explanation,
police scoured the house for fingerprints. While
most items had been cleaned and dusted, a single
print was found on a pickle bottle at the back of
a cupboard in the cellar. It was a match to the
dead body. Horace Manton confessed and was jailed
for life. He died in prison in 1947.

20 November

Darby Sabini was the closest Britain ever came to
having a mafia 'Godfather'. He grew up in London's
'Little Italy' quarter in Clerkenwell and by the
1920s had built a criminal empire based on extor-
tion and blackmail of bookmakers at racecourses
across the country. Sabini made such a name for
himself that it is claimed he was the inspiration
for the gangster Colleoni in Graham Greene's novel
Brighton Rock. And he was not without enemies.
In the early hours of 20 November 1922, Sabini
was standing at the bar of the Fratellanza Club
in Clerkenwell when four brothers of the rival
Cortesi family walked in and asked for a drink.
One of them pulled a gun and aimed it at Sabini,
but the barmaid grabbed it as he pulled the
trigger and the bullet passed harmlessly through a
window. A second Cortesi then shot Darby's younger
brother Harry in the stomach. Yet rather than
take his revenge on the streets, Darby got his own
back in the courts and gave evidence against the
Cortesi brothers at the Old Bailey. Two of them,
Augustus and Enrico Cortesi, were convicted of
attempted murder and jailed for three years.

21 November

At 3 a.m. on 21 November 1931, Peter Queen walked
into his local police station in Glasgow and said:
'Go to 539 Dumbarton Road. I think you will find my
wife dead. I think I have killed her.' Or did he
say, as Queen later claimed in court: 'Don't think
I have killed her'? Either way, officers arrived
at the house to discover 21-year-old nursemaid
Chrissie Gall lying dead in her bed with a clothes-
line tied around her throat. Queen, a 24-year-old
bookmaker's son, was charged with murder. The trial
in January 1932 became a battle between two
theories: murder or suicide. While two experts
for the Crown favoured homicide, Sir Bernard
Spilsbury and Sir Sydney Smith (perhaps the two
most famous pathologists at the time) were of the
opinion that Chrissie strangled herself, not least
because there was no sign of a struggle. After all,
Chrissie had previously threatened suicide: 'Some
day you will come in and find me strung up.' Her
latest threat was made the day before her death.
A majority of the jury decided Queen was guilty of
murder, although they made a recommendation he be
spared execution. Queen was jailed for life.

22 November

The notorious eighteenth-century thief
James Dalton made two trips to the gallows at
Tyburn in his lifetime. The first – to watch the
execution of his father Edward for robbery in
1715 – appears not to have dissuaded him from
crime. He was already a practised pickpocket, wig-
snatcher and housebreaker; his adulthood would
see him robbing an army captain in the street
and raiding a toy shop before being sentenced to
transportation to America in 1720. The ship made
it as far as the coast of Spain before Dalton
led a mutiny, seized the ship and returned to
London. He was sentenced to death for the offence
of 'returning from transportation' but received
a merciful reprieve and sailed once more for
Virginia. Dalton returned to England in 1727 to
recommence his criminal career, but his luck soon
ran out. John Waller, a professional 'affadavit
man' who testified against innocent men for a
reward, claimed that Dalton robbed him of twenty-
five handkerchiefs on the road to Hampstead on
22 November 1729. Dalton was hanged for the crime
but would soon be avenged – Waller was pelted to
death by the mob after being sent to the pillory
in 1732.

23 November

Patrick Carraher, also known as 'The Fiend of
the Gorbals', was a real-life psychopath. By 1945,
the 39-year-old Glaswegian ex-borstal boy had
spent more than sixteen years in prison and
had amassed thirty-eight previous convictions,
ranging from theft to serious violence. One of
them was for 'culpable homicide', after he stabbed
a stranger to death for daring to tell him to be
quiet during a row in the street in 1934. Carraher,
an alcoholic with a fiery temper, was sentenced
to only three years in jail. His reign of terror
continued until he stabbed a demobilised solder,
John Gordon, in the neck with a wood chisel at a
pub in Townhead on 23 November 1945. Detectives
could find no evidence of provocation – this was
violence for the sake of violence, a desire to
start a fight, any fight. As Carraher confessed to
a friend, 'I gave one of them a jag and ran away
when the fight started'. He was convicted of murder
at the High Court in Glasgow and sentenced to
death. His appeal, based on medical evidence of
a 'psychopathic personality' and alcoholism, was
turned down and he was hanged at Barlinnie Prison
in April 1946.

24 November

Titus Oates ranks as one of the most despicable villains in British history. He was also hideous to look at: short, stocky and bow-legged, with a purple face adorned with tiny, sunken eyes and an excessively long chin. It was perhaps the perfect appearance for a perjurer who made a career of hurling false accusations around. Oates produced his criminal masterpiece in 1678, a 68-page pamphlet setting out the 'Popish Plot' against Charles II. Ninety-nine people were named as conspirators, including the queen's physician, and Oates was summoned before Parliament. All of London was in uproar as Jesuits were thrown in jail and Catholic houses were searched for weapons. On 24 November that year, Oates went one step further and accused the queen herself of plotting to kill her husband Charles II. Although this allegation did not stick, at least fifteen people were executed because of his lies. It was only in 1681 that Oates was discredited and convicted of sedition. Four years later James II had him tried for perjury, whipped and placed in the pillory to be pelted with eggs. Oates was pardoned and released after the Glorious Revolution and died in 1705.

25 November

On 25 November 1834, two trade unionists were
executed for the assassination of a Manchester
mill owner. The murder itself took place on
3 January 1831. That evening Thomas Ashton,
the 23-year-old son of a wealthy cotton-spinner,
was making his way from the family home at Pole
Bank Hall in Hyde towards Apethorn Mills when he
was shot in the heart with a pistol from close
range. The killing, at a time of growing unrest
over the condition of the working class, horrified
the local community but remained unsolved for
three years, despite the offer of a £2,000 reward.
The breakthrough came when James Garside, perhaps
hoping to benefit from a royal pardon, revealed
the identity of his two co-conspirators, brothers
William and Joseph Moseley. But when it came to
trial, the Crown preferred the evidence of William
Moseley, who named Garside as the gunman and
trade unionist Samuel Scholfield as the mastermind
behind the plot. The motive, he said, was the
unfair wages paid by the Ashton family. Garside
and Joseph Moseley were convicted of murder at the
Chester Assizes and sentenced to death. They were
both hanged on top of Horsemonger Lane Gaol.

26 November

On 26 November 1712, a Scottish woman called
Susanna Murrey was walking through the fields of
Shoreditch in east London when she fell victim
to the infamous 'Whipping Tom'. True to his name,
the attacker grabbed her, tied her hands together
and lashed her 'unmercifully both Fore and Aft,
which threw her into such a disorder both of Mind
and Body as deprived her of her right senses ever
since'. She was just one of many victims – one
milkmaid claimed Tom stuffed a handkerchief in
her mouth to stifle her cries as he whipped her
in a ditch, while Mary Stroud suffered such a
lashing across her thighs that people thought her
wide-legged waddle was caused by 'the crinkums'
(a sexually transmitted disease). Eventually
Tom was exposed as Thomas Wallis, who happily
confessed that he chastised women for the good of
the country, declaring: 'Unless woman be whipped
out of their wicked pride and baseness, mankind
will become women's slaves.' His punishment was
to 'run the gauntlet' between 200 maids, wives
and widows in Cheapside. But Wallis was not the
original Whipping Tom of around 1681, who famously
smacked passing gentlewomen in the street while
shouting: 'SPANKO!'

27 November

The last hanging for sodomy took place on this day in 1835. James Pratt, 30, and John Smith, 40, were spotted visiting the home of 68-year-old William Bonill in Southwark, south London, on the afternoon of 29 August. The nosey landlord and his wife, suspicious about the number of male visitors, decided to spy on the pair through the keyhole. Outraged at what he saw, the landlord broke open the door before summoning the police. Pratt, Smith and Bonill were all arrested and the following month stood trial at the Old Bailey (Bonill for being an accessory). All three were convicted. Pratt and Smith were condemned to death, while Bonill was sentenced to fourteen years' transportation. On 5 November, Bonill left England for Australia on a convict ship while Pratt and Smith awaited their execution in separate cells at Newgate Prison, where they were observed by the visiting author Charles Dickens. 'No plea could be urged in extenuation of their crime,' he later wrote in *A Visit to Newgate*, 'and they well knew that for them there was no hope in this world.' Pratt and Smith were hanged together in front of the prison three weeks later.

28 November

The flamboyant Victorian fraudster Jabez Balfour
lived a life of luxury on the savings of thousands of ordinary working people before fleeing
the country when his crimes were exposed.
In his early years, Balfour appeared to be the
model 'do-gooder': he served as a Liberal MP for
Tamworth and Burnley; he was elected as Mayor
of Croydon; and, most importantly, in 1867 he
set up the Liberator Building Society to help
investors buy their own homes. By the mid-1880s,
Liberator was a massive financial institution that
kept Balfour in champagne, expensive suits and
plush country houses. Then, in 1892, the company
collapsed, ruining everyone who put money into it,
from young married men to elderly ladies. Some
of Balfour's victims committed suicide. Facing
arrest, the disgraced MP ran away to Argentina.
He spent two years avoiding extradition until
an enterprising Scotland Yard detective decided
to effectively abduct him and bring him back to
the UK to stand trial. Having earned the title
of 'Champion Hypocrite of England', Balfour was
convicted of fraud and jailed for fourteen years
on 28 November 1895. He later wrote a book about
his experience, entitled *My Prison Life*.

29 November

Harold Loughans liked to make confessions to police. When he was caught burgling a house in Lancashire, he claimed he had murdered a 15-year-old girl in Elgin, Scotland. Detectives investigated but found no evidence of a killing of that kind. Two years later, when Loughans was spotted breaking into a cafe in London, he said: 'I am wanted for far more worse than this … I did the big job at Portsmouth where I got the money and strangled the old woman at the beerhouse.' This time it seemed true: a 63-year-old widow named Rose Robinson had been found strangled after a suspected break-in at the John Barleycorn pub in Portsmouth on 29 November 1943. But when he came to trial, Loughans claimed he had made up his confession to annoy police and produced alibi witnesses to prove he was in the Warren Street underground shelter in London at the time of the murder. Loughans was acquitted, only to be jailed for five years for robbing a disabled woman in St Alban's a month later. In 1963, knowing he could not be tried again, he sold his confession to the murder of Rose Robinson to the *People Newspaper*.

30 November

The prospect of seeing a banker swinging from the gallows drew an estimated 100,000 people to Newgate Prison on this day in 1824. Henry Fauntleroy, or 'Fauntleroy the Forger', was accused of embezzling nearly £200,000 from the London firm of Marsh, Stacey Fauntleroy and Graham, over the previous ten years. His arrest led to a run on the bank and its eventual bankruptcy. It was suspected he frittered the money away on a lavish lifestyle but at his trial, Fauntleroy insisted that it was used to prop up the bank. Knowing that forgery carried the death sentence, Fauntleroy spent most of the case in tears and buried his head in his handkerchief as seventeen 'gentleman of the highest respectability' gave evidence about his otherwise impeccable character. The jury took just twenty-nine minutes to find him guilty and, on 30 November 1824, he met the same end as the common murderer. According to one account, 'every window and roof which could command a view of the dreadful ceremony was occupied, and places from which it was impossible to catch a glimpse of the scaffold were blocked up by those who were prevented by the dense crowd before them from advancing farther'.

1 December

Thomas Culpeper, gentleman of the king's privy chamber, was sentenced to death for high treason on this day in 1541 after confessing to adultery with Henry VIII's fifth wife, Catherine Howard. Nine days later, he was dragged from the Tower of London to Tyburn and beheaded. The affair was confirmed by a letter the queen wrote to Culpeper a few months earlier:

> I never longed so much for a thing as I do to see you and to speak with you, the which I trust shall be shortly now. That which doth comfort me very much when I think of it, and when I think again that you shall depart from me again it makes my heart die to think what fortune I have that I cannot be always in your company.

Catherine Howard had also failed to disclose a sexual encounter with another courtier, Francis Dereham, before her marriage to the king. She was beheaded at the Tower of London on 13 February 1542 (her execution was followed by that of her lady-in-waiting Jane Boleyn, Lady Rochford, sister-in-law of Anne Boleyn). The heads of Culpeper and Dereham were mounted on London Bridge. Henry married Catherine Parr the following year.

2 December

In the early hours of 2 December 1925, the last
guests left the party organised by Chinese businessman Lock Ah Tam to celebrate his son's coming
of age. After a drunken argument with his English
wife Catherine, he stormed off and loaded his
shotgun and revolver. He then shot his wife dead
without speaking a word. His horrified 20-year-old
daughter Doris shouted: 'Oh Daddy, what did you do
that for?' Ah Tam then shot her and his youngest
daughter Cecilia before calling the police. He told
officers: 'My wife has not a kind word for me.
My son is the cause of it.' At his trial, it was
argued the real cause lay in the brain injury he
suffered in 1918 when a Russian beat him over the
head with a billiard cue. Ah Tam had until then
led a successful career as a shipping agent and
was a respected leader of the Chinese community
in Liverpool. After the attack, he began drinking
two bottles of whisky a day and lost £10,000 in
a business deal. The jury rejected his claim of
'epileptic automatism' and convicted him of murder.
He was executed at Walton Gaol on 23 March 1926.

3 December

On 3 December 1881, Dr George Lamson called at
Blenheim House School in Wimbledon, south London,
to see his 18-year-old brother-in-law, Percy John.
After a cheerfully blunt greeting ('Why, how fat
you are looking, Percy, old boy'), he presented
his gifts – sweets and a slice of Dundee cake.
The pair were happily munching on the cake when
Dr Lamson took out a box of gelatine capsules.
He extracted one and made a show of filling it
with ordinary sugar before giving it to Percy,
supposedly to demonstrate this new improved way of
swallowing medicine. Dr Lamson then left, claiming
he had a train to catch. Percy fell ill a few
minutes later and before the night was out, he was
dead. Tests of two of the remaining pills revealed
the presence of the poison aconite, from the plant
known as monkshood or devil's helmet. Dr Lamson
must have somehow switched the sugar pill for the
poison by sleight of hand. But why? His aim was
to claim a share of the family inheritance after
Percy's death in order to pay off his increasing
debts. It was a desperate plan which ended in his
execution on 28 April 1882.

4 December

The 'Waltham Blacks' were an eighteenth-century
gang of poachers who darkened their faces with
gunpowder before carrying out their crimes. It was
an effective, and terrifying, disguise which led
Parliament to pass a law (The Black Act) in 1723
banning 'any person appearing in any forest,
chase, park, etc., or in any highroad, open heath,
common or down, with offensive weapons, and having
his face blacked, or otherwise disguised'.
The same law gives a clue to the gang's activities:
stealing deer and fish, robbing rabbit warrens,
vandalising fishponds and trees, attacking cattle,
setting fire to barns and haystacks, shooting
at people, sending anonymous letters demanding
valuables, and rescuing their associates from
prison. So successful were the 'Blacks' that they
were offered a free pardon if they surrendered
by a set date. They managed to avoid capture
for more than a year until they shot dead the
Bishop of Winchester's deer keeper in Waltham
Chase, Hampshire. Seven members of the gang were
convicted of murder and deer stealing: Edward
Elliot, Richard Parvin, Robert Kingshell, Henry
Marshall, brothers John and Edward Pink, and James
Ansel. On 4 December 1723, the Waltham Blacks were
all hanged at Tyburn.

5 December

Chicken farmer Norman Thorne told police that on the night of 5 December 1924, he arrived back at his hut in Crowborough to find his fiancée, Elsie Cameron, hanging from a roof beam:

> I cut the cord and laid her on the bed. She was dead. I then went down to the workshop … I got my hacksaw and some sacks and took them back to the hut. I took off Miss Cameron's clothes and burned them in the fireplace in the hut. I then laid the sacks on the floor and sawed off her legs and the head by the glow of the fire. Next morning, just as it got light, I buried the sacks and a tin containing the remains in a chicken run.

The truth was much more straightforward. Thorne killed Elsie Cameron when she visited him on 5 December because he had started seeing another woman, Bessie Coldicott, and wanted to break off the engagement. When the body was recovered at his farm six weeks later, Thorne came up with the only possible explanation. The jury were unconvinced and convicted him of murder. Thorne was hanged at Wandsworth Gaol on 22 April 1925.

6 December

In the 1950s, George 'Taters' Chatham was hailed as 'one of the cleverest cat burglars in the country'. His most daring feat (according to Chatham himself) was the theft from the National Maritime Museum of the diamond Chelengk, presented to Admiral Nelson by the Sultan of Turkey after the Battle of the Nile. Although it was valued at only £250, the Chelengk was a priceless relic from one of the country's greatest naval victories. The diamonds were never recovered. Two years later, Chatham was arrested for another burglary but escaped from Brixton Prison before his trial. Despite being sought by police, he continued his life of crime by raiding a diamond jeweller's in London's Regent Street by climbing through an upstairs lavatory window and blowing off the door to the safe using explosives. Chatham was eventually arrested and, on 6 December 1954, he was jailed for ten years. It was while serving this prison sentence that he met his partner-in-crime Peter Scott, also known as 'King of the Cat Burglars', 'Burglar to the Stars' or 'The Human Fly', who is perhaps most famous for stealing a £200,000 necklace from the actress Sophia Loren in 1960.

7 December

Robert Kett was a wealthy farmer who took up the grievances of his peasants and led a rebellion in Norfolk during the reign of Edward VI. One of their main complaints was the spread of enclosure, which blocked off common land previously used for grazing. In July 1549, rioters began dismantling the offending hedges and fences. By the 12th, around 16,000 people from surrounding towns had flocked to join the rebels camped on Mousehold Heath on the outskirts of Norwich. Rejecting the offer of a pardon from the King's Council if they dispersed, Kett launched an attack. Although hardly a professional fighting force, his force captured the city and held off a small royal army led by the Marquess of Northampton. During the battle, Lord Sheffield (a second cousin of Henry VIII) was

killed by one of the rebels after falling from his horse. It was not until 27 August that Kett's army was defeated by a larger royal army strengthened with mercenaries from Europe. Kett was captured, imprisoned at the Tower of London and convicted of treason. He was hanged from the walls of Norwich Castle on 7 December 1549.

8 December

Joseph Hunton was a well-known businessman in the
City of London, not least because of his distinctive appearance. 'Hunton is a little man,' wrote
one newspaper, '[who] walks the streets in an
extraordinary erect manner, wears large spectacles
and always appears in Quaker's attire.' He had
worked his way up from Yarmouth slop-seller to
partner in a warehouse firm and was known to
speculate heavily on the Stock Exchange. So it was
a notable scandal when, in 1828, Hunton went on
the run after being accused of forging bills of
exchange in the name of a dead man to cover his
debts. He was traced to Plymouth and was arrested
as he attempted to sail for New York under a false
name. In his pocket there was an unsent letter
to *The Times*, protesting that their report of the
value of his forgeries had been vastly exagger-
ated, and that he would pay back the bank with
interest. He was convicted of forging two bills
totalling more than £250 and sentenced to death.
On 8 December 1828, he was hanged on the gallows
outside Newgate Prison with a blue handkerchief
tied over his eyes (at his own request).

9 December

The one-legged actor, playwright and satirist Samuel
Foote was an eighteenth-
century celebrity with a
tragic demise to rival
the best. He was short,
fat and selfish, but
his comic buffoonery
(catchphrase: 'Hey, hey,
what?') was apparently
irresistible, even to the
stoniest of faces. Then, in
1775, a newspaper accused him
of 'unnatural practices' and
the following year he was prosecuted for sexually
assaulting a man half his age. At his trial at the
King's Bench Court on 9 December 1776, his coachman
Jack Sangster claimed that Foote had attacked him
on two separate occasions, first in a room at the
back of the Haymarket Theatre (which Foote owned
and ran) and later in some stables. Foote, to his
relief, was found not guilty and left court a free,
if broken, man. He plunged back into acting but,
just six months later, collapsed while performing
his play *The Devil on Two Sticks*. Four months
after that, in October 1777, Foote died while on
his way to France to recuperate. His reward was an
unmarked grave at Westminster Abbey.

10 December

One of the suggested origins of the phrase
'the clap' as slang for the sexually transmitted
disease gonorrhoea is said to be a notorious
eighteenth-century brothel-keeper. Margaret Clap,
or 'Mother Clap', ran a coffee house that doubled
as a homosexual meeting place in Holborn, central
London. The authorities placed the brothel under
surveillance for several months before launching
a raid in February 1726. Clap was arrested and
put on trial for 'keeping a House in which she
procur'd and encourag'd Persons to commit Sodomy,
on the 10th of December last and before and after'.
One witness told the Old Bailey how he found
'near 50 men there, making love to one another as
they call it':

> Sometimes they'd sit in one anothers Laps, use
> their Hands indecently Dance and make Curtsies and
> mimick the Language of Women – O Sir! – Pray Sir! –
> Dear Sir! Lord how can ye serve me so! – Ah ye
> little dear Toad! Then they'd go by Couples, into a
> Room on the same Floor to be marry'd.

Clap was convicted and sentenced to two years in
prison, to stand in the pillory and pay a fine of
20 marks.

11 December

On 11 December 1775, the Irish adventurer David 'Tiger' Roche stood trial at the Old Bailey for the murder of Captain John Ferguson in what is now South Africa. It was a highly unusual case, as the killing took place outside the British dominions and Roche had already been acquitted of the charge at a court in the Cape of Good Hope. The solution was a prosecution by 'special commission' before a jury in London, which heard the following facts: Roche, a captain of infantry with the East India Company, fell out with Captain Ferguson during a sea voyage in the summer of 1773 but avoided the challenge to arms until their arrival at the Cape. On 4 September, the two men were seen fighting in the gardens. Ferguson suffered a series of sword thrusts to his chest and died moments later. Roche claimed that Ferguson had chased him ('you rascal, I have found you') and knocked him down with a cane. 'As an officer I was compelled to support my honour, and I did not draw my sword till after I was knocked down,' he added. Roche was acquitted for a second and final time.

12 December

In 1912, Inspector Arthur Walls was shot dead
when he confronted a suspected burglar at the
home of Countess Flora Sztaray in Eastbourne.
The prime suspect was 29-year-old John Williams,
a known criminal who had been seen prowling
the area. It was a circumstantial case with one
major flaw: none of the witnesses were able to
pick out Williams from an identity parade. When
the trial opened on 12 December, the prosecution relied on the evidence of Williams' pregnant
girlfriend, who had been caught by police trying
to recover the gun from its hiding place on the
beach. She had previously told detectives that
Williams disappeared for half an hour at the time
of the murder and returned without his trilby hat
(which was found in a gutter near the scene of the
shooting), but at court she withdrew her statement.
The key evidence proved to be the testimony of
ballistics expert Robert Churchill, who claimed
that the bullet which killed Inspector Walls
had been fired from the recovered gun. The jury
convicted Williams of murder and he was sentenced
to death. Williams appealed after receiving a
letter claiming to identify the real killer, but
was hanged on 30 January 1913.

13 December

The last person to be hanged in public in Britain
was an Irish terrorist, who planted a bomb in a
wheelbarrow outside Clerkenwell Prison in central
London. The attack on 13 December 1867 – which
was compared to the Gunpowder Plot of 1605 –
was intended to bring down the wall and enable
a senior member of the Fenians to escape from
custody, but the explosion was so powerful that
it demolished a row of houses on the other side
of the road. Twelve people were killed and dozens
more were injured. Six Fenians were put on trial
at the Old Bailey but only one was convicted of
murder, 27-year-old Michael Barrett. Before being
sentenced to death, he told the court: 'I love my
country and if it is murderous to love Ireland
dearer than I love my life, then it is true,
I am a murderer.' Barrett was hanged in front of a
crowd of around 2,000 people (who are said to have
sung 'Rule Britannia' as he died) on 26 May 1868.
The Capital Punishment Act brought an end to
public executions three days later.

14 December

The murder of 10-year-old Vera Page in 1931 was
never solved, despite a series of clues that all
pointed to a single suspect. Vera disappeared
while making the short 50-yard journey home from
her aunt's house in London's Notting Hill at around
5 p.m. on 14 December. Two days later, a milkman
discovered her body in a garden in Kensington.
She had been strangled. At the scene, detectives
found a discarded finger bandage which smelled of
ammonia and noted coal dust on her clothing. A few
days later, her red beret was found in an empty
cellar which contained coal dust. Coincidentally
or not, a 41-year-old married man named Percy
Orlando Rush, who knew Vera and regularly visited
the Page house (his parents lived on the top floor),
had until recently worn a bandage over a wound on
left little finger. He also worked with ammonia at a
laundry. Yet suspicion was not enough. Although he
was not charged with murder, Rush was questioned
at the public inquest into Vera's death. He swore
on oath he did not meet Vera Page that night and
the inquest jury returned a verdict of 'murder
against some person or persons unknown'.

15 December

As a member of the Bow Street Runners, the first English detectives, George Vaughan was supposed to bring criminals to justice in the early nineteenth century before the formation of the Metropolitan Police. In fact, the 24-year-old officer had decided to follow the example of Jonathan Wild by joining forces with London's crooks in order to claim the tempting £40 reward for the capture of burglars. In one case, Vaughan was tipped off about a break-in at the home of tailor James Poole on the night of 15 December 1815. He duly alerted the intended victim and lay in wait to arrest the offenders, three men named Batts, Rawley and Farthing. Vaughan gave evidence against them at the Old Bailey and all three were convicted and sentenced to death. The officer was exposed a few months later when one of his accomplices turned against him and a fellow Bow Street Runner testified about the arrangement to share the reward. Vaughan was convicted of conspiracy in relation to a burglary in Hoxton and aiding and abetting the burglary of Mr Poole and sentenced to five years' imprisonment.

16 December

In the early hours of 16 December 1942, Edward
Arnold Chapman parachuted into England from a
German Focke-Wulf bomber. His mission was to
sabotage the De Havilland aeroplane factory in
Hatfield, Hertfordshire, but as soon as he landed,
he handed himself in to police and MI5 and
requested to become a double agent. His handlers
gave him the nickname Agent Zigzag. A plan was
drawn up to fake an attack on the De Havilland
factory to fool Chapman's German controllers
(who nicknamed him Fritz). It was so successful
that the Nazis awarded him the Iron Cross and
tasked him with reporting on the effectiveness
of the V-1 missile. Chapman credulously reported
that they were hitting their targets, when in
fact they were miles off course. As a reward for
his service for MI5, Chapman was granted a pardon
for his previous career as a robber and a thief
in London, Scotland and Jersey, including a stint
with a West End 'Jelly Gang' whose trademark was
to blow up safes with gelignite. After the war, he
was fined £50 for breaching the Official Secrets Act
by publishing his memoirs. Chapman died in 1997.

17 December

In 1902, the murderess Emma 'Kitty' Byron was
spared the death sentence for stabbing her
abusive lover to death thanks to a wave of public
sympathy. The victim, Arthur 'Reg' Baker', was a
married stockbroker with a habit of getting blind
drunk on whisky every day, knocking her down
and abusing her as having 'no class' (she was a
brewer's daughter). Asked by their landlady why
she put up with his behaviour, the 23-year-old
milliner replied: 'Because I love him, and I have
lost my character, and I cannot get any work.'
On 10 November 1902, she sent a messenger to the
Stock Exchange, calling Baker to meet her urgently
at the post office in Lombard Street in the City of
London. Moments after his arrival, Byron pulled
a knife from her muff and plunged it into his
chest. Byron initially told police 'I killed him
willingly, and he deserved it, and the sooner I am
killed the better', but later insisted she did
not mean to kill Baker. At the trial, her lawyers
argued she was provoked but the jury convicted her
of murder on 17 December 1902. Byron was released
after serving only six years in prison.

18 December

On 18 December 1634 a Scotswoman named Anna Tait was arrested after trying to hang herself three times at her own house in Haddington. When questioned by an investigating Commission, she admitted to murdering her first husband with a poisonous brew of foxglove leaves. Then, when her daughter became pregnant, she attempted to abort the child using a cocktail of wine and salt. To her dismay, the concoction killed her daughter as well as the unborn baby. As if that was not enough, Anna admitted she 'had carnal copulation with the Devil in her own bed', first while the Devil was in the form of a black man and secondly when he was in the form of the wind. A few days later the Devil returned to her bedside, grabbed her hair and 'nipped' her cheek. This confession meant that she would not be burnt alive as befitted a witch, but instead mercifully strangled before being set on fire. Attempted suicide remained a crime in English common law until 1961 and was punishable with imprisonment. The offence was rarely prosecuted in Scotland after the eighteenth century.

19 December

The Ratcliffe Highway Murders began on
7 December 1811 when linen draper Timothy Marr,
his wife Celia and 3-month-old son, together
with the apprentice boy, were battered to death
at their home. Twelve days later, at 11 p.m. on
19 December, a scream of 'Murder! Murder!' once
more echoed through the streets of Wapping, east
London. Inside the King's Arms tavern in New
Gravel Lane (about half a mile from the Marrs'
shop on Ratcliffe Highway), 56-year-old publican
John Williamson was found with his head smashed
in and his throat cut. His wife Elizabeth and
maidservant Bridget Harrington were also dead.
Only his 14-year-old granddaughter and the lodger
had survived. The two events were quickly linked
and inspired Thomas De Quincey's essay 'On Murder
Considered as One of the Fine Arts'. A suspect,
27-year-old John Williams (a former shipmate
of Timothy Marr), was arrested but never stood
trial – he hanged himself with his scarf in his
cell at Coldbath Fields Prison on 27 December.
As was customary at the time, he was buried under
a crossroads with a stake through his heart.
The murders were only surpassed in notoriety by
the crimes of Jack the Ripper.

20 December

William Davis managed to lead a double life as a
farmer and a highway robber for forty-two years
before being exposed. None of his neighbours in
Salisbury suspected the truth about the happily
married father of eighteen, although many must
have wondered why he always paid his debts in gold,
so earning his nickname 'The Golden Farmer'. Davis
worked alone and relied only on the assistance
of his trusty pistols and a filthy tongue to cow
his victims into submission. On one occasion he
confronted the wealthy Duchess of Albemarle on
Salisbury Plain. After seeing off her footmen
with a few well-placed shots, he tore the diamond
rings from her fingers and snatched her gold watch.
Noticing her use of makeup, he added: 'You bitch
incarnate, you had rather read over your face in
the glass every moment, and blot out pale to put
in red, than give an honest man, as I am, a small
matter to support him on his lawful occasions
on the road.' He was finally captured in an alley
off Fleet Street in the City of London and hanged
in chains on Bagshot Heath in Surrey on this day
in 1689.

21 December

The nose of Sir John Coventry was slit to the
bone on this day in 1670 after he made a joke
at the expense of King Charles II in Parliament.
During a debate on a tax on theatres, it was
argued that they had been of great service to the
king. Sir John slyly asked the speaker whether
he meant the actors or the actresses – as the
king was known to have taken Nell Gwyn (among
others) as his mistress. Later that night, as Sir
John returned home from the pub at 2 a.m., he was
ambushed by a group of guards led by Sir Thomas
Sandys. The injury to his face so outraged his
fellow politicians that they passed a law making
it a felony to 'unlawfully cut or disable the
tongue, put out an eye, slit the nose, cut off
the nose or lip, or cut off or disable any limb
or member'. The attackers, who were thought to be
acting on the orders of the king's illegitimate
son the Duke of Monmouth (with the approval of
Charles himself), were given a royal pardon.
The law remained in force until 1828 and became
known as the Coventry Act.

22 December

Convicted murderer Charlotte Bryant attempted to avoid her execution by sending a telegram to King Edward VIII:

> Mighty King, Have pity on your lowly, afflicted
> subject. Don't let them kill me on Wednesday.
> From the brink of the cold, dark, grave I am a poor
> helpless woman. I ask you not to let them kill me,
> I am innocent.

Bryant had poisoned her husband at their cottage in Coombe, Dorset. The mother of five was well known in the small village for her extramarital affairs and in the weeks leading up to the murder had been living in a *ménage à trois* with Frederick Bryant and her Gypsy lover. When Mr Bryant died on 22 December 1935, traces of arsenic were found in his body and a tin of weedkiller was found on a nearby rubbish tip. She was found guilty after a trial at Dorset Assizes and spent her remaining days desperately maintaining her innocence. A final note, censored by the authorities, hinted at her guilt: 'It's all fault [censored] I am here. I listened to the tales I was told.' Her appeal was turned down and she was hanged on 15 July 1936.

23 December

1890: Convicted murderer Mary Pearcey, now touted as a candidate for 'Jill the Ripper', was hanged outside Newgate Prison. Pearcey had battered her lover's wife Phoebe Hogg to death after inviting her round to her home in Kentish Town, north London. She also smothered Hogg's baby daughter and used the child's pram to dump the bodies in Hampstead and Finchley. Pearcey tried to explain the bloodstains on her walls, clothing and a poker by claiming she had been 'killing mice'. After her execution, the pram was exhibited at Madame Tussauds.

1952: Leslie Green was executed for the murder of 62-year-old Alice Wiltshaw, the wife of a wealthy pottery manufacturer, at her twelve-roomed house in Barlaston, Staffordshire. Green, who had been sacked as the Wiltshaws' chauffeur for unauthorised use of the car, stabbed and battered Mrs Wiltshaw to death with a poker during a burglary. He was linked to the killing by a pair of bloodstained gloves which had a tear in the left thumb – matching a healed cut on Green's hand. Green had also given some of the £3,000 worth of stolen jewellery to his girlfriend. He was hanged at Winsom Green Prison in Birmingham.

24 December

The phrase 'Sweet Fanny Adams' has its origins in the grisly murder of an 8-year-old girl in Alton, Hampshire. On 24 August 1867, Fanny was playing with three friends near her home when she was abducted by a 29-year-old solicitor's clerk, Frederick Baker. Later that day, her worried mother discovered Fanny's head, arms and legs strewn across the hops fields. Her eyes had been plucked out. Baker, identified by one of Fanny's friends, insisted he had only given the girls some sweets but was undone by a telling entry in his diary for that day which read: 'killed a young girl; it was fine and hot.' He also had blood on his cuffs and a penknife. At the trial at Winchester County Assizes, it was argued that Baker was only recording the fact of the death of the girl, followed by an observation about the weather. The jury found him guilty of murder and he was hanged on Christmas Eve outside Winchester Gaol. Fanny Adams' name entered the language as naval slang for cheap tinned meat and is now used to mean 'nothing at all' (to put it politely).

25 December

The cross-dressing criminal Mary Frith (aka Moll
Cutpurse) became a notorious figure in the early
seventeenth century by wearing baggy trousers,
smoking tobacco, swearing and brawling in the
street. Mary, who was said to be 'so ugly in
any dress as never to be wooed nor solicited
by any man', began her career as a fortune
teller, a pickpocket and a handler of stolen
goods for London's underworld. But it was for
dressing 'indecently' that she was arrested on
25 December 1611 and sentenced to perform public
acts of penance while dressed in a white sheet
at the door of St Paul's Cathedral (although one
observer suspected her weeping was inspired by
a large amount of alcohol). The resulting fame
took her to the stage, where she performed in
male clothing for the entertainment of the public,
and she became known as 'The Roaring Girl'. Mary
is also said to have turned to have turned to
highway robbery during the English Civil War and
specialised in targeting Roundheads. One story
involves her shooting General Fairfax in the
arm and having to pay him £2,000 to avoid the
death sentence.

26 December

Boxing Day 1856 was the last day in the criminal career of master forger 'Jim the Penman', the alter ego of barrister James Townsend Saward. For thirty years, Saward skilfully replicated signatures on cheques and money orders to claim up to £1,000 a time. The scam relied on a network of errand boys and girls (usually recruited from newspaper advertisements for 'situations wanted'), to collect the money, thereby concealing Saward's identity. He was caught thanks to the blundering incompetence of accomplice William Hardwicke, who used the wrong name at Barclay's bank and had to write to Saward asking for advice. The reply, which included a quotation from Ovid (*cavendo tutus*, or 'safe through caution'), was intercepted by the police and Saward was arrested on 26 December. At the trial, Saward was convicted of forging a £100 money order after Hardwicke gave evidence for the Crown. Asked if he had anything to say in his defence, the 58-year-old replied: 'I shall leave the case in the hands of your Lordship, as far as I am concerned; I am quite unprepared, being quite unrepresented.' In March 1857 he was sentenced to transportation for life to Australia.

27 December

The eight men waiting to be hanged were offered a
deal: if one of them volunteered to carry out the
execution of the others he would be pardoned and
set free. They were all 'Covenanters', members
of a Presbyterian group which had refused to
accept Charles II as head of the Scottish Church.
So strong were their beliefs in the face of state
persecution that they had taken part in a rebellion against the king in 1666. Their defeat was
as inevitable as their conviction for treason and
the sentence of death. Less predictable was the
flight of the hangman at Ayr and the refusal of
his replacement (despite the threat of torture)
to carry out the punishment. So would any of the
eight god-fearing men break ranks and take up the
offer? It seemed unlikely, but Cornelius Anderson,
having begged the others for forgiveness, grasped
the poisoned chalice. On 27 December 1666, his
resolved stiffened with brandy, Anderson hanged
his seven fellow Covenanters on the gallows at Ayr.
He was then set free. It is said that he fled into
obscurity in Ireland, consumed by guilt, only to
burn to death in a house fire.

28 December

The Swing Riots of 1830 were the agricultural
equivalent of the Luddite protests earlier in
the century. Workers, fearing that they would
lose their jobs or forced to accept lower wages,
destroyed threshing machines, burnt down barns and
sent threatening letters signed 'Captain Swing'.
The protests spread from Kent across the rest of
England as far north as Yorkshire and special
commissions had to be set up to deal with all the
arrests. In Berkshire, on 28 December, William
Oakley, William Winterburne, Daniel Bates and
Edmund Steele appeared in court accused of robbing
Magistrate John Willes Esq of 5 sovereigns. Having
joined a mob of 300 rampaging through Hungerford,
they demanded that the workers were granted 12
shillings a week in wages and a reduction of house
rent. Bates, armed with a sledgehammer, then
demanded Willes hand over £5, and Oakley added:
'You gentlemen have been living long enough on the
good things – now is our time, and we will have
them.' Steele was acquitted but the other three
were found guilty. Winterburne, the leader of the
gang, and Oakley, a carpenter who appears to have
little connection to the rioters' complaints, were
both sentenced to death.

29 December

'Will no one rid me of this turbulent priest?'
Did King Henry II (1133–89) utter these words
as a cry of despair, or an order of assassination? Either way, by the end of the year 1170,
the Archbishop of Canterbury, Thomas Becket, was
dead. On 29 December, four sword-wielding knights
rushed into Canterbury Cathedral and seized him
as he headed for evening prayer. The first blow
shaved off the top of his head. After a second and
a third blow, Becket said: 'For the name of Jesus
and the protection of the church I am ready to
embrace death.' According to an eyewitness, the
fourth blow:

… shattered the sword on the stone and his crown,
which was large, separated from his head so that
the blood turned white from the brain yet no less
did the brain turn red from the blood; it purpled
the appearance of the church with the colours of
the lily and the rose, the colours of the Virgin
and Mother and the life and death of the confessor
and martyr.

Becket, a popular figure across Europe, was made
a saint just three years later and in 1174, King
Henry confessed his sins and allowed the bishops
and monks of the cathedral to beat him with a rod
more than 240 times.

30 December

1818: The execution of convicted robber Robert Johnston in Edinburgh was interrupted after the crowd surged on to the scaffold, attacked the executioner, cut the rope and carried the half-strangled man into the middle of the High Street to recover. Johnston's respite did not last long, for the local constables regrouped, seized him back from the mob and dragged him to the police office. He was then taken back to the scaffold for the noose to be placed around his neck a second time, only for his trousers to fall down. It took several minutes for him to die as the crowd shouted: 'Murder!' and 'Shame!'

1902: The dismembered bodies of missing grocer William Darby, his wife Beatrice and their baby daughter Ethel were discovered in the back garden of a house in Leyton, east London. They had been beaten to death by hot-headed businessman Edgar Edwards, who might have got away with the murders if he had not subsequently attacked another grocer, John Garland, with the same type of weapon, a lead sash weight. Edwards' motive appears to have been simple greed. He pleaded insanity but was convicted of murder at the Old Bailey and hanged in March 1903.

31 December

It took five carts and a mourning coach to carry
all fifteen prisoners to the gallows at Tyburn on
31 December 1750. They were Benjamin 'Ben the Coal-
heaver' Beckenfield, convicted of robbing a man of
his hat on the King's Highway; Anthony Byrne, who
broke into a haberdasher's to steal fifty hats;
John Newcombe, another highway hat robber; William
Tidd, a burglar with a taste for pewterware; John
Ross, Thomas Proctor and Derby Long, teenage
burglars of gold and silver jewellery; John Watlin
and John 'Cock-eye' Carbold of Norfolk, smugglers
of tea and brandy; John Richardson, an apprentice
carpenter who stole from his master; Adam Dawson,
William 'Little Will' Knight and John Foster,
highway robbers; William Baker, a prosperous and
well-educated grocer who forged a warrant for the
delivery of three chests of Chinese tea to obtain
a loan of £1,000; and 17-year-old Catherine Conner,
who was convicted of presenting a will forged in
the name of a dead mariner. It was noted that all
'behaved very decently' except William Tidd, who,
having already once escaped the death sentence
for robbing a sheep drover, 'shewed some Levity,
unbecoming a Person so near his last Moments'.

Also from The History Press

MURDER & CRIME

This series brings together numerous murderous tales from history. Featuring cases of infanticide, drowning, shooting and stabbing, amongst many other chilling killings, these well-illustrated and enthralling books will appeal to everyone interested in true crime and the shadier side of their hometown's past.

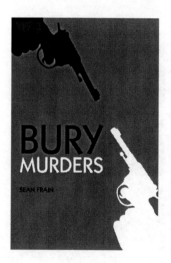

Find these titles and more at
www.thehistorypress.co.uk

Also from The History Press

BLOODY BRITISH HISTORY

Britain has centuries of incredible history to draw on – everything from Boudica and the Black Death to the Blitz. This local series, harking back to the extraordinary pulp magazines of days gone by, contains only the darkest and most dreadful events in your area's history. So embrace the nastier side of British history with these tales of riots and executions, battles and sieges, murders and regicides, witches and ghosts, death, devilry and destruction!

Find these titles and more at
www.thehistorypress.co.uk

Also from The History Press

GRIM ALMANAC

The *Grim Almanac* series is a day-by-day catalogue of ghastly tales from history. Full of dreadful deeds, macabre deaths and bizarre tragedies, each almanac includes captivatingly diverse tales of highwaymen, smugglers, murderers, bodysnatchers, duellists, poachers, witches, rioters and rebels, as well as accounts of old lock-ups, prisons, bridewells and punishments. All these, plus tales of accidents by land, sea and air, and much more, are here. If you have ever wondered about the nasty goings-on of yesteryear, then look no further – it's all here. But do you have the stomach for it?

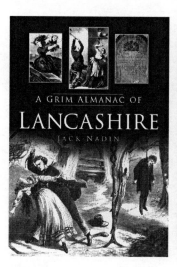
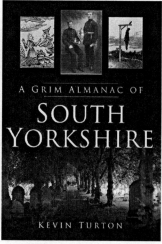

Find these titles and more at
www.thehistorypress.co.uk

Lightning Source UK Ltd.
Milton Keynes UK
UKOW04f0304250714

235741UK00001B/1/P

9 780750 956543